mastering american english

D1212624

Legal Deposit 4th Trimester 1973
National Quebec Library   Printed and bound in Canada
        12 13 14 PDM 73 8 7 6
ISBN 0-07-077553-2

GRANT TAYLOR
Formerly, Director of
American Language Institute,
New York University

PATRICK J. COLLINS, M.A.
École des Roches International School
Bluche-sur-Sierre
Switzerland

mastering american english

McGRAW-HILL, EDITEURS — MONTREAL

Toronto • New York • Düsseldorf • Johannesburg • Kuala Lumpur
London • Mexico • New Delhi • Panama • Paris • Rio de Janeiro
Singapore • Sydney.

PRÉFACE

Mastering American English *est un manuel d'anglais langue seconde qui convient tout aussi bien aux étudiants du niveau moyen qu'à ceux du niveau avancé. La présente édition a été préparée à l'intention des Canadiens de langue française qui sont appelés à perfectionner cette langue.*

Nous avons divisé le manuel en deux sections, une pour le niveau moyen et l'autre pour le niveau avancé. Ainsi peut-on passer de la première section à la deuxième sans devoir changer de livre ou se réhabituer à une autre méthode. La première section traite des éléments grammaticaux de base tels que la conjugaison, les formes négatives et interrogatives, la syntaxe, les contractions, etc. Au niveau avancé, on étudie les aspects plus complexes de la langue. Arrivé à la fin du livre, l'étudiant devrait avoir une connaissance bien assise de l'anglais et une bonne compréhension de ses particularités linguistiques les plus difficiles à maîtriser.

On remarquera que nous avons peu insisté sur l'explication grammaticale comme telle ; la raison en est double. D'abord, l'étudiant connaît déjà la grammaire de base, et ensuite il devrait s'appliquer à mettre en œuvre ses connaissances acquises et à se sensibiliser davantage à la syntaxe anglaise. Si nous avons employé une terminologie grammaticale au début de certains exercices, ce n'est que pour mieux orienter l'enseignant. L'étudiant n'aura à se préoccuper de la grammaire qu'à travers les quelques exemples cités au début des exercices. Mais ceux-ci se suffisent à eux-mêmes et ne demandent pour ainsi dire pas d'explications.

L'étudiant arrive ainsi à perfectionner son anglais en faisant un nombre considérable d'exercices au lieu d'apprendre les règles de la grammaire comme telles. Quoique ces trois cent douze exercices constituent des unités d'enseignement indépendantes, ils sont placés selon un ordre bien établi que l'enseignant peut respecter.

Les nombreux exercices de récapitulation permettent aux étudiants de revoir les questions qui les ennuient le plus souvent et de les travailler en profondeur tout au long du cours. Celui qui veut maîtriser une langue étrangère se doit de réviser continuellement les notions acquises.

Bien que ce livre porte essentiellement sur l'anglais écrit, nous avons aussi tenu compte de la pratique orale de la langue dans la préparation des exercices. Nous recommandons d'ailleurs aux enseignants de mettre l'accent sur une méthode d'enseignement orale afin que les étudiants acquièrent la maîtrise de la

PREFACE

Mastering American English is a comprehensive ESL textbook designed for students who have attained intermediate and advanced levels of proficiency. This edition has been specifically adapted to the needs of French-speaking Canadians.

The text has been divided into two sections : intermediate and advanced. This enables the " intermediate " student to graduate to the Advanced Section without the necessity of changing to another book and having to familiarize himself with a different format. The Intermediate Section contains exercises that cover such basic points as tenses, the use of negatives, questions, word order, contractions, etc. The Advanced Section is composed of the more complex features of the English language. Thus, by the time the student reaches the end of the book, he should have a firm grasp of the fundamentals of English and an authoritative awareness of its more difficult characteristics.

It will be noted that there is little grammatical explanation in this book. There are two reasons for this : (1) it is presumed that the student knows his English grammar, and (2) to make him apply this knowledge, so that he will become more aware of the sentence patterns used in English. Grammatical terminology has been used in some of the titles of the exercises, but this is intended as a guide for the teacher. The student's attention is only drawn to the grammar through the few examples given at the beginning of the exercises. These examples, however, should certainly be adequate as they are essentially self-explanatory.

Thus, the student's knowledge of English is furthered through the employment of a large number of exercises rather than through grammatical rules. While these exercises may be taught as separate units, all 312 of them have been arranged in a deliberate sequence which the teacher may wish to follow.

Throughout both sections, there are many review exercises. Not only do these exercises deal with areas which generally cause problems for intermediate and advanced students, but they also give the student continual and thorough practice in these areas. Repetition is imperative for mastering a language.

While the emphasis in this book has been placed on written English, the exercises have also been constructed with oral practice in mind. The teacher

langue parlée et qu'ils aient confiance en eux-mêmes. C'est ainsi que le magné-tophone peut rendre de très bons services. L'étudiant aura l'occasion de s'écou-ter parler, de reconnaître ses faiblesses et de se reprendre lui-même.

Nous avons mis l'accent sur la langue courante, celle que l'on est suscepti-ble de parler, d'écrire et de lire tous les jours, y compris les idiotismes les plus usuels de l'anglais, car il est très important que l'étudiant soit familier avec la langue de tous les jours. Cela fait, il se doit d'approfondir son vocabulaire, par-ce que ce n'est qu'à ce moment-là qu'il aura acquis une connaissance fonda-mentale des structures de l'anglais.

Nous avons partout employé des graphies américaines plutôt qu'anglaises puis-que de nos jours l'américain s'utilise de plus en plus au Canada.

On trouvera un guide de solutions à la fin du volume. La plupart du temps, nous n'avons fourni que les réponses aux premières questions d'un exercice don-né. L'étudiant peut ainsi vérifier le début de l'exercice sans toutefois succomber à la tentation de reproduire les solutions dans ses propres travaux. Les réponses à toutes les questions sont fournies seulement dans les exercices qui portent sur les temps composés et les prépositions, car dans ces cas-là l'étudiant peut diffici-lement contrôler ses progrès d'une autre façon.

Nous espérons que l'étudiant pourra approfondir aisément sa connaissance de l'anglais grâce à cette nouvelle édition. Afin d'agrémenter la tâche parfois difficile de l'apprentissage d'une langue étrangère, nous nous sommes efforcés de placer l'étudiant dans des situations d'apprentissage qui reflètent la vie cou-rante et de mettre en relief des événements auxquels il est confronté dans sa vie de tous les jours.

Bluche-sur-Sierre,   *P.J.C.*
Suisse   *G.T.*
1973

is strongly advised to use the oral method of instruction as often as possible as this will give the student a more comprehensive grasp of the language and an added confidence. In this respect, a tape recorder will be extremely useful. It will also give the student the opportunity of hearing himself speak and of recognizing his oral mistakes himself.

Mastering American English stresses the more common, day-to-day words and expressions. The text includes several exercises based on idioms. It is more important for the student to master the vernacular first. Once he has achieved this, he may, and certainly should, concentrate on broadening his vocabulary, because he will then have a strong foundation on which to build.

American spelling has been used throughout this book as this form of spelling, rather than the English form, is becoming increasingly more common in Canada.

An Answer Section has been included at the end of the book. For most exercises, however, only the first few answers have been given. This enables the student to check that he has started his work correctly and avoids the obvious temptation to copy the answers. Complete answers have only been given for the exercises on two-word verbs and prepositions, because it is difficult for students to obtain this information.

We hope that this edition will bring both enjoyment and edification to the student. In order to make the sometimes laborious task of language learning more palatable, much of this material deals with situations and events that a student commonly experiences from day to day.

Bluche-sur-Sierre, Switzerland, 1973 P.J.C.
G.T.

CONTENTS

                    APPENDIX

INTERMEDIATE SECTION

1

NORTH AMERICA

Read this story. Study the verbs carefully.

James Johnson is my name. I work in the main office of a big company. Twenty people work in that office every day. Mr. Wilson is my boss. He works very hard. Almost everyone works hard. Of course, a few people don't work hard.

Mr. Wilson has a private office. He also has a secretary. Her name is Miss Stewart. She helps Mr. Wilson. She doesn't help me. I don't have a private office, but I do have my own secretary. She is called Mary Peters.

Mr. Wilson meets all of the important visitors. I don't meet any important visitors. Miss Stewart doesn't meet any important visitors either. I occasionally talk to other visitors, though.

Mr. Wilson writes many letters every day. He sends many letters to customers. I write letters too. I send letters to other companies, but I don't send letters to customers.

I often study statistics. Then I write reports for Mr. Wilson. He studies the reports carefully. I get the statistics from my assistants. I have two assistants, Smith and Green. They help me very much. They don't write letters. They collect information from other people. Then they give the information to my secretary. She collects information from other people too. Then she gives the information to me.

My secretary doesn't write reports, but she writes many letters for me. She also opens my mail. She gives me the important letters. I read these important letters carefully. Then I answer them. My secretary doesn't give me the other letters. She answers them herself.

Use the simple present tense of each verb. Write the verb in the blank space.

1 (*work*)   I <u>work</u> in the main office.
2 (*work*)   Mr. Wilson <u>works</u> very hard.
3 *(work)*   Almost everyone .... very hard.
4 (*work*)   We .... from 9:00 a.m. to 5:00 p.m.
5 (*have*)   Mr. Wilson .... a private office.
6 (*have*)   I .... my own secretary.
7 (*write*)   Miss Peters .... letters for me.
8 (*write*)   I .... reports for Mr. Wilson.
9 (*study*)   Mr. Wilson .... the reports.
10 (*study*)   I .... the information carefully.
11 (*read*)   My secretary .... all of the mail.
12 (*read*)   I .... only the important letters.
13 (*collect*) Smith and Green .... information.
14 (*collect*) Miss Peters .... information too.

Change the word *I* to *he* or *she*. Notice the examples.

1   I go to the office every day.
    He goes to the office every day.
2   I write many letters every day.
    She writes many letters every day.
3   I read all of the important letters.
4   I study the reports very carefully.
5   I have a private secretary too.
6   I usually work in the main office.
7   I meet all of the important visitors.
8   I get the information from Miss Peters.
9   I always give the reports to Mr. Wilson.
10 I answer all of the important letters.
11 I send letters to many other companies.
12 I talk to Smith and Green every day.

Answer these questions about the story. "Every Day". Answer the questions with a full sentence.

1   Does Mr. Johnson work for a big company ?
    Yes, Mr. Johnson works for a big company.

2   Do the two men work in the same room ?
    No, the two men don't work in the same room.

3   Does Mr. Johnson have a private office ?
4   Do the two men have secretaries ?
5   Does Miss Stewart help Mr. Johnson ?
6   Does she help Mr. Wilson or Mr. Johnson ?
7   Do Mr. Wilson and Mr. Johnson work hard ?
8   Does Mr. Wilson meet the important visitors ?
9   Does Mr. Johnson meet the important visitors too ?
10 Do Mr. Wilson and Mr. Johnson write many letters ?
11 Do the two secretaries write letters too ?
12 Does Mr. Johnson send letters to customers ?
13 Do Mr. Wilson and Mr. Johnson write reports ?
14 Does Mr. Johnson study the reports carefully ?
15 Does Mr. Johnson study the statistics carefully ?
16 Does Mr. Johnson have two assistants ?
17 Do Smith and Green give the information to Johnson ?
18 Do they give the information to his secretary ?
19 Does Miss Peters give the information to her boss ?
20 Does she give the information to Wilson or Johnson ?
21 Does Miss Peters write reports every day ?
22 Do Smith and Green write reports too ?
23 Does Mr. Johnson open the mail every day ?
24 Does Miss Peters open all of the mail ?
25 Do Smith and Green open the mail too ?
26 Does Mr. Johnson read all of the mail ?
27 Does Mr. Johnson answer all of the letters ?
28 Does Mr. Johnson answer only the important letters ?

Write *do* or *does* in the blank space in each sentence.

1   *Do*   the students study hard every day ?

2   *Does*   Mr. Brown go to his office every day ?

3 .... you want cream and sugar in your coffee ?

4 .... the children go to bed very early ?

5 .... that girl come from St.-Sauveur ?

6 .... you know that Italian student ?

7 .... Miss Stewart prefer coffee or tea ?

8 .... your English lessons seem very difficult ?

9 .... you have a good English dictionary ?

10 .... Mr. Moore teach English or history ?

11 .... the Johnsons watch television every night ?

12 .... Johnson and Wilson work in the same office ?

13 .... you write reports for your boss every day ?

14 .... those two students understand that lesson ?

Write *don't* or *doesn't* in the blank space in each sentence.

1 We .... listen to the radio every night.

2 Mr. Johnson .... have a private office.

3 The boys .... study at the library every day.

4 These exercises .... seem very difficult.

5 It .... rain very much in June and July.

6 The men .... always eat at that cafeteria.

7 I .... eat at that cafeteria every day.

8 Miss Peters .... write reports for her boss.

9 The Wilsons .... watch television every night.

10 Smith and Green .... teach English at this school.

11 That tall man .... work for this company.

12 The people .... speak English very well.

13 Mrs. Moore .... go to the store every day.

14 Yvonne .... enjoy that history class.

Read this story. Study the verbs carefully.

My name is James Johnson. I am the office manager of the Bideford Company. I am in my office now. I am sitting at my desk right now.

I am working on a report for Mr. Wilson. He is my boss. Miss Peters is helping me with the report. She is my secretary. She is sitting beside my desk, but she isn't writing in her notebook. I am not dictating to her at this moment. We are not working. We are resting for a few minutes. I am looking around the office at the moment.

Mr. Wilson isn't working in his office. I see four people at the end of the room. Mr. Wilson is with these people. He is taking them through our office. He is telling them about our methods. They are listening to Mr. Wilson carefully.

Miss Stewart is wearing a blue pantsuit today. She is sitting at her desk. She is talking over the telephone. She is writing in her notebook at the same time. Someone is giving important information to her over the telephone right now.

There are twenty people in the room. Everyone is working hard right now. Three or four people are writing letters. Some people are studying important papers. Smith and Green are not here at the moment. They are now writing reports. They are collecting information for me.

I hear some noise in the hall. There are three workmen there. The three men are fixing the floor in the hall. They are talking and laughing. They are also hitting the floor with hammers.

Write *am*, *is*, or *are* in the blank space in each sentence.

1 Mr. Wilson _is_ talking to visitors right now.
2 I _am_ sitting at my desk right at this moment.
3 Miss Peters .... helping me with a report now.
4 We ....working on the report right now.
5 I ....looking around the office at this moment.
6 The people .... listening to Mr. Wilson carefully.
7 He .... telling the people about our methods.
8 Someone .... talking to Miss Stewart at the moment.
9 She .... talking and writing at the same time.
10 Everyone .... working very hard right now.
11 Some people .... studying important papers now.
12 Smith and Green .... collecting information now.
13 The men .... fixing the floor in the hall right now.
14 They .... also making much noise at this moment.

Use the continuous present tense of each verb. Write the verb in the blank space.

1 (*work*)   He _is working_ on a report right now.
2 (*study*)   We _are studying_ some important papers.
3 (*help*)   She .... me with the report now.
4 (*sit*)   The men .... at their desks now.
5 (*write*)   The two girls .... letters now.
6 (*work*)   Everyone ....very hard right now.
7 (*watch*)   I .... my boss and the visitors.
8 (*listen*)   They .... to Mr. Wilson carefully.
9 (*talk*)   Someone ....to Miss Stewart now.
10 (*dictate*)   Mr. Adams ....letters at the moment.
11 (*collect*)   Smith and Green ....information.
12 (*talk*)
     (*write*)   She .... and .... at the same time.
13 (*talk*)
     (*laugh*)   The men .... and .... right now.

Answer these questions about the story, "Right Now". Answer the questions with a complete sentence.

1 Is Mr Johnson the office manager ?
   Yes, Mr. Johnson is the office manager.

2 Is Mr. Wilson in his private office now ?
   No, Mr. Wilson isn't in his private office now.

3 Is Mr. Johnson sitting at his desk right now ?
   Yes, Mr. Johnson is sitting at his desk right now.

4 Is Mr. Wilson working on a report at the moment ?
   No, Mr. Wilson isn't working on a report at the moment.

5 Is Miss Peters helping Mr. Johnson right now ?
6 Is Miss Peters sitting at her own desk now ?
7 Is Mr. Johnson dictating to Miss Peters now ?
8 Is Miss Peters writing in her notebook right now ?
9 Are Mr. Johnson and Miss Peters working on a report ?
10 Are they working on the report right at this moment ?
11 Are they resting for a few minutes ?
12 Is Mr. Johnson looking around the office now ?
13 Is Mr. Wilson in his private office right now ?
14 Does Mr. Johnson see many people in the office ?
15 Are the four customers with Mr. Wilson now ?
16 Is Mr. Wilson with the four visitors now ?
17 Is Mr. Wilson talking to the four people right now ?
18 Are the people listening to Mr. Wilson carefully ?
19 Is Miss Stewart sitting beside Mr. Johnson right now ?
20 Is Miss Stewart talking to someone at the moment ?
21 Are there very many people in the office now ?
22 Are Smith and Green in the main office now ?
23 Are Smith and Green helping Mr. Johnson now ?
24 Does Mr. Johnson hear some noise in the hall now ?
25 Are the three workmen talking and laughing ?
26 Are they also hitting the floor with hammers ?

Write *don't, doesn't, isn't, aren't,* or *am not* in the blank space in each sentence.

1 He _isn't_ listening to the radio right now.
2 He _doesn't_ listen to the radio every evening.
3 We .... watching a television program now.
4 We .... watch television every day.
5 They .... study their lessons after class.
6 They .... studying their lessons right now.
7 It .... raining very hard right at the moment.
8 It .... rain very much during the summer.
9 Mr. Johnson .... eating his lunch now.
10 Mr. Johnson .... always eat at that place.
11 I .... see any students in that room.
12 I .... hear anyone in the hall now.
13 They .... like milk with their meals.
14 They .... have enough money for a new car.

Write *do, does, is, are,* or *am* in the blank space in each sentence.

1 _Do_____ the men come to work at 9:00 every morning ?
2 _Are_____ the men coming into the room right now ?
3 .... you learn the new words in each lesson ?
4 .... you learning the new words right now ?
5 .... Mr. Johnson work for the Bideford Company ?
6 .... Mr. Johnson working on a report right now ?
7 .... she usually sit in the third row ?
8 .... she sitting in the fourth row today ?
9 .... you read many books every year ?
10 .... you reading an interesting book now ?
11 .... the students need help with their lessons ?
12 .... this lesson seem very difficult to you ?
13 .... you remember the name of that book ?
14 .... you understand all of the words very well ?

Use the correct tense of the verb in each sentence. Choose between the simple present tense and the continuous present tense.

1 He (*work*) hard every day.   *He works hard every day.*

2 He (*talk*) to Tom now.   *He is talking to Tom now.*

3 Miss Steward (*look*) at the newspaper now.
4 The children (*sleep*) for two hours every afternoon.
5 Those two fellows (*fix*) the car right now.
6 Anne-Marie (*speak*) English very well.
7 Uncle Walter (*eat*) dinner with us every Sunday.
8 My friend (*enjoy*) hamburgers very much.
9 John and Frank (*write*) letters at this moment.
10 Mr. Johnson (*work*) thirty-five hours a week.
11 My sister (*need*) some money for her books.
12 It (*rain*) very much in England.
13 Mr. Brown (*pay*) his bills once a month.
14 The student (*look up*) that new word right now.
15 Mr. Moore (*teach*) English from 2:00 to 4:00 p.m.
16 Mr. Moore (*begin*) the new lesson right now.
17 I (*owe*) my friend two dollars and fifty cents.
18 Smith (*watch*) a baseball game every Saturday.
19 Miss Peters (*talk*) to Mr. Johnson right now.
20 Pierre (*know*) all of the new words very well now.
21 We always (*do*) our English lessons carefully.
22 We (*do*) exercise thirteen right at the moment.
23 The sun (*get*) very hot during the afternoon.
24 Alice and Mary (*put away*) the dinner dishes right now.
25 Mr. Harris (*read*) an interesting book about Quebec.
26 The Moores often (*attend*) our Tuesday night meetings.
27 Henri (*talk*) to his teacher about that mistake.
28 I frequently (*do*) my homework on the bus.
29 I (*do*) the next to last sentence right now.
30 The teacher (*close*) the door at nine o'clock sharp.

Choose *this* or *these*.   Choose *that* or *those*.

1 *This* is your briefcase.   15 *Is that* man here now ?
2 *These* are your books.   16 Are *those* students ready ?
3 .... book is interesting.   17 Is .... your notebook ?
4 .... questions are hard.   18 Are .... your gloves ?
5 .... is very difficult.   19 Is .... boy reading now ?
6 .... are quite easy.   20 Are .... students working ?
7 .... seem very hard.   21 Does .... seem difficult ?
8 .... seems very easy.   22 Do .... feel comfortable ?
9 .... lesson is simple.   23 Are .... children here ?
10 .... words are new.   24 Do .... men speak English ?
11 .... are very heavy.   25 Does .... woman know you ?
12 .... is very pretty.   26 Is .... lesson very easy ?
13 .... goes on .... lines. 27 Do .... belong on .... desk ?
14 .... go on .... line.   28 Does .... go in .... drawers ?

Use *there is* and *there are* and *in the room* with these words. Make statements and questions. Notice the examples.

1 a table   *There is a table in the room.*
                Is there a table in the room ?

2 chairs   *There are chairs in the room.*
                Are there chairs in the room ?

3 a picture   11 two doors   19 a big table
4 desks   12 a closet   20 some women
5 a blackboard   13 some men   21 a pretty picture
6 chairs   14 three maps   22 many people
7 a telephone   15 a wastebasket   23 a small man
8 windows   16 children   24 four chairs
9 a rug   17 many chairs   25 much light
10 people   18 an ashtray   26 many lamps

Substitute pronouns for the italicized words in each sentence. Notice the first two examples.

1 *The boy* is reading *the book.*   *He is reading it.*
2 *The students* are talking to *Tom.*   *They are talking to him.*
3 *Marie* is studying her lesson with *Yvan.*
4 *Mr. and Mrs. Johnson* enjoy *television* very much.
5 *That fellow* understands *the lesson* completely.
6 *The children* like *their teachers* very much.
7 Do *Georges and Marie* like *that English book* ?
8 Is *Miss Brown* explaining the lesson to *the students* ?
9 *The women* are talking about *the party.*
10 *The man* is moving *the furniture* into the other room.
11 *Those people* need *the money* as soon as possible.
12 *John and Frank* are writing *the letter* right now.
13 *Frank and I* usually meet *our friends* at the corner.
14 *The two girls* are putting *the food* on the table now.
15 Are *the men* speaking to *Mr. Wilson* at this moment ?
16 *The teachers* spoke to *the students* about *that matter.*
17 *Pierre, Françoise, and I* are studying *the new words* now.
18 *The waitress* always washes *the tables* carefully.
19 Does *Mrs. Brown* buy *her groceries* at that store ?
20 *All of the students* enjoy *hockey* very much.
21 *Betty* sends a letter to *her parents* every week.
22 *Mr. Harris* is helping *that student* with *the lesson.*
23 Do *Bill and you* read *that newspaper* every morning ?
24 *The people* don't like *the news* very much.
25 *The student* is writing *the explanation* in his notebook.
26 *The police* protect *the city* day and night.
27 *The policeman* is giving a ticket to *that woman.*
28 *Canada* is made up of *ten provinces and two territories.*
29 *The teacher* is explaining *the words* to *Thérèse.*
30 *His friends* always enjoy *his jokes* very much.

Write the correct possessive form of each word in parentheses.

1 *(Helen)*   hat is pretty. *Helen's hat is pretty.*
2 The   *(boys)*   books are here. *The boys' books are here.*
3 *(Philippe)*   English isn't very good.
4 That   *(girl)*   summer suit is beautiful.
5 Those *(girls)* new apartment is lovely.
6 Mr.   *(Brown)*   son knows Bill and Tom well.
7 That   *(man)*   brother works for a small company.
8 Those   *(men)*   coats are in the other closet.
9 The   *(student)*   books are on his desk.
10 The   *(students)*   papers are in that drawer.
11 *(Tom)*   *(friend)*   sister lives in Charlottetown.
12 *(Fred)*   *(parents)*   house is at the end of the next block.

Show possession with *'s* or *s'* or *of.* Add *the* if necessary. Notice the first two examples.

1 *(man)*   *(name)*   is unusual.   *The man's name is unusual.*
2 *(book)*   *(title)*   is short.   *The title of the book is short.*
3 *(doctor)*   *(office)*   is on the tenth floor.
4 *(table)*   *(legs)*   are not very strong.
5 Does Mr. Johnson know   *(price)*   *(car)* ?
6 Do Alice and Betty know *(boys)*   *(friend)* ?
7 Does anyone know   *(height)*   *(that wall)* ?
8 *(coats)*   *(women)*   are in the closet in the hall.
9 *(table)*   *(surface)*   is not very smooth.
10 *(cover)*   *(book)*   is yellow and black.
11 The students usually write on   *(paper)*   *(both sides)*.
12 All of our suitcases are in   *(trunk)*   *(car)*.
13 Mr. Harris is talking to   *(student)*   *(father)*.
14 Mrs. Edna Wilson is   *(aunt)*   *(Miss Stewart)*.
15 The two workers are repairing   *(house)*   *(roof)*.
16 *(new car)*   *(Claude)*   is certainly very beautiful.

14

Refer to the italicized word or words with the correct possessive adjective. Notice the first two examples.

1 *The student* is studying _his_ English assignment now.
2 *Miss Peters* is writing in _her_ notebook right now.
3 *They* usually eat .... lunch at a cafeteria.
4 *We* always study .... English lessons very carefully.
5 *That girl* always takes very good care of .... clothes.
6 *The children* are playing with .... toys right now.
7 *I* always put .... pens and pencils in the second drawer.
8 *You* don't do.............. English lessons very carefully.
9 *Tom and Bill* are walking home with .... friends.
10 *Mr. Brown* seldom drives .... car to .... office.
11 *Miss Davis* is using .... sister's book today.
12 *We* write letters to .... friends once or twice a month.
13 *Mr. and Mrs. Wilson* are sitting in .... living room now.
14 *You and I* don't spend .... money very wisely.

Substitute a possessive pronoun for the words in parentheses in each sentence. Notice the first two examples.

1 That book is   (*my book*).   That book is *mine.*
2 Those are   (*her pictures*).   Those are *hers.*
3 All of these magazines are   (*his magazines*).
4 Those cigarettes on the table are   (*my cigarettes*).
5 Are all of these papers   (*your papers*) ?
6 That newspaper on the desk is   (*her newspaper*).
7 That big white house on the corner is   (*their house*).
8 Is this your purse or   (*Miss Brown's purse*) ?
9 Are those my overshoes or   (*his overshoes*) ?
10 Are these two books (*your books*) or (*my books*) ?
11 Edward's new suit and   (*my new suit*) are very similar.
12 Their house and   (*our house*) are both on the same block.
13 That red car in front of   (*your car*) is (*my brother's car*).
14 Is this English book ¨ (*your book*) or (*his sister's book*) ?

mine
yours
his
hers
ours
theirs

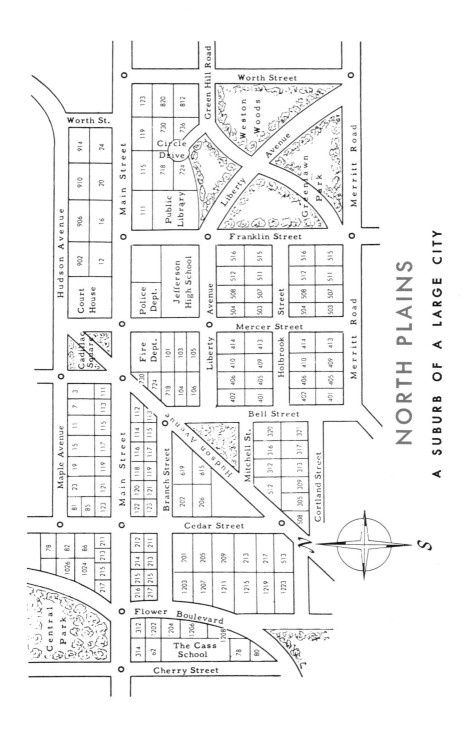

NORTH PLAINS

A SUBURB OF A LARGE CITY

Follow these directions carefully. Use the map of North Plains. Then look in the answer section for the correct address of each location.

1 *Where do Mr. and Mrs Smith live ?*
   You are at the corner of Main Street and Cherry Street. Drive east to the third stop light. Turn right. Turn left at the next light. Drive to Holbrook Street, and turn to your left. Stop at the third house on your right.

2 *Where is the Booth Shoe Store ?*
   You are at the corner of Main Street and Worth Street. Walk west to the third stop light. Turn left. Then turn right at the next corner. Go to the third store on your right.

3 *Where do the Browns live ?*
   You are in front of Jefferson High School. Drive west on Liberty to Bell. Make a right turn. Cross Hudson Avenue and take Branch Street to Cedar. Turn left on Cedar Street. It's the second house on your left.

4 *Please give me the directions to Mr. Johnson's house.*
   You are at the corner of Bell Street and Cortland Street. Go north on Bell to Liberty Avenue. Make a right turn on Liberty. Take Liberty to Green Hill Road. Then make a left turn. His house is on the northwest corner of Worth Street and Green Hill Road.

Give the correct directions for the following places.

1 I'm at the corner of Cedar Street and Branch Street. Please give me the directions to *Greenlawn Park.*

2 I'm at Franklin Street and Merritt Road. Please direct me to *The Cass School.*

3 I'm at the corner of Maple Avenue and Cedar Street. How do I get to *Jefferson High School ?*

4 I'm at the corner of Worth Street and Hudson Avenue. Please give me the directions to the *Public Library.*

5 I'm at the corner of Bell Street and Holbrook. How do I get to the *Court House ?*

6 I'm at the corner of Merritt Road and Liberty Avenue. Where is the *North Plains commercial section ?*

Change these orders and directions to polite requests. Use two forms. Notice the first two examples.

1 Open the door.
   Please open the door.
   Would you please open the door ?
2 Come at 7:30.
   Please come at 7:30.
   Would you please come at 7:30 ?
3 Give me the magazine.
4 Shut that window.

5 Finish your work.
6 Come back soon.
7 Call me before 5:30.
8 Mail the letter today.
9 Pass the sugar.
10 Tell me the answer.
11 Bring it to me.
12 Return those books.

Change these orders and directions to polite requests. Use two forms. Notice the first two examples.

1 Shut the door.
   Don't shut the door.
   Please don't shut the door.
2 Sit on the sofa.
   Don't sit on the sofa.
   Please don't sit on the sofa.
3 Put the box there.
4 Move the chairs.

5 Call me after 5:30.
6 Bring your friend today.
7 Tell them about that.
8 Put your coat there.
9 Turn off the light.
10 Turn on the radio.
11 Push the table back.
12 Talk to me now.

Change these orders and directions to suggestions with *let's*. Write the negative form also. Notice the first two examples.

1 Call Fred tonight.
   Let's call Fred tonight.
   Let's not call Fred tonight.
2 Study that lesson now.
   Let's study that lesson now.
   Let's not study that lesson now.
3 Visit Mr. and Mrs. Moore.
4 Learn those words now.

5 Read the newspaper.
6 Walk to school today.
7 Listen to the radio.
8 See that movie.
9 Watch television tonight.
10 Finish the work now.
11 Go to the store.
12 Study those two lessons.

Change the verb in each sentence to the past tense.

1 He *is* in his office.
   He *was* in his office.
2 We *are* almost ready.
   We *were* almost ready.
3 You *are* very late.
   You *were* very late.
4 They *are* at work.
5 It *is* in that drawer.
6 She *is* in Montreal.
7 I *am* very tired.
8 That *is* a surprise.
9 The men *are* angry.
10 Mr. Harris *is* there.
11 You *are* on time.

12 *Is* the teacher here ?
13 *Are* you very tired ?
14 *Am* I right or wrong ?
15 *Are* the lessons easy ?
16 *Is* the sandwich good ?
17 *Are* you in that class ?
18 *Is* that book interesting ?
19 He *is* not in the room.
20 I *am* not very tired.
21 The man *is* not busy.
22 They *ar* not hungry.
23 Miss Brown *is* not here.
24 Those *are* not very easy.
25 That *is* not difficult.

Use the past tense form of the verb in parentheses in each sentence.

1 We (*finish*) the work yesterday. *We finished the work yesterday.*
2 Frank (*borrow*) some money from his friend last night.
3 Mr. Harris (*explain*) the lesson to us very carefully.
4 I (*like*) that movie about life in the Gaspé.
5 That company (*hire*) twenty new workers last year.
6 The students (*study*) those two lessons yesterday.
7 Everyone (*enjoy*) the party very much last night.
8 The driver (*stop*) the bus very quickly.
9 The clerk (*count*) the money two or three times.
10 My friend (*help*) me with my homework this afternoon.
11 André (*describe*) his trip to us after class yesterday.
12 My sister (*stay*) in Europe for two and a half months.
13 All of the students (*copy*) the assignment carefully.
14 The secretary (*omit*) two or three names from the list.

Use the past tense form of the verb in parentheses in each sentence. Check your work with the list of irregular verbs in the appendix.

These irregular verbs are difficult!

1 We (*go*) to a concert.   *We went to a concert.*
2 He (*bring*) his friend.   *He brought his friend.*
3 Antoine (*take*) a course in Spanish last year.
4 We (*find*) Miss Stewart's purse under a chair.
5 Paul (*speak*) to the teacher right after class.
6 Mr. Johnson (*put*) all the papers in his briefcase.
7 You (*make*) several mistakes in the last exercise.
8 I (*drink*) two cups of coffee at breakfast today.
9 Mr. Harris (*tell*) the students the answer to the question.
10 Charles (*leave*) for Sherbrooke three days ago.
11 Mr. and Mrs. Wilson (*sell*) their old house at a low price.
12 The Wilsons (*build*) a new house in Outremont.
13 All of the students (*read*) the assignment carefully.
14 We (*eat*) lunch at the cafeteria with our friends.

Use the past tense form of the verb in parentheses in each sentence.

1 They (*sell*) their house.   *They sold their house.*
2 They (*walk*) to the corner.   *They walked to the corner.*
3 We (*listen*) to that radio program last night.
4 Mr. Johnson (*ride*) downtown with his friend today.
5 The two men (*carry*) the furniture very carefully.
6 Professor Taylor (*teach*) a different class last year.
7 The students (*practice*) the new words after their class.
8 We (*spend*) two and a half weeks in Los Angeles.
9 Everyone in the audience (*enjoy*) the professor's speech.
10 Mr. Wilson (*drive*) his car to work this morning.
11 I (*repeat*) each new word four or five times.
12 The secretary (*put*) the dictionary beside the typewriter.
13 The rain (*stop*) in the middle of the afternoon.
14 The Browns (*receive*) a letter from them several days ago.

Change the following statements to questions. Study the first three examples carefully.

1 They finished the work.   *Did they finish the work ?*
2 They spoke to John.   *Did they speak to John ?*
3 They were in their office.   *Were they in their office ?*
4 Mr. and Mrs. Wilson visited their friends in Chicoutimi.
5 The teacher told the students the answer to the question.
6 That movie about birds in the Arctic was interesting.
7 Mr. Harris explained the meaning of the word to her.
8 Those men from Nova Scotia were at the meeting.
9 The students studied carefully for the examination.
10 The Wilsons sold their house at a low price.
11 The last lesson was very difficult for the students.
12 Their friends watched that television program last night.
13 The man read the instructions in the book very carefully.
14 There were many people at the party last Friday night.

Change the following statements to negatives. Study the first three examples very carefully.

1 He worked very hard.   *He didn't work very hard.*
2 He drove very carefully.   *He didn't drive very carefully.*
3 He was at the meeting.   *He wasn't at the meeting.*
4 The secretary copied the names from the list carefully.
5 Alice ate lunch at the cafeteria with her friends.
6 The students were ready for the examination.
7 Mr. Harris taught at Loyola last summer.
8 The teacher noticed the mistake in that sentence.
9 The last two lessons were very difficult for me.
10 The students brought their dictionaries to class yesterday.
11 The director agreed with his assistants on that matter.
12 There were many people in the audience last night.
13 Mr. Johnson prepared that report for Mr. Wilson.
14 Our friends went to the movies with us on Saturday night.

Use the past tense form of the verb in parentheses in each sentence.

1 The Browns (*take*) a trip last summer.
2 They (*want*) to go out West.
3 First, they (*drive*) to Dorval airport.
4 They (*fly*) to Calgary.
5 Then they (*spend*) one week in Banff.
6 After that, they (*have*) a wonderful time in Vancouver.
7 Next the Browns (*leave*) for San Francisco.
8 They (*see*) many interesting things in Southern California too.
9 The Browns (*buy*) gifts for their friends and relatives.
10 They (*send*) many postcards to their friends and relatives as well.
11 After two weeks, they (*go*) back by air to Montreal.
12 The whole trip (*cost*) them about two thousand dollars.

Use the past tense form of the verb in parentheses in each sentence.

1 Fred (*buy*) a camera from his friend Bill last month.
2 His friend Bill (*sell*) the camera to him for eighty dollars.
3 Fred (*pay*) for the camera in cash.
4 Fred (*know*) almost nothing about photography at the time.
5 Bill (*give*) Fred a book with complete instructions.
6 Fred (*read*) all of the instructions very carefully.
7 Fred (*keep*) the camera in a case for protection.
8 Then Fred (*take*) pictures of all of his friends.
9 Of course, Fred (*hold*) the camera very carefully.
10 Fred (*leave*) the films at a camera store the next day.
11 Fred (*get*) the pictures back two or three days later.
12 All of the pictures (*come out*) very clearly.
13 Fred (*bring*) all of the pictures to class yesterday.
14 Bill (*see*) all of Fred's photographs.
15 Bill (*say*) all of the pictures were very good.
16 Fred (*put*) two or three photographs in his wallet.
17 Fred (*send*) the other photographs to his mother and father.

Use the past tense form of the verb in parentheses in each sentence.

1 My wife and I (*go*) to the party at Bill's house last night.
2 My wife (*wear*) her new silk dress to the party.
3 The party (*begin*) at eight-thirty, but we (*leave*) at eight.
4 We (*meet*) our friends at their house before the party.
5 We (*drive*) our car to their house.
6 Our friends (*ride*) to the party in our car.
7 Fortunately, I (*know*) almost everyone at the party.
8 My wife and I (*speak*) to most of the guests.
9 Everyone (*eat*) lots of sandwiches and cake at the party.
10 Everyone (*drink*) a lot of coffee and beer at the party.
11 Mr. Brown (*tell*) us all about his trip out West.
12 Michael (*bring*) a guitar and an accordion to the party.
13 We (*sing*) all of our favorite songs at the party.
14 Everyone (*have*) a very good time at Bill's party.
15 After the party, my wife and I (*feel*) tired and sleepy.

Use the past tense form of the verb in parentheses in each sentence.

1 Yesterday (*be*) a very bad day for me.
2 I (*begin*) the day with an accident.
3 I (*cut*) my hand with a razor blade.
4 I (*forget*) about the meeting.
5 Then I (*tear*) my new suit.
6 I (*bet*) on a baseball game next.
7 Unfortunately, I (*lose*) my money.
8 Then a thief (*steal*) my wallet.
9 Fortunately, the police (*catch*) the thief a little while later.

10 Later I (*fall*) on some slippery steps and (*hurt*) my arm.
11 Then a little boy (*throw*) a ball and (*hit*) me accidentally.
12 Next an angry dog (*bite*) me and (*tear*) the seat of my pants.
13 After that, I (*fall down*) again and (*break*) my new watch.
14 As a climax, I (*find*) a ten-dollar parking ticket on my car!

QUESTIONS ABOUT "THE BROWNS' TRIP"

1 Did the Browns take a trip last summer ?
2 Did the Browns drive to Calgary ?
3 Did Mr. and Mrs. Brown spend much time in Southern California ?
4 Did they have a good time in Vancouver ?
5 Did the Browns send postcards to their friends ?
6 Did they buy gifts for their friends and relatives ?

37 QUESTIONS ABOUT "THE PHOTOGRAPHER"

1 Did Fred buy a camera from his friend Bill ? (Hold it, please!)
2 Did Fred pay very much for the camera ?
3 Did Fred know a lot about photography at that time ?
4 Did Bill give Fred a book with complete instructions ?
5 Did Fred take a lot of pictures of his friends ?
6 Did Fred put any photographs in his wallet ?

38 QUESTIONS ABOUT "THE PARTY"

1 Did you go to a party at Bill's house last night ?
2 Did you meet your friends before the party ?
3 Did the party begin at seven-thirty or eight-thirty ?
4 Did everyone eat sandwiches and drink coffee at the party ?
5 Did everyone have a good time at the party last night ?
6 Did Michael bring musical instruments to the party ?
7 Did you feel very tired and sleepy after the party ?

39 QUESTIONS ABOUT "MY BAD DAY"

1 Was yesterday a very bad day for you ?
2 Did you cut your hand with a razor blade ?
3 Did you forget about that important meeting in the morning ?
4 Did you lose all of your money on the baseball game ?
5 Did you fall on those slippery steps and hurt your arm ?
6 Did a dog bite you and tear the seat of your pants ?
7 Did you get a parking ticket from a policeman ?

Select the correct verb for each sentence. Use each verb only once. Use only the past tense form of the verb.

choose	1	The boys _went_ home an hour ago.
feel	2	That tree .... three feet last year.
take	3	Bill .... a red tie from the rack.
send	4	I .... a course in Canadian history.
go √	5	The little boy .... the glass window.
meet	6	Alice .... her pen at school yesterday.
lose	7	Mother .... very sick this morning.
stand	8	They .... a letter to Walter yesterday.
fall	9	We .... his speech on the radio.
blow	10	The wind .... very hard last night.
grow	11	I .... on the corner for half an hour.
break	12	We .... our friends there at 5:00 p.m.
hurt	13	He .... on the ice and .... his arm.
hear		

Select the correct verb for each sentence. Use each verb only once. Use only the past tense form of the verb.

build	1	Last year, this class _began_ at 8:30 p.m.
put	2	Mary .... on the slippery steps today.
fall	3	The Browns .... a new house last year.
feel	4	The thief .... jewelry from that store.
fly	5	Miss Davis .... to Sydney with Jane.
bite	6	Frank .... us a long letter last week.
steal	7	He .... his hand with a sharp knife.
tear	8	Mary .... her new dress to the party.
cut	9	Bill .... me fifteen dollars yesterday.
begin √	10	The man .... the door very quietly.
write	11	Mr. Wilson .... the car carefully.
drive	12	She .... the dictionary beside the typewriter.
lend	13	We .... happy because of the news.
shut	14	The dog .... me and .... my clothes.
wear		

Choose the correct verb for each sentence. Use each verb only once. Use only the past tense form of the verb.

sleep	1	Jean .... the answers to the questions.
find	2	I .... the back door a few minutes ago.
speak	3	He .... for ten hours last night.
drive	4	Guy .... to the teacher about that.
know	5	I .... to work by bus this morning.
bring	6	Fred .... quite sick last night.
tell	7	Betty .... the dishes on the shelf.
shut	8	Mr. Harris .... that class last year.
ride	9	We .... ten dollars over the weekend.
spend	10	Charles .... a friend to the party.
feel	11	The teacher .... the students the answer.
put	12	Frank .... the car very carefully.
teach	13	I .... the answer in the appendix.

Choose the correct verb for each sentence. Use each verb only once. Use only the past tense form of the verb.

teach	1	The men .... for Chicago last Tuesday.
win	2	Frank .... to school with his friend.
ride	3	Mr. Moore .... Canadian history last year.
tear	4	They .... the news from their friend.
begin	5	The students .... the story carefully.
leave	6	Our car .... the other car very hard.
hear	7	Fred .... his old car to Mr. Brown.
pay	8	She .... her bracelet under a chair.
find	9	Fred .... the camera from Bill.
speak	10	Fred .... for the camera in cash.
buy	11	He .... to his boss about that matter.
hit	12	The meeting .... at eight-thirty.
sell	13	She .... the paper into two pieces.
read	14	Miss Davis .... a prize in the contest.

Select the correct verb for each sentence. Use each verb only once. Use only the past tense form of the verb.

bring	1 Our team .... the hockey game yesterday.
cut	2 Mr. Smith .... his job last Thursday.
break	3 The other suit .... me very well.
catch	4 The man .... the rope with a knife.
throw	5 The boy .... the butter on his bread.
drive	6 My brother .... me twenty-five dollars.
fit	7 The boys .... the window with a ball.
win	8 He .... the ball to me, and I .... it.
buy	9 The teacher .... in front of the blackboard.
quit	10 Fred's new camera .... eighty dollars.
spread	11 The Browns .... a new house last month.
cost	12 We .... to Toronto in six hours.
stand	13 The students .... their dictionaries to class.
lend	

Select the correct verb for each sentence. Use each verb only once. Use only the past tense form of the verb.

stand	1 He .... the name of the book.
throw	2 She .... the paper into the wastebasket.
sit	3 The meeting .... at eight o'clock sharp.
make	4 He .... the money under the books.
cut	5 I .... in the seat right behind Frank.
hold	6 You .... some mistakes on the test.
cost	7 They .... us fifteen dollars yesterday.
fit	8 We .... on the corner for half an hour.
begin	9 The boys .... the big box very carefully.
forget	10 His new suit .... eighty-five dollars.
keep	11 Tom and Ed .... dinner with Mr. Harris.
lend	12 Fred .... his hand with a sharp knife.
have	13 We .... our car in a garage last winter.
hide	14 Edward's new suit .... him very well.

Change the following statements to questions. Study the first three examples carefully.

1 The men are here now.   *Are the men here now ?*
2 The men are working now.   *Are the men working now ?*
3 There are students in the room. *Are there students in the room ?*
4 René is taking a course in German this semester.
5 The house right next to theirs is Mr. Johnson's.
6 The last lesson was difficult for the students.
7 Miss Peters is writing letters for Mr. Johnson right now.
8 There were a lot of people at Bill's party last night.
9 The men were very tired after all of that hard work.
10 Smith and Green are collecting information for Mr. Johnson.
11 There are many clerks in that big department store.
12 It is raining very hard right now.
13 The man in front of Frank is Mr. Anderson.
14 Mr. Brown is reading the evening newspaper right now.

Change the following statements to questions. Study the first three examples carefully.

1 The man drives very fast.   *Does the man drive very fast ?*
2 The man worked very hard.   *Did the man work very hard ?*
3 The man spoke very fast.   *Did the man speak very fast ?*
4 Mr. Wilson flies to Los Angeles once a month.
5 Those two women come from Lachine.
6 The secretary understood Mr. Wilson's instructions completely.
7 Mr. and Mrs. Johnson borrowed the money from a bank.
8 They watch television every night of the week.
9 Mr. Moore teaches English from nine o'clock to eleven o'clock.
10 Françoise always does her homework very carefully.
11 Tom's friend put his hat and overcoat in the closet.
12 Mr. Johnson works thirty-five hours a week.
13 Miss Peters wrote all of the reports for Mr. Johnson.
14 The two mechanics did that work very quickly.

Use the future tense of the verb in parentheses in each sentence. Use only the future tense with *will*. Study the first three examples carefully.

1 He (*leave*) early tomorrow.   *He will leave early tomorrow.*
2 We (*see*) him next week.   *We will see him next week.*
3 They (*be*) here in ten minutes. *They will be here in ten minutes.*
4 The meeting (*begin*) at nine o'clock tonight.
5 I (*give*) Mr. Brown your message tomorrow night.
6 Mr. Moore (*read*) that story to the students next Monday.
7 The janitor (*lock*) the door to the office at 6:30 p.m.
8 We (*have*) an important holiday two months from now.
9 The men (*be*) here at one-thirty this afternoon.
10 I (*remind*) Mr. Wilson of his appointment with you tonight.
11 Mr. Johnson's wife (*buy*) refreshments for the party.
12 Everyone (*be*) ready at ten o'clock tonight.
13 Mr. Bouchard (*return*) a week from tomorrow.
14 Our friends (*meet*) us at the subway station at five o'clock.

USING THE FUTURE TENSE (1)   49

Change the verb in each sentence to the future tense with *will*. If necessary, change the expression of time (change *yesterday* to *tomorrow*, etc.).

1 We ate lunch with John.   *We will eat lunch with John.*
2 I returned and asked him.   *I will return and ask him.*
3 John spoke to the director's secretary about that matter.
4 Charles went to the movies with his friends last night.
5 The Wilsons flew to Switzerland last year.
6 The clerk wrapped the package and gave her the change.
7 Our guests saw almost all of the city during their vacation.
8 The student wrote a description of his city for the teacher.
9 My friend Edward lent me the money a week ago.
10 Bill sold his camera to Fred and bought a new one.
11 They read that historical novel three weeks ago.
12 Mr. Johnson wore his new winter overcoat to work.
13 My secretary got to the office on time this morning.
14 We got up early and had our breakfast at 7:30.

29

Use the future tense of the verb in parentheses in each sentence. Use only the future tense with *go*. Study the first four examples carefully.

1 I (*finish*) it next week.   *I am going to finish it next week.*
2 He (*go*) there tomorrow.   *He is going to go there tomorrow.*
3 We (*be*) at the meeting.   *We are going to be at the meeting.*
4 I (*return*) and (*ask*) him.   *I am going to return and ask him.*
5 The teacher (*explain*) the next lesson to us tomorrow.
6 We (*attend*) that conference in Quebec City next month.
7 I (*study*) my English lesson with my friends tonight.
8 Mr. Wilson and Mr. Johnson (*be*) in the office all afternoon.
9 We (*go*) to the movies with our friends tomorrow night.
10 Miss Anderson (*invite*) all of her friends to her party.
11 Mr. Harris (*teach*) a different English class next year.
12 My brother (*go*) to Winnipeg with me next week.
13 The men (*repair*) the roof of the house the day after tomorrow.
14 There (*be*) an important meeting here next Thursday evening.

Change the verb in each sentence to the future tense with *go*. If necessary, change the expression of time (change *yesterday* to *tomorrow*, etc.).

1 We went there last night. *We are going to go there tomorrow night.*
2 I saw him two days ago. *I am going to see him two days from now.*
3 The students read the assignment carefully yesterday.
4 Marc spoke to Professor Taylor about that last Thursay.
5 Mr. and Mrs. Brown bought a new house last year.
6 Mr. Foster quit his job last month.
7 I sent my friend a letter and told him about everything.
8 Mr. Moore was the teacher of this class last year.
9 She picked up the paper and threw it into the wastebasket.
10 Tom and Bill had dinner with Mr. Moore and Mr. Harris.
11 Mrs. Johnson wore her new spring coat to the party yesterday.
12 The president made an important announcement on television.
13 My wife bought a new winter overcoat this week.
14 The Browns sold their old house last year and bought a new one.

Change the following statements to questions. Notice the examples.

1 He will go by train.   *Will he go by train ?*
2 They will be there.   *Will they be there ?*
3 Mr. and Mrs. Wilson will arrive in Montreal on Monday.
4 You will finish all the work before tomorrow.
5 Many people will attend the meeting tomorrow night.
6 There will be enough food and coffee for everyone.
7 All of the students will copy the list of words from the book.
8 Normand and Jeanne will be in Halifax a week from now.
9 Your friends will help you with your homework tonight.
10 Mr. Johnson will mail that important letter tomorrow.
11 Dinner will be ready at 7:00 p.m. tonight.
12 The messenger will deliver the package to your house.
13 There will be an important announcement on television tonight.
14 Mr. and Mrs. Robertson will return from Toronto by train.

Change the following statements to questions. Notice the examples.

1 He is going to leave early.   *Is he going to leave early ?*
2 They are going to be there.   *Are they going to be there ?*
3 Gilles is going to eat lunch with us today.
4 Mr. Foster is going to quit his job with the Sandhurst Company.
5 All of the students are going to go to the lecture tonight.
6 You are going to accept his offer for a job with that company.
7 There is going to be a party here next Friday night.
8 His friends are going to leave here the day after tomorrow.
9 Professor Moore is going to explain that lesson to them.
10 We are going to watch that television program tonight.
11 Both Fred and Tom are going to be at the meeting tomorrow.
12 Mrs. Johnson is going to wear her new dress this evening.
13 Mr. Brown is going to take his vacation in August.
14 Frank's friends are going to go to the movies with us tonight.

Change the following statements to negatives. Study the examples.

1 He will explain that lesson.   *He won't explain that lesson.*
2 He will be at the meeting.   *We won't be at the meeting.*
3 Our friends will go to that part of the city tomorrow.
4 The Pronovosts will leave California before January tenth.
5 Mr. Johnson's secretary will be in the office today.
6 Réjean will attend his English class tomorrow afternoon.
7 There will be a meeting here next Thursday evening.
8 The Robertsons will stop in Kingston on their way to Toronto.
9 Miss Peters will finish those reports before Wednesday.
10 Frank and I will be at the library this afternoon.
11 Uncle Dan will eat dinner with us next Sunday.
12 We will need your help with that work tomorrow.
13 The students will be ready for the examination next week.
14 Mr. Wilson will read Mr. Johnson's reports this afternoon.

Change the following statements to negatives. Study the examples.

1 They are going to return. *They aren't going to return.*
2 She is going to be there. *She isn't going to be there.*
3 The Browns are going to buy a new house this year.
4 I am going to answer John's letter this evening.
5 My friend Frank is going to join that club.
6 Miss Stewart and I are going to go shopping this afternoon.
7 The Johnsons' friends are going to be at the party.
8 I am going to ask Mr. Wilson for his advice in this matter.
9 The workmen in that company are going to join a union.
10 Pierre is going to work for a degree at the university.
11 The boss is going to hire another assistant.
12 There are going to be many people here tomorrow night.
13 Smith is going to accept Mr. Wilson's offer for a job.
14 We are going to watch that television program this evening.

Use the future with *go* in place of the future with *will*.

1   I will leave very soon.   *I am going to leave very soon.*
2   He will be ready at five.   *He is going to be ready at five.*
3   I will mail the letter to my brother this afternoon.
4   The president will make an important speech tomorrow.
5   There will be a concert in the park on Friday night.
6   We will eat dinner at six or six-thirty tonight.
7   Mr. Smith will meet us right here after the meeting.
8   Will you be at the library until four o'clock ?
9   She won't clean the house until next Monday morning.
10 Our guests will leave tomorrow night.
11 Will you stop in Trois-Rivières on your way to Quebec City ?
12 Will Mr. Wilson and Mr. Johnson be in the office tomorrow ?
13 There won't be many people in the office this afternoon.
14 The plumber will fix the leak in the bathroom tomorrow.

Use the future with *will* in place of the future with *go*.

1   We are going to go tonight.   *We will go tonight.*
2   She is going to be there too.   *She will be there too.*
3   Our teacher is going to help us with that lesson.
4   Anne-Marie is going to meet us after class today.
5   Are you going to accept Mr. Wilson's offer for a job ?
6   I'm going to study my assignment with Antoine tonight.
7   His friend isn't going to leave until next Thursday or Friday.
8   There's going to be an important meeting here tomorrow.
9   Are you going to be in your office tomorrow afternoon ?
10 No, I'm not going to be in my office tomorrow afternoon.
11 Is Mr. Wilson going to hire a new secretary next week ?
12 Mr. Johnson is going to ride to work with Mr. Smith today.
13 We aren't going to go to Ottawa by train this time.
14 I'm going to return all of the books to you tomorrow morning.

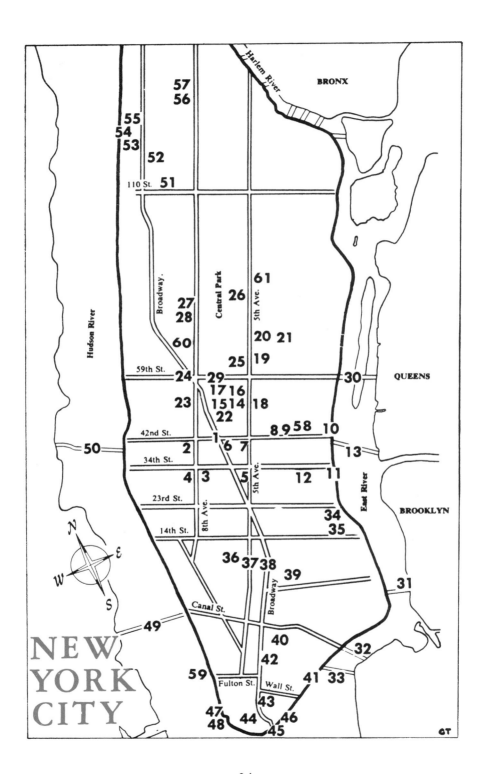

57
56

55
54
53

52

110 St. 51

BRONX

Harlem River

Hudson River

Broadway.

Central Park

5th Ave.

61

26

27
28

60

25

59th St.

24

29

17 16
15 14
22

23

42nd St.

50

2

1

6 7

34th St.

4

3

5

5th Ave.

23rd St.

8th Ave.

14th St.

N
W   E
S

36 37 38

39

Canal St.

49

NEW
YORK
CITY

59

Fulton St.

47
48

44

43

45 46

20 21

19

30

18

QUEENS

8 9 58

10

13

12

11

East River

34

35

BROOKLYN

31

40

42

Wall St.

41

33

32

GT

34

Read this story. Study the use of the verbs carefully.

Mr. and Mrs. Lafleur *are going to take* a trip to New York. They *will leave* Montreal on Sunday. They *are going to fly* on an Air Canada D C 9. They *will arrive* at Dorval airport at 2:00 Sunday afternoon. The plane *will leave* for New York at 2:30. They *will arrive* in New York an hour later. They *are going to stay* at a hotel near Times Square.

They *will get up* early on Monday. They *will eat* breakfast and *leave* the hotel before nine o'clock. They *are going to walk* through the area between 34th Street and 42nd Street. They *will start* at Pennsylvania Station at 34th Street. Then they *will go* to Macy's and Gimbel's, two of New York's largest department stores, on Sixth Avenue. They *will* also *visit* one of the tallest buildings in New York, the Empire State Building (1250 ft.). They *are going to go* up to the top of the building. They *will see* all of New York City from there. Then they *are going to walk* to the Metropolitan Opera House and the famous New York Public Library. They *are going to go* to bed early that night. They *will be* very tired.

They *are going to walk* to First Avenue and 42nd Street on Tuesday. On the way, they *will pass* the Air Canada office at 80, East 42nd Street. Then they *will see* the beautiful United Nations buildings along the East River. They *will go* on a guided tour through the buildings. Next they *will walk* down the street to the New York University Medical Center between 34th Street and 30th Street. Then they *will return* to their hotel. They're *going to eat* dinner with some old friends that evening.

They *are going to walk* along Park Avenue and Fifth Avenue on Wednesday. Mrs. Lafleur *is going to buy* presents for her relatives in

GUIDE TO MAP OF NEW YORK CITY : 1 Times Square. 2 the Port Authority Bus Terminal. 3 Pennsylvania Station. 4 the U.S. General Post Office. 5 the Empire State Building. 6 the Metropolitan Opera House. 7 the New York Public Library. 8 Grand Central Terminal. 9 the Chrysler Building. 10 the United Nations. 11 the New York University Medical Center. 12 the East Side Airlines Terminal. 13 the Queens-Midtown Tunnel. 14 Rockefeller Center. 15 Radio City Music Hall. 16 the Museum of Modern Art. 17 the Whitney Museum of American Art. 18 St. Patrick's Cathedral. 19 Temple Emanu-El. 20 the Frick Collection. 21 Hunter College. 22 Quebec House. 23 Madison Square Garden. 24 the New York Coliseum. 25 the Central Park Zoo. 26 the Metropolitan Museum of Art. 27 the Hayden Planetarium. 28 the American Museum of Natural History. 29 Carnegie Endowment Center. 30 the Queensboro Bridge. 31 the Williamsburg Bridge. 32 the Manhattan Bridge. 33 the Brooklyn Bridge. 34 Peter Cooper Village. 35 Stuyvesant Town. 36 Greenwich Village. 37 Washington Square. 38 New York University (downtown section). 39 the Bowery. 40 Chinatown. 41 the Fulton Fish Market. 42 City Hall. 43 the New York Stock Exchange. 44 Battery Park. 45 Brooklyn Battery Tunnel. 46 the Ferry to Staten Island. 47 the Ferry to Ellis Island. 48 the Ferry to the Statue of Liberty. 49 the Holland Tunnel. 50 the Lincoln Tunnel. 51 Cathedral of St. John the Divine. 52 Columbia University. 53 Riverside Church. 54 Grant's Tomb. 55 the International House. 56 City College of New York (C.C.N.Y.) 57 Lewisohn Stadium. 58 Air Canada Office. 59 World Trade Center. 60 Lincoln Center. 61 Guggenheim Museum.

some of the Fifth Avenue stores. After that, they *will go* west to the theater district between 40th Street and 46th Street. They *are going to attend* a popular Broadway play that evening.

Mr. and Mrs. Lafleur *will see* the area north of 46th Street on Thursday. They *will spend* several hours at Rockefeller Center. Just before they *will get* there, they *will see* Quebec House at 17, West 50th Street. At the Rockefeller Center, they *will see* the Radio City Music Hall. In this same general area, they *will* also *visit* the Museum of Modern Art, the Whitney Museum of American Art, the Temple Emanu-El, St. Patrick's Cathedral, and Hunter College. Perhaps they *will* also *have* time to see the Guggenheim Museum. Finally, they *will go* crosstown to Madison Square Garden and the New York Coliseum at Columbus Circle.

They *are going to visit* the zoo in Central Park on Friday. Their other stops on that day *will be* at the Metropolitan Museum of Art, the American Museum of Natural History, the Lincoln Center, and the Hayden Planetarium. They *are going to attend* a concert at the Carnegie Endowment Center that evening.

They *are going to drive* through downtown New York on Saturday. They *will see* several large bridges along the East River. They *will go* through Greenwich Village. At nearby Washington Square, they *are going to visit* the downtown section of New York University, one of the largest universities in the world. After that, they *will visit* the Bowery, Chinatown, City Hall, Wall Street, and Battery Park. They *will finish* their day with a trip by ferry boat to the Statue of Liberty on Liberty Island. From the ferry boat, they *will be able to see* the new World Trade Center.

The Lafleurs *are going to visit* Columbia University at 116th Street and Broadway on Sunday. They *will* also *see* the Cathedral of St. John the Divine, the Riverside Church, Grant's Tomb, and the International House, all in the same area. They *will meet* students and visitors from all over the world at the International House. Later in the day, they *are going to drive* to C.C.N.Y., Lewisohn Stadium, the Polo Grounds, Yankee Stadium, and the Cloisters at 198th Street. They *will end* their day at the world-famous Bronx Zoo.

Mr. and Mrs. Lafleur *are going to return* to Montreal by train. In this way, they *will see* the countryside. They *will visit* some more friends on Monday and Tuesday. They *will go* back on Wednesday. Of course, they *are going to describe* their wonderful trip to all of their friends.

Give a complete answer for each of the following questions.

1   Are Mr. and Mrs. Lafleur going to take a trip ?
2   Will they leave Montreal on Saturday or Sunday ?
3   Are they going to go to New York by train or by air ?
4   Will the plane leave for New York at 8:45 or 9:15 ?
5   Are they going to stay at a hotel on Park Avenue ?
6   Are they going to eat breakfast and leave the hotel early ?
7   Will they have much trouble with directions in New York ?
8   Are they going to see the Empire State Building ?
9   Will they go to the zoo in Central Park on Monday ?
10   Are they going to visit the New York Public Library ?
11   Will they be very tired at the end of their first day ?
12   Are they going to go to bed very late on Monday night ?
13   Will they go through the United Nations Building ?
14   Are the Lafleurs going to go to their hotel after that ?
15   Are they going to eat dinner with friends on Tuesday night ?
16   Will they stay at their hotel on the following day ?
17   Are they going to go to the downtown section on Wednesday ?
18   Are they going to walk along Park Avenue and Fifth Avenue on Wednesday ?
19   Is Mrs. Lafleur going to buy presents for her relatives ?
20   Will the Lafleurs attend a Broadway play that night ?
21   Are they going to spend time at Rockefeller Center too ?
22   Will they visit any museums in this same area ?
23   Are they going to visit the zoo in Central Park on Friday ?
24   Are they going to drive through downtown New York ?
25   Will they see Columbia University or New York University ?
26   Are they going to drive through Greenwich Village ?
27   Will the Lafleurs return to Montreal on Saturday ?
28   Are they going to see the downtown section on Sunday ?
29   Are the Lafleurs going to visit the International House ?
30   Will the Lafleurs describe their trip to all of their friends ?
31   Are they going to return to Montreal by plane ?
32   Will they get back on Wednesday ?

Use *much, many,* or *very* in the blank space or spaces in each sentence.

1 We made .... sandwiches.
2 Did you buy .... meat ?
3 The food was .... delicious.
4 We bought .... food for the party.
5 The guests drank .... coffee.
6 Was the coffee .... strong ?
7 I enjoy coffee ....
8 I don't drink .... milk.
9 You didn't invite .... guests.

10 There were .... glasses on the table in the dining room.
11 There was .... milk and coffee in the kitchen.
12 There weren't .... people at the party last night.
13 Mary and Louise bought .... bread for the sandwiches.
14 The two girls used .... pieces of bread for the sandwiches.

Use *much, many,* or *very* in the blank space or spaces in each sentence.

1 Our last two English lessons were .... long.
2 The students had .... difficulty with the last lesson.
3 Did you have .... trouble with the homework today ?
4 The last lesson was .... difficult for everyone.
5 Did you spend .... time on your homework last night ?
6 I wrote each new word in the lesson .... times.
7 Does your English teacher give you .... homework ?
8 Mr. Harris, our teacher, has a .... clear voice.
9 Our teacher speaks .... slowly and .... clearly.
10 We learn .... new English words in class every day.
11 Does your friend Marcel speak .... English ?
12 Do Hélène and Jeanne speak English .... well ?
13 On the whole, the English language is .... easy.
14 .... people all over the world speak English these days.

Substitute the expressions *a lot of* and *lots of* for *much* or *many* in each sentence.

1 Guy spends *much* time on his assignments.
   Guy spends *a lot of* time on his assignments.
   Guy spends *lots of* time on his assignments.
2 There are *many* people in the auditorium now.
   There are *a lot of* people in the auditorium now.
   There are *lots of* people in the auditorium now.
3 The students learn many new words every day.
4 Georges drinks much coffee every day.
5 There are many short words in the English language.
6 Miss Lemieux puts much cream in her coffee.
7 That student from Spain has many friends.
8 Frank receives many letters from his friends and relatives.
9 There are many students in the classroom right now.
10 We had much trouble with the sentences on that page.

Use *too, too much,* or *too many* in the blank space in each sentence.

1 The waitress put .... cream and sugar in my coffee.
2 You made .... mistakes. Write the lesson again.
3 Mr. Duncan gave us .... homework. It was .... difficult.
4 There are .... people in this room. It's .... hot !
5 You spoke .... fast and used .... hard words for me.
6 There are .... pictures and .... different colors in this room.
7 The radio is .... loud now. It's making .... noise.
8 I drank .... coffee and ate .... sandwiches last night.
9 There are .... things in the suitcase. Its .... heavy.
10 You put .... water in the glasses. They're .... full.
11 That old house is .... large and has .... rooms.
12 That program has .... advertising and .... interruptions.
13 That work took .... time. It was .... trouble for us.
14 That fellow was .... impatient. He made mistakes .... times.

Use *some* or *any* in the blank space in each sentence. Study the examples.

1 There are *some* students in the room now.
2 Are there *any* students in the classroom now ?
3 I had *some* trouble with my homework last night.
4 I didn't have *any* trouble with my homework last night.
5 There were .... beautiful pictures on the wall.
6 The students didn't have .... difficulty with the lesson.
7 The children are eating .... ice cream in the kitchen.
8 Jacques doesn't want .... dessert after dinner tonight.
9 Are there .... cigarettes in the box on the table ?
10 Mr. Duncan didn't give us .... specific instructions.
11 Are there .... extra chairs in the other classroom ?
12 Your secretary has .... important messages for you.
13 I'm sorry. I don't have .... information about that.
14 Did the teacher make .... comments on your paper ?

Use *something* or *anything* in the blank space in each sentence.

1 Is there .... on Mr. Cromwell's desk right now ?
2 Yes, Mr. Cromwell put .... there a few minutes ago.
3 Did you say .... to Mr. Lewis about our plans ?
4 No, I didn't say .... at all to him about our plans.
5 Is there .... in the middle drawer of that desk ?
6 There isn't .... there. I looked in the drawer.
7 Did Mrs. Drouin find .... in the boxes in the closet ?
8 Yes, she did. She found .... in the small red box.
9 Is Mr. Evans going to tell us .... about his trip ?
10 Yes, he's going to tell us .... about his trip.
11 Did the girls buy .... at that department store ?
12 No, Alice and Louise didn't buy .... at the store today.
13 Did the mailman bring .... for me this morning ?
14 Yes, he did. There's .... for you on the desk in your room.

Choose *someone* or *anyone* for the blank space in each sentence.

1 Listen ! There is .... at the front door now.
2 Mr. Grégoire didn't tell .... about his suggestion.
3 Did you see .... in the hall outside my office ?
4 Paul doesn't have a book. He lent his to ....
5 There will be .... in this office before 9:00 a.m.
6 Please don't tell .... about this matter until later.
7 Did you ask .... to help you with the work tomorrow ?
8 .... left this package on your desk this morning.
9 Please give this envelope to .... in Dean Tallard's office.
10 Do you know .... in the advanced class ?
11 There wasn't .... in the office after 5:30 p.m.
12 .... told Mr. Duncan the news a few minutes ago.
13 Mr. Lamb didn't talk to .... about his problem.
14 The secretary is speaking to .... on the telephone now.

Choose *anyone* or *no one* for the blank space in each sentence.

1 There was .... at the information desk this morning.
2 There isn't .... in Mr. Tallard's office now.
3 .... finished the examination before three o'clock.
4 Jean didn't see .... in Dean Tallard's office.
5 Jean saw .... in the hall outside the office either.
6 He didn't notice .... in the other room. He's sure of that.
7 .... in the whole class knew that word.
8 Please don't tell .... about this until next Friday.
9 I will tell .... about your plans until that time.
10 .... knows a thing about this except you and me.
11 I don't know .... in the other two English classes.
12 I saw .... from our class at the meeting yesterday.
13 .... said anything to me about it at the meeting.
14 The chairman didn't get suggestions from .... in the audience.

PART ONE : THE INDIRECT OBJECT WITH *TO*

Change the position of the word or words in italics (the indirect object) and omit the word *to*. Study the first two examples carefully.

  1 Philippe gave the money to *me*.   *Philippe gave me the money.*
  2 I wrote a letter to *Mr. Hill*.   *I wrote Mr. Hill a letter.*
  3 The agent sold the house to *Mr. and Mrs. Hanson*.
  4 We gave a birthday present to *Jean* yesterday.
  5 Mr. Johnson sent a letter to *the Apollo Company*.
  6 Did the boy throw the baseball to *his friend*?
  7 Tom handed the books and envelopes to *me*.
  8 Miss Wilson sent some beautiful flowers to *us*.
  9 Mrs. Baker wrote a letter to *her son* last Friday.
 10 Please give your paper to *me* right now.
 11 Our friends sent the package to *us* the next day.
 12 The teacher told an interesting story to *the students*.
 13 I showed all of the photographs to *my friends*.
 14 Professor Moore gave some excellent advice to *all of us*.

PART TWO : THE INDIRECT OBJECT WITHOUT *TO*

Change the position of the word or words in italics (the indirect object) and add the word *to*. Study the first two examples carefully.

  1 I told *him* the story.   *I told the story to him.*
  2 We wrote *them* a letter.   *We wrote a letter to them.*
  3 Dr. Davis gave *Charles* the tickets.
  4 Did the manager offer *that fellow* the job?
  5 Mr. Houle told *us* the story of his narrow escape.
  6 Ruth and Betty sent *Mary* a birthday gift last week.
  7 Did Mr. Kennedy lend *his brother* the money?
  8 Mr. Filion told *us* an interesting story last night.
  9 Are you going to write *George* a letter soon?
 10 Please lend *me* your pen and pencil for a few minutes.
 11 My wife sent *them* the package last Thursday or Friday.
 12 The Bakers read *us* all of those interesting letters.
 13 Are you going to show *the people* your photographs tonight?
 14 Mr. and Mrs. Brown mailed *us* a lovely gift from Vancouver.

Write the correct form of the verb in parentheses in each sentence. Use only the
simple present tense (examples : *he works, they study*) or the continuous present
tense (examples : *he is working, they are studying*).

1 I often   (*leave*)   town over the weekend.
2 Miss Peters   (*use*)   the telephone now.
3 The children always   (*go*)   to bed early.
4 Mrs. Johnson   (*prepare*)   dinner now.
5 Look ! That boy   (*run*)   into the house.
6 Jean-Guy   (*understand*)   those words.
7 The students   (*finish*)   their papers now.
8 I   (*need*)   some money for my textbooks.
9 The guests   (*watch*)   that television program now.
10 We   (*review*)   the use of the tenses in English this week.
11 Yes, Marjorie   (*want*)   some cake and coffee.
12 I   (*go*)   to bed around eleven o'clock during the week.
13 We never   (*go*)   to the library in the evening.
14 Mr. Harris   (*teach*)   English from 2:00 to 5:00 p.m.
15 Mr. and Mrs. Stewart   (*fly*)   to California every winter.
16 Jacques Bouchard   (*work*)   thirty-eight hours a week.
17 I   (*hear*)   the sound of a car outside.
18 Our English class always   (*start*)   at 8:30 p.m.
19 I   (*read*)   an interesting book about Expo 67.
20 Mr. Smith's secretary   (*sit*)   at another desk today.
21 The weather   (*get*)   very hot here in July and August.
22 My friend   (*study*)   his English lesson one hour every night.
23 Mr. Rockwell   (*pay*)   his bills at the end of every month.
24 That tall fellow in my class   (*come*)   from Châteauguay.
25 Professor Moore   (*write*)   another book about English.
26 It   (*rain*)   very much in this region in the spring.
27 Frank   (*have*)   a bad cold. He   (*take*)   some medicine for it.
28 That department store   (*have*)   a big sale on shoes today.
29 Listen ! I   (*think*)   someone   (*knock*)   at the front door.
30 I   (*see*)   the airplane now. It   (*come*)   in this direction.
31 Pierre always   (*do*)   his English lessons very carefully.
32 The students   (*do*)   Exercice 69 right now.

Change the following sentences to simple questions. Notice the examples.

  1 That man is Mr. Harris.   *Is that man Mr. Harris ?*
  2 There are chairs in that room.   *Are there chairs in that room ?*
  3 He is studying right now.   *Is he studying right now ?*
  4 They will return soon.   *Will they return soon ?*
  5 The last lesson was very difficult for the students.
  6 Mr. Chase is listening to the radio right now.
  7 The Andersons will travel to Greece by air.
  8 Danielle is taking a course in history this semester.
  9 Mr. and Mrs. Kennedy are going to stay at a hotel.
10 There were a lot of people at the party last night.
11 His friends will get the train at 9:00 a.m.
12 The men were very tired after all of the hard work.
13 Miss Stewart is going to be busy this afternoon.
14 There will be a meeting here next Thursday night.

Change the following statements to simple questions. Notice the examples.

  1 Fred drives carefully.   *Does Fred drive carefully ?*
  2 They study every evening.   *Do they study every evening ?*
  3 She bought a new dress.   *Did she buy a new dress ?*
  4 Mr. Harper walked downtown with his friend.
  5 The students in that class always work very hard.
  6 Mr. Williams knows Professor Moore very well.
  7 Tom's friend finished all of the work for him.
  8 Miss Stewart wore her new spring dress yesterday.
  9 The students had trouble with the first part of the lesson.
10 Françoise does her homework for this class in the evening.
11 The two plumbers did the work in the basement quickly.
12 André always comes to this class on time.
13 Miss Cunningham put the money in the top desk drawer.
14 All of the students understand the last two lessons.

Change the following statements to simple questions.

1 The men are waiting in the other room now.
2 Carole learned all of the new words by heart.
3 Our teacher will explain that lesson to us tomorrow.
4 That department store is having a big sale today.
5 Mr. and Mrs. Grégoire are going to write to us from Italy.
6 Mr. Kennedy usually leaves his car in the alley.
7 The students are copying the sentences from the blackboard.
8 That fellow lost his temper during the argument.
9 The mechanic did all of the work very carefully.
10 The students' papers will be on Mr. Cromwell's desk.
11 Your friend had a good time at the party last night.
12 The men will finish all of their work before next Friday.
13 Mrs. Wilson took her sister downtown in her car.
14 His secretary sent the letter to that company by airmail.

Change the following statements to negatives. Study the examples carefully.

1 François knows that word. *François doesn't know that word.*
2 Lucien is studying his lessons now. *Lucien isn't studying his lessons now.*
3 He will be there tomorrow. *He won't be there tomorrow.*
4 There were many people at the meeting yesterday.
5 My friend always studies his lessons at the library.
6 Mr. Harris taught this same English class last year.
7 Fred's cousin will get back here before two-thirty.
8 Professor Moore put some papers on his desk.
9 The students are talking to their teacher right now.
10 Jacques has his English lessons in the afternoon.
11 You had the right answer to that question on your paper.
12 Mr. Johnson's secretary is writing letters for him right now.
13 I am working on my English assignment right now.
14 Mrs. Franklin called her friend and told her the news.
15 My assistant will have enough time for that this week.

Give short answers to these questions. Use personal pronouns (*you, it, they,* etc.) or *there* in the short answer. Use contractions only for short answers with *no.*

QUESTION	SHORT ANSWER
1 Is Mrs. Smith in the other room ?	Yes, *she is.*
2 Does the man like strong coffee ?	No, *he doesn't.*
3 Will you be ready before three o'clock ?	No, *I won't*
4 Is there going to be a meeting tonight ?	Yes, *there is.*
5 Is the alarm clock ringing right now ?	No, *it isn't.*
6 Are the students ready for the test ?	Yes, ...
7 Do these students work very hard ?	No, ...
8 Were the last two lessons difficult ?	Yes, ...
9 Do you want a cheese sandwich ?	Yes, ...
10 Was there a book on Mr. Cromwell's desk ?	No, ...
11 Did Mrs. Burke's sister go with you ?	Yes, ...
12 Will Marjorie answer the phone for us ?	Yes, ...
13 Did the men move the furniture ?	No, ...
14 Are you going to study Italian ?	No, ...
15 Were there many people at the concert ?	Yes, ...
16 Do you know the answer to that question ?	No, ...
17 Does the bus stop at the next corner ?	Yes, ...
18 Will Dr. Duncan's speech be interesting ?	Yes, ...
19 Did that woman find her purse ?	No, ...
20 Was there a chair in the other room ?	No, ...
21 Will the Browns travel to Spain by boat ?	No, ...
22 Is the weather warm in the spring ?	Yes, ...
23 Are you working on your assignment ?	Yes, ...
24 Does Henri study every night ?	No, ...
25 Will this be enough money for everything ?	Yes, ...
26 Were there enough sandwiches on the plate ?	No, ...
27 Do your friends like the United States ?	Yes, ...
28 Did the women attend the meeting too ?	No, ...
29 Are the children sleeping right now ?	Yes, ...
30 Was this a very difficult assignment ?	No, ...

William Colin Hill was born in Vancouver in 1923. He lived there with his parents until 1929. Then his parents moved to Toronto. He and his two brothers finished elementary school in Toronto. He finished in 1936. His father started a business in Hamilton the next year. Therefore, he attended high school in that city. He received his diploma in 1941. Unfortunately, he didn't have enough money for a university education. His first job was working in the office of a shoe factory. He worked there for two years. He was the assistant bookkeeper. He married Miss Rosemary White in 1942. In 1943, he became a salesman for a metal products company. He didn't enjoy that job at all. Therefore, he quit the job six months later. He and his wife moved to Quebec that year, and he found a job. He started his own business in

William Colin Hill

Montreal in 1945. Unfortunately, his business failed after only six months. He lost almost $10,000. Then he was sales manager for a small container corporation for seven years. Between 1944 and 1951, Mr. Hill and his wife had four children. The first child was born in 1944, and the last child was born in 1950. In 1953, Mr. Hill started another business. He called his business the Hilltop Company. His business was very successful this time and he made a lot of money. Between 1959 and 1961, he and his wife traveled across Canada and through the northern United States. He learned much valuable information for his business. Their eldest son, Thomas, went to McGill in 1963. Mr. Hill retired from active business life in 1967. After that, he and his wife moved to Europe for four years. Their daughter, Linda, lived in Europe with them for a year. While she was there, she learned Spanish in only eight months. Their other two sons, Philip and Kevin, graduated from Queens University in 1970 and 1971 respectively. Thomas got married in 1967 and has two children now. Linda is still going to university. She is working for a degree at Laval. Mr. Hill is going to school now too. He is going to a university because he wants to complete his education. He started two years ago. He will finish his university courses two years from now. Then he will finally have his degree, like his children.

Answer the following questions about the story on the previous page.

1 Where was William Colin Hill born? 2 When was he born? 3 How long did he live in Vancouver? 4 Where did he finish elementary school? 5 When did he finish elementary school? 6 Who finished elementary school with him? 7 In what city did he go to high school? 8 Why did he attend high school there? 9 When did he receive his high school diploma? 10 Why didn't he go to university? 11 Where was his first job? 12 How long did he work at the shoe factory? 13 What was his position there? 14 Whom did he marry? 15 What was his wife's maiden name? 16 When did he marry her? 17 What did he do after that? 18 What kind of company did he work for? 19 What did he do for that company? 20 How did he like his job there? 21 How many months did he work there? 22 What province did he and his wife move to? 23 When did he start his own business? 24 Where did he start his own business? 25 When did his business fail? 26 How much money did he lose? 27 What kind of company did he work for next? 28 How long did he work for that company? 29 When was the Hills' first child born? 30 When were their other children born? 31 How many children do the Hills have? 32 What did Mr. Hill do in 1953? 33 What did he name his business? 34 How did his business do? 35 Where did the Hills travel after this? 36 When did they go? 37 What did Mr. Hill learn? 38 Where did Thomas go in 1963? 39 When did Mr. Hill retire from active business life? 40 Where did the Hills move then? 41 When did they move? 42 Who went with them? 43 Where were the other children? 44 How long did Linda live in Europe with them? 45 What language did Linda learn? 46 How long did it take her? 47 When did their two other sons graduate from Queens University? 48 When did Thomas get married? 49 How many children do Thomas and his wife have now? 50 Where is Linda going to university? 51 What is Mr. Hill doing at present? 52 Why is he doing it? 53 When will he graduate? 54 Whom will he then be like?

Answer these questions about your English class. Read the questions carefully. Notice the position of all the words in the question. Compare the position of the words in the questions with the position of the words in your answers.

1 Why are you studying English? 2 Why are you going to this school? 3 When did you start your English course? 4 How long ago did you start to learn English? 5 At what school are you studying English now? 6 Where did you study English before this? 7 How many years did you study English before this? 8 What is your teacher's name? 9 Where does your teacher live? 10 How do you like your English class? 11 What is the title of your textbook? 12 At what time does your English class begin? 13 How long does your English class last? 14 How long is each class period? 15 What do you do during the first ten minutes? 16 What are you doing right now? 17 What is your teacher talking about right now? 18 At what time is your class over? 19 How many classes do you attend each week? 20 What lesson are you studying this week? 21 When do you usually study your homework? 22 How much time do you spend on your homework? 23 Whom do you study your lessons with? 24 With whom do you practice pronunciation? 25 How many sentences do you write every day? 26 What did your teacher talk about yesterday? 27 What is your teacher going to talk about tomorrow? 28 How many hours are you going to study at home next week? 29 How often do you speak English outside this class? 30 When is your teacher going to give an examination? 31 Which lesson was the most difficult for you? 32 Why was it the most difficult for you? 33 Do you find that lesson easier now? 34 How many new words did you learn yesterday? 35 How many English words do you know in all? 36 How many exercises are there in this book? 37 How many pages are there in this book? 38 How many mistakes did you make on the last exercise? 39 How often does your teacher dictate sentences to you? 40 How often does your teacher give you a vocabulary test? 41 How many exercises does your teacher assign each week? 42 How often do you write letters in English? 43 Which exercise are you writing right now? 44 At what time did you get to school today? 45 How did you get to school today? 46 How do you usually get to school? 47 Who sits beside you in your classroom?

Answer these questions about your life. Read the questions carefully. Notice the use of the question words (*when, why, how, how many, how long*, etc.)

1   When were you born?   2   How old are you now?   3   In what town or city were you born?   4   Where did you go to elementary school?   5   What other schools did you go to?   6   How big is your family?   7   How many brothers and sisters do you have?   8   How old are they?   9   Where do your brothers go to school?   10   Where do your sisters go to school?   11   How long did you attend your last school?   12   What subjects did you study?   13   What was your favorite subject?   14   How well do you speak and write English?   15   How long are you going to stay at this school?   16   How long are you going to study English?   17   Where do you live?   18   What is your address?   19 Who is your best friend?   20 What do you plan to do in the future?   21   Why do you want to do that?   22   Where do you usually go over the weekend?   23   What do you usually do on Saturday and Sunday?   24   What did you do last weekend?   25   What are you going to do next weekend?   26   What is your favorite sport?   27   What is your hobby?   28   Do you have more than one hobby?   29   What are your other hobbies?   30   How much time do you spend on your hobby, or hobbies, each week?   31   Do you know many people in this town?   32   How many of the students in your English class do you know?   33   When did you have your last vacation?   34   Where did you go on your last vacation?   35   When are you going to take your next vacation?   36   Where are you going to go on that vacation?   37   What are you going to do after this semester?   38   At what time do you usually get up in the morning?   39   At what time do you get up on Saturday and Sunday?   40   What kind of breakfast do you usually eat?   41   At what time do you usually leave home for school?   42   Where do you generally eat lunch?   43   What is your father's profession?   44   Where does he work?   45   How does he get to work?   46   How long has he worked there?   47   When does he get home?   48   What is the first thing he does when he gets home?   49   What do your parents do over the weekend?   50   How many uncles and aunts do you have?   51   What are their names?   52   How many cousins do you have?   53   How old are they?   54   What are their names?

Choose *where, when,* or *why* for each question. Read the short answer at the right. Then choose the appropriate question word.

	QUESTION	ANSWER
1	.... did you put your books ?	On the desk.
2	.... did you speak to Mr. Adams ?	Two days ago.
3	.... do you need the money now ?	To buy a suit.
4	.... will they arrive at the airport ?	About ten o'clock.
5	.... did that accident happen ?	At the intersection.
6	.... are you going to go home now ?	Because it's late.
7	.... do you keep your car ?	In our garage.
8	.... did you go to the library ?	To get a book.
9	.... does summer start in Canada ?	In June.
10	.... were you late for class today ?	I missed my bus.
11	.... will you spend your vacation ?	In New England.
12	.... are you going to tell them the news ?	Tomorrow night.
13	.... is there a telephone in this building ?	Beside the elevator.
14	.... are you taking a course in English ?	I need practice.

(a) Change each statement to a simple question. (b) Change the simple question to a question with the word *why.* Study the first example.

1 Susanne went downtown after school today.

   (a) *Did Susanne go downtown after school today ?*

   (b) *Why did Susanne go downtown after school today ?*

2 Christian borrowed a dictionary from his friend.

3 The Drouins are going to travel by train.

4 Mr. Slater sold his house in Pierrefonds.

5 Those two men were late for work today.

6 Mr. Moore usually comes to school by bus.

7 That student spoke to the teacher after class.

8 They sent the letters to the wrong address.

9 Your friend took those two books back to the library.

10 Marjorie called her sister and told her the news.

11 Luc will be absent from his English class tomorrow.

12 Bill gets off the bus there and transfers to another one.

13 I'm going to leave my house early tomorrow morning.

Why will ..
Why did ...
Why are ...

Read this schedule carefully. Then answer all the questions in the next exercise. For additional practice, change all the verbs in the schedule to the past tense.

He gets up at 7:30 in the morning. He takes a shower at 7:45 a.m. He gets dressed at 8:00 a.m. He eats his breakfast at 8:20 a.m. He leaves for the office at 8:40 a.m. He takes a taxi at the corner at 8:45 a.m. He gets to the office at 9:00 a.m. He dictates letters to his secretary at 9:30 a.m. He reads the morning mail at 10:00 a.m. He goes out for coffee at 10:30 a.m. He returns to the office at 11:00 a.m. He has a conference with the other executives at 11:30 a.m. He leaves the office at 12:30 p.m. He has his lunch at the Old Hotel at 1:00 p.m. He returns to his office at 1:30 p.m. He calls his secretary into his office at 1:45 p.m. He dictates answers to the morning mail at 1:45 p.m. He meets important visitors between 2:00 p.m. and 3:00 p.m. He discusses problems with his two assistants between 3:00 p.m. and 3:30 p.m. He makes most of his important telephone calls after 3:30 p.m. He goes over the company reports between 4:00 pm. and 4:30 p.m. He catches a taxi in front of his office at 5:45 p.m. He gets back home at 6:00 p.m. He eats dinner with his wife and children at 6:30 p.m. He reads the evening newspaper between 7:30 pm. and 8:30 p.m.

Supply the correct words for the blank spaces in each question. Note : In this type of question, the word *at* is often omitted.

1 At what time   *does*   *he*   *get up*   in the morning ?
2 At what time .... a shower ?
3 At what time .... his breakfast ?
4 At what time .... for the office ?
5 At what time .... a taxi at the corner ?
6 At what time .... to the office ?
7 At what time .... letters to his secretary ?
8 At what time .... his lunch at the hotel ?
9 At what time .... answers to the mail ?
10 At what time .... important visitors ?
11 At what time .... his telephone calls ?
12 At what time .... the company reports ?
13 At what time .... the evening newspaper ?
14 At what time .... dinner with his family ?

Study these questions and short answers carefully. Pay special attention to the order of words. Some of the questions have statement word order. Indicate with a check the questions with statement word order.

QUESTION ANSWER

1	Who invited George to dinner ?	The Taylors.
2	Whom did the Taylors invite to dinner ?	George.
3	What did the Taylors serve for dinner ?	Roast beef.
4	What happened after dinner ?	Nothing special.
5	Who used Pierre's dictionary in class ?	Philippe.
6	Whose dictionary did Philippe use in class ?	Pierre's.
7	Whose dictionary is on my desk ?	Mine.
8	Which dictionary is yours ? There are two.	The small one.
9	What is the name of your dictionary ?	"Word Guide."
10	Who is going to speak to Dr. Duncan ?	I am.
11	Whom are you going to speak to ?	Dr. Duncan.
12	To whom is Mr. Burke going to send a letter ?	To the editor.
13	Who is going to send a letter to the editor ?	Mr. Burke.
14	What is Mr. Burke going to send to the editor ?	A letter.
15	What supplies the power for this motor ?	A generator.
16	Who supplies the electricity for this building ?	The Electric Co.
17	What color did you paint your house ?	Blue and white.
18	Which color did you use more ?	White.
19	Who sent that package to Miss Davis ?	I sent it.
20	To whom did you send that package ?	To Miss Davis.
21	What did you send to Miss Davis ?	That package.
22	Whose books are on that table ?	Dick's.
23	Which is Tom's : the red one or the blue one ?	The red one.
24	Whom did your friends meet at the corner ?	Mr. Kennedy.
25	With whom did your friends ride to school ?	With Mr. Fox.
26	Whom did they ride downtown with ?	With George.
27	Who drove them back home afterwards ?	George.
28	What kind of car does George have ?	A Ford.
29	What model does he have ?	A Pinto.
30	Whose car is in front of your house now ?	Mr. Kennedy's.

Study these questions with *how*. Notice the short answers at the right.

QUESTION	ANSWER
1 How did you do that work ?	With some tools.
2 How is the weather today ?	Quite chilly.
3 How often do you watch television ?	Twice a week.
4 How did you get here this morning ?	By bus.
5 How do you like the weather here ?	Very much.
6 How long will you stay in Nova Scotia ?	Two months.
7 How many students are there here ?	Twenty-one.
8 How much coffee did you drink today ?	Three cups.

Use adjectives (*big, cold, often, far,* etc.) after *how* in these questions.

1 How .... will your friends stay in Quebec ?

2 How .... is your classroom (in square feet) ?

3 How .... is Montreal from Vancouver ?

4 How .... does it get in June, July, and August ?

5 How .... is the Empire State Building in New York ?

6 How .... do you go to concerts or lectures ?

7 How .... is your English teacher ?

8 How .... were the last two reading assignments ?

Use *much* or *many* after *how* in each of these sentences.

1 How .... students are there in your English class ?

2 How .... bread is there in the kitchen now ?

3 How .... letters do you write to your parents each week ?

4 How .... sugar do you want in your coffee ?

5 How .... cups of coffee did you drink during the day ?

6 How .... did you pay for your new winter overcoat ?

7 How .... times did you write the words on the list ?

8 How .... time do you spend on your homework ?

Read the answer to the question. Then supply the appropriate question word (*why, who, which, how far*, etc.) in the blank space in each sentence.

QUESTION ❓ ANSWER

	QUESTION	ANSWER
1	.... are you going now ?	To the library.
2	.... English book is this ?	It's Pierre's.
3	.... time is it now ?	It's eight-fifteen.
4	.... money do you have ?	Seventy-five cents.
5	.... one did Bill take ?	The small one.
6	.... was that tall boy ?	My friend, Jean.
7	.... did you talk to ?	The chairman.
8	.... is your brother ?	Twenty years old.
9	.... flour did you buy.?	Two pounds.
10	.... did you get to school ?	By car.
11	.... girl is your sister ?	The thin one.
12	.... color is her hair ?	Light brown.
13	.... will she get here ?	Probably Monday.
14	.... do they come here ?	Twice a year.
15	.... does "peculiar" mean ?	It means "strange".
16	.... is there a bus stop ?	At the next corner.
17	.... put the chair here ?	Roger, I think.
18	.... are you going to buy ?	A pair of shoes.
19	.... is Fred talking to now ?	Mr. Kennedy.
20	.... were you in the army ?	Three years.
21	.... did you meet yesterday ?	Betty's cousin.
22	.... do you do that ?	Because I enjoy it.
23	.... is Sept-Îles ?	A hundred miles.
24	.... people are there here ?	About thirty-five.
25	.... do you want your coffee ?	With cream.
26	.... will you get to Chicago ?	By air.
27	.... do you travel so much ?	I like it.
28	.... will you be in Sweden ?	Several months.
29	.... is your brother ?	Five feet eleven.
30	.... kind of cloth is that ?	It's silk.

Read the answer to the question. Then supply the appropriate question word (*what, whose, when, how much,* etc.) in the blank space in each sentence.

	QUESTION	ANSWER
1	.... did you put my book ?	On the desk.
2	.... does school usually start ?	In September.
3	.... gave Mr. Green the money ?	His sister.
4	.... did he need the money ?	To buy a ticket.
5	.... books are these ?	Jim's.
6	.... are your friends now ?	At Jim's (house).
7	.... did Smith leave for Boston ?	Last Friday.
8	.... is it to Lachute ?	Fifty-five miles.
9	.... is going to help you tonight ?	My friend Bill.
10	.... is he going to help ?	All of us.
11	.... did Mr. Brown say to you ?	Nothing important.
12	.... dictionary will you use ?	Jean-Paul's.
13	.... cups of coffee did you drink ?	Two or three.
14	.... color did you paint your house ?	White.
15	.... gasoline do you need ?	Ten gallons.
16	.... did you go there yesterday ?	To see Thomas.
17	.... of these do you prefer ?	That one.
18	.... kind of material is that ?	It's wool.
19	.... did the accident happen ?	At the corner.
20	.... is the nickname for "Robert" ?	It's "Bob".
21	.... did you speak to Yvan ?	Yesterday.
22	.... did you pay for that jacket ?	Sixty dollars.
23	.... does that word mean ?	It means "easy".
24	.... ago did Mr. Johnson leave ?	A week ago.
25	.... are your friends leaving now ?	Because it's late.
26	.... one did you finally buy ?	The red one.
27	.... do you want to get it now ?	I need it.
28	.... do you like this city ?	Very well.
29	.... do you call that in English ?	A "suitcase".
30	.... do you pronounce that word ?	Like this.

Write a question about the italicized part of each sentence. Begin each question with a question word (*where, what, how much*, etc.) Notice the examples.

1 Alice went *to the movies* last night.   *Where did Alice go last night ?*
2 They will be there *for two weeks*.   *How long will they be there ?*
3 *Miss Peters* wrote those letters.   *Who wrote those letters ?*
4 Bill's birthday is *on the twelfth of August*.
5 There are *twenty-one* floors in that building.
6 John is coughing *because he has a bad cold*.
7 The Browns left for home *at six o'clock*.
8 The students studied *the irregular verbs*.
9 That is *Professor Moore's* briefcase.
10 There were *fourteen guests* at the party.
11 Mr. Burke bought his new car *last Saturday*.
12 Oka is *ninety miles* from there.
13 Their classes usually begin at *nine o'clock*.
14 I'm going to go *because the game will be interesting*.
15 That customer wants *four* packs of cigarettes.
16 Dorothy bought *the pink* dress *with the blue stripes*.
17 We call those things *"gadgets"* in English.
18 My friends helped me *very* much yesterday afternoon.
19 *Mr. Wilson* gave the annual report to Mr. Johnson.
20 The whole trip takes about *twenty-two hours*.
21 We're going to look for *winter coats* at that department store.
22 Those two dictionaries belong to *Jean-Claude*.
23 Our friends stayéd in California *for three weeks*.
24 The messenger gave the packages to *Mr. Wilson's secretary*.
25 Mother put the cups and saucers *in the cupboard*.
26 The word "rapid" means *"fast" or "quick"*.
27 The doctor will come *within fifteen or twenty minutes*.
28 The price of that car is *four thousand dollars*.
29 Dr. Duncan's mother is *sixty-eight years* old.
30 There will be another meeting *next Thursday or Friday*.
31 Edward has about *two thousand dollars* in the bank now.
32 Mr. Green wrote to his brother *because he needed some money*.

Write a question about the italicized part of each sentence. Begin each question with a question word (*who, why, how many*, etc.). Notice the examples.

1 The Hills have *four* children. *How many children do the Hills have ?*

2 The accident happened *right here. Where did the accident happen ?*

3 Mr. and Mrs. Hanson are going to go *to Holland* next year.

4 Their guests left for home *because it was very late.*

5 Our classroom is *twenty-eight feet* wide.

6 It's about *twelve blocks* to the post office from here.

7 The two men returned to the office at *three o'clock.*

8 That modern chair costs *forty-four dollars plus tax.*

9 The secretary gave Mr. Green *a lot of* information.

10 The name of that book by Mark Twain is *"Tom Sawyer".*

11 Mr. and Mrs. Smith will return to St. John *by train.*

12 *The tall* man *on the left* is Mr. Brown's brother.

13 Those two students are talking about *the last lesson.*

14 Mr. Kennedy will leave for Edmonton *after the holidays.*

15 Miss Stewart chose *the black* dress *with the lace.*

16 Her sister bought *three* pairs of stockings yesterday.

17 I'm looking for *my briefcase and my books.*

18 The thief got into the house *through a basement window.*

19 *Those young boys* broke Mr. Flynn's front window.

20 Mr. Davis goes to Montreal *two or three times a year.*

21 The Slaters' daughter looks like *her grandmother.*

22 Charles got into trouble *because he didn't follow instructions.*

23 The meaning of that word is *"sad" or "unhappy".*

24 Mr. Smith put the reports *on Mr. Johnson's desk.*

25 The Taylors painted their house *blue and white.*

26 Charles asked his father and mother for *some money.*

27 That student has a *very poor* attitude toward his studies.

28 Jacqueline addressed her letter to *the stamp company.*

29 It's about *four hundred* miles to Ottawa from here.

30 The old bridge is *near the park.*

31 *Mr. Trudeau's* car is in the alley behind our house.

32 John's brother is going to study at *Loyola* next year.

Change these statements to simple negative questions. Make a contraction in each question. Study the two examples carefully.

1 He is in his office now. *Isn't he in his office now ?*
2 They studied the lesson. *Didn't they study the lesson ?*
3 Marie is going to go to the movies tonight.
4 Ruth wore her new spring dress to the party.
5 There are some shelves in that closet.
6 The students knew the answers to the questions.
7 Mr. Anderson never drinks coffee in the morning.
8 The Smiths will arrive in Los Angeles tomorrow.
9 There is some milk in the refrigerator.
10 Professor Moore walked to school this morning.
11 Mr. Johnson will be in his office this afternoon.
12 René understands the instructions in the book.
13 That girl does all of her homework carefully.
14 The vice-president was at the meeting last Thursday.

Change these *negatives* to negative questions with *why*. Make a contraction in each question. Study the two examples carefully.

1 He wasn't in class yesterday. *Why wasn't he in class yesterday ?*
2 She didn't write that letter. *Why didn't she write that letter ?*
3 Mr. Foster and Mr. Green weren't at the meeting.
4 Mr. Smith didn't get to work on time this morning.
5 Serge didn't go to the lecture with the other students.
6 His secretary wasn't in the office at that time.
7 The Browns aren't going to go to Europe this year.
8 The students didn't write the last two lessons.
9 Those boys didn't study their English assignment last night.
10 There won't be anyone in this office tomorrow.
11 Guy doesn't know the irregular verbs yet.
12 Frank and John didn't do their share of the work.
13 That fellow didn't tell me about his suggestion until today.
14 Your paper wasn't on my desk before class this morning.

Write the correct form of the verb in parentheses in each sentence. Use only the perfect present tense. Study the examples carefully.

1 We *(visit)* that museum. *We have visited that museum.*
2 Bill *(finish)* the work. *Bill has finished the work.*
3 I *(travel, never)* by air. *I have never traveled by air.*
4 Mr. Moore *(explain)* those two lessons to us already.
5 I *(live)* in this city almost all of my life.
6 That company *(hire)* twenty new workers since June.
7 The boys *(mention, already)* that matter to Mr. Brown.
8 We *(follow)* the instructions in the book carefully so far.
9 Pierre's English *(improve)* a great deal since July.
10 Betty *(copy)* all of the new words into her notebook.
11 The men *(try)* that method several times already.
12 Mr. Smith *(travel, never)* across the Atlantic by plane.
13 The company *(increase)* its production by twenty percent.
14 Up to now, we *(study)* almost every lesson in this book.

Write the correct form of the verb in parentheses in each sentence. Use only the perfect present tense. The verbs in these sentences are irregular verbs. Check your answers carefully with the list of irregular verbs in the appendix.

1 We *(see)* that movie. *We have seen that movie.*
2 He *(have)* his lunch already. *He has had his lunch already.*
3 I *(be, never)* there before. *I have never been there before.*
4 Henri *(take)* three different courses in English.
5 Michelle *(fly)* in an airplane only two other times.
6 The two girls *(do, already)* the dinner dishes.
7 I'm sorry. I *(forget)* the name of that new song.
8 Mr. Bouchard *(be)* in this city for six months.
9 We *(know)* Mr. and Mrs. Smith for over twelve years.
10 I *(fall)* on these steep steps several times this week.
11 I think Mr. Harris *(have, already)* his lunch.
12 I *(read, already)* his letter and *(write)* a reply to him.
13 Carole and Yvonne *(have)* lots of practice in English so far.
14 We *(see, already)* Mr. Duncan and *(speak)* to him about that.

Change these statements to simple questions. Study the examples carefully.

1 Mr. Green has quit his job.   *Has Mr. Green quit his job ?*
2 We have already done that lesson.   *Have we already done that lesson ?*
3 Luc has already given his homework to Mr. Harris.
4 Mr. and Mrs. Burke have heard the good news.
5 Anne has copied all of the new words from the blackboard.
6 The students have already studied that lesson.
7 Your English has improved very much since September.
8 Those men have done their share of the work.
9 The director has mentioned his plan to the committee.
10 The weather has been very bad this past week.
11 Mr. and Mrs. Slater have taken good care of their car.
12 We have heard that radio program several times.
13 My friend Tom has always enjoyed that kind of work.
14 There have been some bad storms in this area recently.

Change these statements to negatives. Study the examples carefully.

1 We have seen that movie.   *We haven't seen that movie.*
2 Yvan has taken that course.   *Yvan hasn't taken that course.*
3 The students have written the last two lessons.
4 Miss Peters has finished those letters for Mr. Johnson.
5 Mr. Jarris and Mr. Moore have eaten lunch.
6 That student has had much practice in conversation.
7 Mr. Moore has explained that part of the lesson.
8 Our friends have decided on a name for their baby.
9 My boss has hired some new workers in the past week.
10 We have discussed that part of the lesson very thoroughly.
11 Mr. Benson and his wife have been here since last August.
12 Tom's sister has told her parents about her plan.
13 There have been some bad storms in this area recently.
14 We've repaired the hole in the roof of our house.
15 Mr. Smith has said something to Mr. Fox about that problem.

Change the verbs in these sentences (a) to the past tense, (b) to the future tense, and (c) to the perfect present tense. Study the examples carefully.

1 I spend my money.
  (a) *I spent my money.*
  (b) *I will spend my money.*
  (c) *I have spent my money.*

2 They use that one.
3 We study English together.
4 They discuss their work.
5 They have enough time.
6 I do all of the lessons.

7 He sits in that row.
8 I drive my car.
9 She hides her money.
10 We go to school.
11 He takes much time.

12 Does he eat there ?
  (a) *Did he eat there ?*
  (b) *Will he eat there ?*
  (c) *Has he eaten there ?*

13 Do you enjoy that work ?
14 Does he write many letters ?
15 Do you send many letters ?
16 Do they explain everything ?
17 Does she attend that class ?

18 Do you have enough time ?
19 Do they copy the sentences ?
20 Does she have much trouble ?
21 Does she do good work ?
22 Do the students practice ?

23 I don't stay there.
  (a) *I didn't stay there.*
  (b) *I won't stay there.*
  (c) *I haven't stayed there.*

24 He doesn't work hard.
25 I don't have any energy.
26 He doesn't pay his bills.
27 We don't see that fellow.

28 She doesn't use this one.
29 They don't remember it.
30 I don't do much work here.
31 He doesn't listen carefully.

Write the correct form of the verb in parentheses in each sentence. Use only the perfect present tense. Check your answers with the list of irregular verbs in the appendix.

1 *Mr. Harris has taught English at this school for five years.*
2 I (*write*)   three or four letters to that company.
3 The students in this class   (*do*)   those two lessons already.
4 I (*know*)   Professor Moore for more than twelve years.
5 Henri (*take*)   three courses in English at this school.
6 These steps are dangerous. I (*fall*)   on them several times.
7 Mr. Kramer (*be*)   in the United States for three years.
8 The janitor (*shut, already*)   the back door.
9 The students (*read*)   all of the stories in that book.
10 Marjorie (*choose*)   a pantsuit for the party.
11 I (*speak*)   to my boss about the problem several times.
12 That tree (*grow*)   at least five feet since last year.
13 Mr. Dupuis (*spend*)   over eighteen hundred dollars since May.
14 Mr. and Mrs. Smith (*buy*)   a new house in North Plains.
15 The real estate agent (*sell*)   the Smith's old house.
16 Charles (*have*)   a bad cold for a whole week.
17 I'm sorry. I (*forget*)   the name of that book.
18 We (*hear, already*)   that new song several times.
19 Mr. Wilson isn't here. He (*go*)   out of town for the weekend.
20 Mr. Kennedy (*wear*)   his blue suit to the office only twice.
21 I (*sit*)   in this same seat since the first day of classes.
22 The money isn't in this drawer. Someone (*steal*)   it !
23 Up to now, I (*understand*)   every lesson in the book.
24 We (*have*)   absolutely no trouble with our car so far.
25 No one (*find*)   that girl's purse and gloves yet.
26 The weather (*be*)   very warm ever since last Thursday.
27 Mr. Anderson and Mr. Brown (*have*)   lunch already.
28 I (*see*)   Place Ville Marie hundreds of times.
29 We (*speak, already*)   to the director and (*give*)   him the message.
30 Grandmother (*fly, never*)   in an airplane before.
31 You (*tear*)   your shirt! There's a hole in the left sleeve.
32 I (*read, already*)   the customer's letter and   (*write*)   a reply to him.

Write the correct form of the verb in parentheses in each sentence. Choose only the simple past tense (examples : *I worked, he took*) or the perfect present tense (examples : *I have worked, he has taken*). Notice the two examples. For additional practice, refer to Exercise 128.

1 I (*see*) that movie already.   *I have seen that movie already.*

2 I (*see*) that movie yesterday.   *I saw that movie yesterday.*

3 I (*read*) that novel by Hemingway several times before.

4 I (*read*) that novel again during my last vacation.

5 Philippe (*study*) Spanish last year.

6 Philippe (*study*) English in this class since last September.

7 Miss Gagnon (*live*) in Oka from 1966 to 1970.

8 Miss Gagnon (*live*) in Montreal since that time.

9 Our guests (*have*) a good time at the party last night.

10 Our guests (*have*) a good time ever since their arrival.

11 Dr. and Mrs. Duncan (*see*) the Coliseum in Rome in 1971.

12 Dr. Duncan (*see*) St. Joseph's Oratory several times.

13 The Browns (*be*) in Toronto twice since Christmas.

14 The Browns (*be*) in San Francisco the week before last.

15 My wife and I (*travel*) by air many times in the past.

16 My wife and I (*travel*) to Mexico by air last summer.

17 The students (*finish, finally*) that hard exercise.

18 The students (*start*) that exercise about three hours ago.

19 We (*receive*) the boy's telegram at 8:00 p.m. last night.

20 We (*send, already*) them a special delivery reply.

21 Mr. and Mrs. Hanson (*visit*) Niagara Falls in 1970.

22 Mr. and Mrs. Hanson (*visit*) Niagara Falls several times since then.

23 We (*study*) almost every lesson in this book so far.

24 We (*study*) a very hard lesson the day before yesterday.

25 I (*have*) a little trouble with my car last week.

26 However, I (*have*) no trouble with my car since then.

27 We (*watch, never*) that television program.

28 We (*watch*) an interesting program on television last night.

29 That tall fellow (*work*) here for the past three weeks.

30 Formerly, he (*work*) for a company in Boston.

31 Mr. Shaw is my English teacher. He (*teach*) here for six years.

32 He (*finish*) his Ph.D. at McGill seven years ago.

Use the correct form of the verb in parentheses in each sentence. Choose only the simple present tense (example : *he writes*), the continuous present tense (example : *he is writing*), or the perfect present tense (example : *he has written*). For additional practice, refer to Exercise 127.

1 We (*study*)   English in this class since last September.
2 My teacher (*teach*)   English at this school for six years.
3 Listen ! I (*think*) someone (*knock*)   at the front door.
4 Mr. Smith (*pay*)   all of his bills at the end of the month.
5 I (*see*)   the Rocky Mountains a few times.
6 It (*rain, usually*)   very much in that part of the United States.
7 Mr. and Mrs. Girouard (*be*)   in Montreal for two months.
8 Those students (*make*)   much progress since October.
9 My friend Frank (*owe*)   David Foster fifty-five dollars.
10 I (*be*)   sorry. I (*forget*)   that fellow's name already.
11 Mr. Johnson's secretary (*sit*)   at a different desk today.
12 I (*have*)   no trouble with my English lessons up to now.
13 Richard (*look*)   forward to his vacation next June.
14 The tall girl in the front seat (*come*)   from Longueuil.
15 Yes, we (*hear*)   that new song several times already.
16 My wife and I (*live*)   in this city for almost nine years.
17 The boys (*study*)   their lessons together every afternoon.
18 Thomas (*have*)   a good time here ever since his arrival.
19 I (*need*)   some more money for my books and tuition.
20 At present, that author (*write*)   a historical novel.
21 Our present teacher (*live*)   in this city all of his life.
22 Miss Fox (*talk*)   to someone on the telephone at the moment.
23 My friend Jean-Pierre (*be*)   everywhere in Quebec.
24 Up to the present, Georges (*do*)   good work in this class.
25 Those four people (*be*)   here since eight o'clock.
26 Laurent Rousseau (*work*)   thirty-eight hours a week.
27 We (*write*)   almost every exercise in this book up to now.
28 The weather (*get, generally*)   very hot in July and August.
29 So far, you (*make*)   no mistakes in this exercise.
30 At the moment, I (*read*)   a book about the Voyageurs.
31 Mr. Kent (*have*)   that job in Winnipeg since June first.

Complete these questions with the correct question phrase. Also, give the expected short answer to each question. Study the examples very carefully.

	QUESTION	ANSWER
1	The sun is shining now, *isn't it ?*	*Yes, It is.*
2	Mr. Wilson lives there, *doesn't he ?*	*Yes, he does.*
3	The men haven't done it yet, *have they ?*	*No, they haven't.*
4	Mrs. Fox didn't speak to you, *did she ?*	*No, she didn't.*
5	That is Mr. Kennedy's car, *isn't it ?*	*Yes, It is.*
6	There wasn't anyone in the room, *was there ?*	*No, there wasn't.*
7	Miss Peters wasn't in the office,................... ?	......, ...
8	Mr. Moore speaks French very well,........... ?	......, ...
9	Your friend didn't see you yesterday,........... ?	......, ...
10	Anne has written the letter already,............. ?	......, ...
11	They will be at your house tonight,............. ?	......, ...
12	There were some keys on the desk,............. ?	......, ...
13	Miss Kent doesn't have a car,...................... ?	......, ...
14	Your guests had a very good time,............. ?	......, ...
15	The Browns aren't eating right now,............. ?	......, ...
16	The men haven't done that yet,.................. ?	......, ...
17	That isn't Mr. Johnson's briefcase,.............. ?	......, ...
18	That bus goes to Pointe-Claire.................... ?	......, ...
19	You have already seen that movie,............. ?	......, ...
20	Mary didn't leave the front door open,........ ?	......, ...
21	Mr. Green went home very late,.................. ?	......, ...
22	Bill is studying at McMaster,.................... ?	......, ...
23	These aren't your cigarettes,.................... ?	......, ...
24	Ed's brother finished school last year,......... ?	......, ...
25	There will be enough coffee for everyone,... ?	......, ...
26	That last lesson wasn't very difficult,........... ?	......, ...
27	You study each vocabulary list carefully,...... ?	......, ...
28	The students did their work together,........... ?	......, ...
29	Luc had enough money for his books,......... ?	......, ...
30	The students haven't done that lesson,......... ?	......, ...

Choose *before, after, from,* or *ago* for the blank space in each sentence.

1 Our friends will arrive in this city a week .... now.

2 Mr. Benson was here the week .... last.

3 The men are leaving for Halifax the month .... next.

4 Jean-Guy's brother finished school several years ....

5 Bill and I went to that meeting the night .... last.

6 Pierre will return to this country two years .... now.

7 Our school year ended the month .... last.

8 Mr. and Mrs. Fox left there two weeks .... yesterday.

9 I'm going to go back to school the week .... next.

10 Did you speak to Miss Davis the day .... yesterday ?

11 My friends will arrive here a week .... next Sunday.

12 Mr. and Mrs. Taylor will get back the day .... tomorrow.

13 I am leaving for St. John's a week .... tomorrow.

14 I'll get back to Quebec a month .... now.

15 My friends left for Belgium a week ....,.. yesterday.

EXPRESSIONS OF TIME (1)   103

month year day season hour

Choose *in, on,* or *at* for the blank space in each sentence.

at in on
in on at

1 The mailman delivered the letter .... 1:45 p.m.

2 I woke up .... three o'clock .... the morning.

3 The weather is pleasant here .... the spring.

4 Mr. Johnson's birthday is .... February 20.

5 We saw Thérèse in Quebec City .... September.

6 Mr. and Mrs. Brown are leaving for England .... Saturday.

7 The flight from Toronto arrived in Montreal .... noon.

8 Mr. Anderson plans to return to Ottawa .... the third of April.

9 Réjean Gilbert graduated from university .... 1970.

10 My English class starts .... ten minutes after three.

11 Mr. Foster will get back from Chicago .... the tenth of January.

12 Many people take their vacations .... June, July, and August.

13 Are you going to study .... the afternoon or .... night ?

14 We had a wonderful time at that party .... Friday night.

Choose *in, on,* or *at* for the blank space in each sentence.

1 This English class seemed very easy .... first.
2 .... present, we are studying the use of prepositions.
3 Did you get to work .... time yesterday morning ?
4 Did you get to the meeting .... time for the movie ?
5 Both of us were in Miami .... that time.
6 .... the future, please write the exercises more carefully.
7 I go to Place des Arts once .... a while.
8 .... the beginning, the work seemed very difficult to me.
9 My friend came back with the money .... no time .... all.
10 From now ...., please study .... least two hours a day.
11 We went out for coffee .... the middle of the afternoon.
12 I've mentioned it to him .... several different occasions.
13 You're making too much noise. Stop that .... once !
14 Why don't you call him ? I'll wait here .... the meantime.

Choose *in, on,* or *at* for the blank space in each sentence.

1 My wife and I will return to Shawinigan .... the fifth of August.
2 Mr. Kramer and his family came to Quebec .... 1969.
3 He had a lot of trouble with English .... the beginning.
4 .... present, we are using a different English book.
5 Our visitors are going to go to that museum .... Thursday.
6 Our English teacher closes the door .... ten minutes after two.
7 Do you usually get to work .... time .... the morning ?
8 The weather generally gets quite hot .... July and August.
9 We plan to leave for Europe early .... the spring.
10 The students finished those two exercises .... no time .... all.
11 Our baby was born .... two o'clock .... the afternoon .... May 2.
12 Please get ready now. .... the meantime, I'll call our friends.
13 This English book seemed very easy to me .... first.
14 Our friends are going to visit us here .... Sunday night.
15 Well, I've finished this terrible exercise .... last !

In each section, choose one of the two indicated words for each sentence.

SINCE vs. FOR

1 Marcel has studied English in this class .... eight months.
2 My friend has studied English in this class ....last October.
3 The Browns have lived in this city .... 1966.
4 The Wilsons have lived in Chomedey .... six years.
5 Mr. Smith worked for that company .... one year.
6 Mr. Smith has worked for our company .... that time.
7 Marie-Claire has been here .... the beginning of the year.
8 Her sister has been in Vancouver .... a long time.

SINCE vs. IN

1 Mr. and Mrs. Hanson lived in Sherbrooke .... 1963.
2 Mr. and Mrs. Hanson have lived in this city .... 1970.
3 We haven't seen our friends the Flynns .... August.
4 Mr. and Mrs. Flynn left for Yugoslavia .... August.
5 Frank's parents returned to Canada .... the fall.
6 Frank's parents have lived in their new apartment .... last fall.
7 Mr. Johnson hasn't had any free time .... this morning.
8 Mr. Johnson had several important meetings .... the morning.

FOR vs. IN

1 Mr. Smith worked for the Container Corporation .... 1968.
2 Mr. Smith worked for the corporation .... one year.
3 My wife and I usually take our vacation .... the summer.
4 We usually stay in Vermont or Maine .... a whole month.
5 Professor Moore came to this university .... 1956.
6 Professor Moore has taught here .... seventeen years.
7 Antoine's sister has had her diploma .... over six weeks now.
8 She received her diploma from the University of Montreal ....
June.

In each section, choose one of the two indicated words for each sentence.

BY vs. *IN*

  1 Thomas and Richard will be there .... ten o'clock.
  2 My friends will be there .... two or three hours.
  3 Will you finish the work .... September 10 ?
  4 I'll finish all of the work .... three months.
  5 I'll lend you my dictionary .... a day or two.
  6 Don't bother, I'll have my own dictionary .... then.
  7 We'll go there at six-thirty. .... that time, Tom will be there.
  8 I'm sure you will not finish the work .... that amount of time.

BY vs. *UNTIL*

  1 Bill is there now. He'll be there .... ten o'clock.
  2 Bill isn't there now. But he'll be there .... ten o'clock.
  3 Don't hurry. The train won't leave .... 5:45 p.m.
  4 We'll certainly get to the station .... 5:40 p.m.
  5 Please return in an hour. I'll be ready .... then.
  6 I'll be back very soon. Wait right here .... then.
  7 Our guests stayed here .... twelve o'clock last night.
  8 .... twelve o'clock, we were practically asleep in our chairs.

BY vs. *FOR*

  1 We'll have that report ready for you .... 4:00 p.m.
  2 We'll work on that report .... the next two hours.
  3 I'm leaving now, but I'll be back here .... noon.
  4 I'll be away from my office .... several hours today.
  5 The highway department will finish that road .... 1975.
  6 The construction company has already worked on it .... one
     year.
  7 Please don't tell my friends the news .... a few days.
  8 Why not ? Your friends will know all about it .... that time.

In each section, choose one of the two indicated words for each sentence.

UNTIL vs. *FOR*

1 I waited for you right there .... five o'clock.
2 I waited for you right there .... an hour and a half.
3 Mr. and Mrs. Carson will be in London .... September.
4 The Carsons are going to stay in London .... two months.
5 Our guests will remain with us .... one more day.
6 They are going to stay here .... the day after tomorrow.
7 Mr. Wilson won't be away from the office .... very long.
8 Why don't you wait here in the office .... then ?

UNTIL vs. *IN*

1 The train will leave the station .... ten minutes.
2 The train won't leave the station .... 2:30 p.m.
3 Mr. Burke will be back here .... nine or ten days.
4 Mr. Burke will stay in Saskatoon .... a week from Friday.
5 You will probably finish all of the work .... an hour.
6 However, you will probably be very busy with it .... that time.
7 Miss Stewart will be ready to leave .... a little while.
8 Miss Stewart won't be ready to leave .... eight o'clock.

FOR vs. *IN*

1 The train to Kingston will leave .... five minutes.
2 The train will stay in the station .... five minutes more.
3 Are your friends going to be in Alberta .... a long time ?
4 No, they'll be back .... a week or two.
5 We usually go from Montreal to Toronto .... six hours.
6 My brother and his wife lived in Corner Brook .... three years.
7 Are you leaving now ? -No, I'll leave .... a little while.
8 Are you leaving now ? -Yes, I'll be away .... a little while.

Choose *for, until, by,* or *in* for the blank space in each sentence.

1 I'm going to stay there .... a year and a half.
2 I'll complete all of the work .... noon tomorrow.
3 The man waited .... eight o'clock. Then he left.
4 Will you get back from Thetford Mines .... tomorrow night ?
5 He's not here now, but he'll be back .... a little while.
6 Mr. and Mrs. Kirby lived in Cowansville .... three years.
7 .... this time, the Smiths have already arrived in Miami.
8 Are they going to remain in Florida .... a long time ?
9 They're going to return to Lachine late .... the spring.
10 I worked on my assignment .... eleven o'clock last night.
11 Mr. Clark came to Canada .... 1971.
12 The entire office staff worked .... six-thirty last night.
13 I'm going to stop .... a few minutes and take a rest.
14 Our friends will stay in Europe .... April or May.

Choose *for, until, since,* or *at* for the blank space in each sentence.

1 The report won't be ready for us .... noon tomorrow.
2 Everything will be ready for you .... 12:00 p.m. sharp.
3 I've been in this class .... the beginning of the semester.
4 .... that time, everything seemed very easy to me.
5 My friends, Jacques and Serge, went hitchiking .... four months.
6 Frank won't get back here .... later this afternoon.
7 He'll probably get back to the office .... four or four-thirty.
8 Mr. and Mrs. Paquette lived in Boucherville .... 1968.
9 Then they moved to New Brunswick .... a year or two.
10 They have lived in Montreal .... then.
11 They are going to stay in Montreal .... 1976.
12 Bill hasn't mentioned that matter .... the last election.
13 He probably won't say anything about it .... the next election.
14 .... two days ago, practically everyone agreed with you.
15 .... that time, everyone has changed his mind about it.

Select the correct preposition for each blank space. Use only the prepositions *since, for, ago, in, on, at.*

Mr. Christian Bernard Vocat was born .... Lausanne, Switzerland .... the year 1931. He was born .... Tuesday, March 15, ... midnight. He lived .... Lausanne .... eight years. Then he moved to Geneva .... 1939. He fell in love with that city .... that time. He has written a lot of stories about Geneva .... that time. However, it has been quite a long time .... his last year .... that city. He went to school .... Geneva .... eight years. He quit school there .... June, 1947. .... July 15, he left .... Holland. He arrived .... The Hague late .... night two days later. He went to a private school .... that city .... two years. Today, he often speaks about the wonderful time he had .... that school many years .... the end of those two years, he left .... France. .... first, he felt very homesick. However, he finally got a job .... the staff of a large newspaper. It was hard work .... the beginning. He didn't have much experience .... that time. That was .... 1949. Of course, he has gained a great deal of experience .... then. But .... those days, he was only a beginner .... that field. .... the beginning of the next year, he got a job .... a publishing house. He worked .... that concern .... ten years. Mr. Vocat came to Canada .... the spring of 1960. He became a Canadian citizen .... the twentieth of April, 1965. He has had a house .... Montreal .... that time. .... all, he has lived in Canada .... quite a long time. Mr. Vocat took a course .... English a number of years .... He started his course .... October, 1963. He studied English .... two years. Mr. Vocat went to the United States six years .... for a national magazine, and he stayed there .... three years. Then he returned to Canada .... good. He has written many things about the United States that he learnt .... that trip. Mr. Vocat has been a professional writer .... 1949. He wrote his first article .... 1949. .... then, he has written almost 500 articles and stories.

Re-read the story about Mr. Vocat. Then write the correct form of the verb in each of the following sentences.

 1 Mr. Vocat (*be*)   in the year 1931.
 2 Mr. Vocat (*write*)   almost five hundred articles.
 3 Mr. Vocat (*come*)   to Canada in the spring of 1960.
 4 Mr. Vocat (*live*)   in Canada since 1960.
 5 Mr. Vocat (*study*)   English for two years.
 6 Mr. Vocat (*gain*)   much experience since his first job.
 7 Mr. Vocat (*be, never*)   in England or Scotland.
 8 Mr. Vocat (*leave*)   Lausanne, Switzerland, after eight years.
 9 Mr. Vocat (*fall*)   in love with Geneva.
10 Mr. Vocat (*take*)   English courses from 1963 to 1965.
11 Mr. Vocat (*live*)   in the United States for only three years.
12 Mr. Vocat (*become*)   a Canadian citizen in 1965.
13 Mr. Vocat (*have*)   a house in Montreal since 1965.
14 Mr. Vocat (*be*)   a professional writer since 1949.

Give a complete answer to each question about "A Brief History of C.B. Vocat".

1 When was Mr. Vocat born ?   2 How long ago was he born ?   3 How long did he live in Lausanne ?   4 When did he leave Lausanne ?   5 How long did he go to school in Geneva ?   6 When did he quit school in Geneva ?   7 When did he leave for Holland ?   8 How long has he been in Canada ?   9 How many years ago did he leave France ?   10 When did he leave for the United States ?   11 How many years did he go to school in The Hague ?   12 When did he get his first job on the staff of a newspaper ?   13 When did he finish his English course ?   14 How many years ago did he get his job in the French publishing house ?   15 In what year did he leave that job in the publishing house ?   16 Where did Mr. Vocat go in 1949 ?   17 When did Mr. Vocat become a Canadian citizen ?   18 How many years has he been a writer ?   19 When did he return to Canada for good ?   20 How many years ago did he leave Switzerland ?   21 How old is Mr. Vocat today ?   22 How many articles and stories has Mr. Vocat written ?   23 Where was Mr. Vocat five years ago ?

Choose *in*, *on*, or *at* for the blank space in each sentence.

1 Mr. and Mrs. Kennedy live .... West End Avenue.
2 Did you buy your new car .... Ontario or here ?
3 The Browns were .... Greece and Italy two years ago.
4 Mr. Foster works .... 667 Sherbrooke Street West .... Montreal.
5 The Johnsons' garage is .... the back of their house.
6 Would you please park your car .... the driveway.
7 Mr. and Mrs. Smith stayed .... the Lincoln Hotel .... Boston.
8 I'll meet you .... the corner of Main Street and Oak Road.
9 How did you enjoy your vacation .... Europe last year ?
10 Françoise isn't .... home right now. She's .... school.
11 There are national parks .... every section of the country.
12 The Empire State Building is one of the tallest buildings ....
   the world.
13 How many floors are there .... that building ?
14 Mr. and Mrs. Johnson's house is .... Jean-Talon Boulevard.
15 Turn left .... the corner. The house is .... the left side.
16 Don't walk .... the street ! Walk here .... the sidewalk.
17 Our friends are going to meet us .... Lafontaine Park.
18 Our friends arrived .... New York the week before last.
19 Mr. Carson arrived .... the airport half an hour early.
20 Have you and your wife ever traveled .... a large ocean liner ?
21 My friend and I always ride to school .... the bus.
22 We usually study our English lessons .... the way to school.
23 Please move over. You are standing .... my way.
24 Mr. Johnson's office is .... the sixth floor of the building.
25 Mrs. Roland is sitting .... the desk .... front of the door.
26 Listen ! I think there is someone .... the front door.
27 Are you and Claude .... the same literature class ?
28 Yes, ... fact he and I sit together .... the first row.
29 Did you put those two packages .... the table .... the hall ?
30 No, I didn't. Did you look .... the top drawer of your desk ?
31 Someone probably put the packages .... the shelf .... the closet.
32 There's paper .... the floor. Please put it .... the wastebasket.

Select the correct preposition for the blank space in each sentence.

1 When do you plan to leave .... Charlottetown ?
2 Mr. Adams went .... a walk .... the park this afternoon.
3 Miss Peters is going to ask her boss .... some advice.
4 Tom's friends are laughing .... his funny answer.
5 Why don't you and Guy ever listen .... classical music ?
6 Don't worry .... that matter. It's not very important.
7 Those books and papers belong .... someone else.
8 We all looked .... Dick's wallet. We finally found it.
9 How much did your friend pay .... those theater tickets ?
10 When do the Lafleurs expect to arrive .... New York ?
11 Mr. and Mrs. Lafleur will arrive .... the airport .... 2:00 p.m.
12 Mr. Vocat is working .... an article .... a national magazine.
13 Mrs. Burke's brother borrowed some money .... her.
14 Why did Mrs. Burke lend the money .... her brother ?
15 I don't want to argue .... you .... that matter .... this time.
16 Our visitors complained .... the bad weather .... this region.
17 The company insisted .... an immediate reply .... their letter.
18 Jeanne's sister is shopping .... a new spring hat today.
19 Frank always depends .... his brother for assistance.
20 This English book consists .... two separate sections.
21 Have Don and Dorothy decided .... a name for their baby yet ?
22 Mary reminded Mr. Fox .... his appointment the next day.
23 Would you please substitute his name .... mine .... that list.
24 Mr. Filion is translating that book .... French .... English.
25 Professor Moore glanced .... his wrist watch quickly.
26 We introduced our guests .... Maurice and Henri.
27 All of the members objected .... the chairman's suggestion.
28 The men will probably rely .... you .... some assistance.
29 That fellow constantly boasts .... his influential friends.
30 I think you have confused that word .... another one.
31 I hope the director will cooperate .... us .... that matter.
32 We don't want to interfere .... our visitors' plans .... any way.

Select the correct preposition for the blank space in each sentence.

1 Are you ready .... the English examination ?
2 My friend Roger is very excited .... his new job.
3 Mr. and Mrs. Brown are proud .... their new house.
4 Marie has been absent .... the last two classes.
5 Why were those girls mad .... Frank and you ?
6 They were mad .... our attitude .... their suggestion.
7 Luc is more interested .... history than English.
8 Please be careful .... this tool. It's very delicate.
9 I am very sorry .... my mistake. I wasn't careful enough.
10 Everyone feels very sorry .... that poor old man.
11 All of the members were pleased .... the final result.
12 We're not accustomed .... this very cold weather yet.
13 Everyone .... the group was very polite .... our guests.
14 I'm angry .... Richard Lamarre .... a very good reason.
15 Lucien wasn't very sure .... the answers .... his paper.
16 We have plenty .... time. We'll get .... school .... time.
17 Mr. Talbot and his wife are quite fond .... strong coffee.
18 I hope you are prepared .... a great deal .... criticism.
19 I think that young girl is afraid .... cats and dogs.
20 That author is famous .... his novels .... the sea.
21 That restaurant .... Tenth Street is known .... its fine food.
22 Those two pails are full .... water .... the rain last night.
23 The police are very suspicious .... those two fellows.
24 I'm getting tired .... that student's constant excuses.
25 Your example is similar .... mine but different .... André's.
26 That man's face seems very familiar .... me.
27 Are you familiar .... that peculiar expression ?
28 They are not aware .... my strong feelings .... that matter.
29 Tom and I are grateful .... you .... all of your assistance.
30 That kind of dress is not suitable .... certain occasions.
31 Judy is always very considerate .... other people's feelings.
32 The quality of this shirt is not equal .... the quality of that one.

Choose *still* or *any more* for the blank space in each sentence. Observe the word order in each sentence carefully. Study the first four examples.

1   My friend William is *still* at the library.
2   Mr. Foster *still* plans to leave as soon as possible.
3   My wife and I *still* haven't found an apartment.
4   Professor Moore doesn't walk to school *any more.*
5   Mr. Johnson is .... talking to his two assistants.
6   Doesn't Elizabeth's father smoke cigarettes .... ?
7   Are the Hiltons .... staying with their friends in Calgary ?
8   Mr. Benson isn't the chairman of that committee ....
9   Fred .... doesn't agree with you and me on that point.
10   Are you fellows .... worrying about the same problem ?
11   Richard and I don't eat lunch at the cafeteria ....
12   Mr. Green .... hasn't spoken to Mr. Wilson about my plan.
13   Don and Dorothy Burke don't watch that television program ....
14   Are Lucien and Jean-Guy .... studying English at this school ?

Choose *already* or *yet* for the blank space in each sentence. Observe the word order in these sentences carefully. Study the first three examples.

1   We have *already* spoken to the men about the problem.
2   Most of the guests have gone home *already.*
3   My friends haven't arrived from Halifax *yet.*
4   Some of the students were .... in the classroom.
5   We haven't started the advanced section of this book ....
6   The Browns have .... had their new car for two weeks.
7   Mr. Green has had no opportunity to mention it ....
8   Most of the students have done those two lessons ....
9   Not many people in this neighborhood have heard the news ....
10   The students have learned a lot of things about English ....
11   Have you seen the movie at the Paramount Theater .... ?
12   My secretary has .... written a reply to that inquiry.
13   Miss Peters is sitting at her desk .... , isn't she ?
14   Those two students have done that work .... , haven't they ?
15   René and Richard haven't done their part of it .... , have they ?

Choose *still, already,* or *yet* for the blank space in each sentence.

1 Jean-Pierre and Laurent have .... done exercises 119 and 120.
2 The other students haven't done those two exercises ....
3 As a matter of fact, they're .... doing Exercise 118.
4 Don't you know the meaning of that word .... ?
5 I think your English vocabulary is .... much too small.
6 Do you .... do your assignments with your friend Yvan ?
7 You have .... spoken to Mr. Johnson, haven't you ?
8 No, I .... haven't had a chance to speak to Mr. Johnson.
9 Does Mr. Johnson know anything about our problem .... ?
10 Miss Peters is .... Mr. Johnson's secretary, isn't she ?
11 Has the company bought an electric typewriter for her .... ?
12 That isn't necessary. Miss Peters has got one ....
13 My wife and I .... live in the same apartment.
14 We .... don't have enough money to buy a house in North Plains.
15 Haven't you and your wife saved enough money for a house .... ?

THE WORDS "ALSO, TOO," AND "EITHER"   120

Choose *also, too,* or *either* for the blank space in each sentence. In some cases, both *also* and *too* are possible. Study the first four examples. For short additions with *too* and *either,* see Exercise 180.

1 I enjoy classical music. I *also* enjoy popular music.
2 Richard is working now. Thomas is working now *also.*
3 Richard is working now. Thomas is working now *too.*
4 Alice didn't do that work. I didn't do that work *either.*
5 They watched television. We watched television ....
6 Frank collects stamps. He .... collects interesting coins.
7 Mr. Smith won't be at the meeting. I won't be there ....
8 She has already seen that movie. I've seen that movie ....
9 Louis plays tennis very well. He .... plays golf very well.
10 I don't like American coffee, and I don't like hot dogs ....
11 Paul's going to go in your car. I'm going to go with you ....
12 I haven't had any free time. She hasn't had any free time ....
13 I was in Europe last year. Were you in Europe last year .... ?
14 I haven't finished the work yet. Haven't you finished .... ?

Read each sentence aloud. If possible, use a contraction (for example : *she is — she's, they did not — they didn't*, etc.). In some sentences, there are two possibilities. Contractions are not possible in a few sentences.

what's
that's
there's

were n't
did

1 He does not like it.
2 I am not a student.
3 She has seen it.
4 It will be ready for you.
5 She is not a teacher.
6 Where is the office ?
7 I am very busy now.
8 They did not write it.
9 John was not absent.
10 When are you leaving ?
11 They do not know that.
12 We are very unhappy.
13 It is very cold outside.
14 She was not late.
15 What is that ?
16 There is a salesman here.
17 That is a very big house.
18 It did not rain very hard.
19 Who will do that work ?
20 We have finished it.
21 It was not very good.
22 She is not here now.
23 Those are ours.
24 He will help us soon.

25 They have been in Regina.
26 Who are those people ?
27 We are going to go soon.
28 I will not have any time.
29 It is not ready yet.
30 That was interesting.
31 That is a suitcase.
32 There is not a thing here.
33 They have not done it.
34 What is this ?
35 He does not know it.
36 She is not ready yet.
37 Whose are those ?
38 They were not angry.
39 You did not come.
40 You have not heard it.
41 There are books here.
42 I do not see it yet.
43 It was not difficult.
44 There is a man here.
45 They will not be here.
46 It did not rain hard.
47 Who is that fellow ?
48 We have not been there.
49 That is very good.
50 I have eaten already.
51 There was a party there.
52 They are not going to go.
53 She is not very nervous.
54 It is very pretty.
55 That is very interesting.
56 I was not in the room.
57 I am ready now.
58 They were not here.

Put each frequency word in the correct position in the following sentences. Study the first four examples carefully.

 1 [*always*]   That man is late.   *That man is always late.*
 2 [*usually*]   Is it cold in the winter?   *Is it usually cold in the winter?*
 3 [*seldom*]   He returns before 2:30.   *He seldom returns before 2:30.*
 4 [*never*]   I have seen that statue.   *I have never seen that statue.*
 5 [*usually*]   Jean-Pierre works very hard.
 6 [*often*]   The children are very active after meals.
 7 [*seldom*]   The food at that restaurant is good.
 8 [*usually*]   Is Mr. Rochefort at home in the evening?
 9 [*always*]   Do you study your English lessons at night?
10 [*never*]   Dorothy and I watch television during the afternoon.
11 [*ever*]   Why doesn't that student write his lessons carefully?
12 [*rarely*]   Mr. Wilson has time to see visitors in the morning.
13 [*usually*]   Don't you keep your important papers in that drawer?
14 [*ever*]   Have you watched that television program?
15 [*always*]   The director is in his office between 2:00 and 4:00 p.m.
16 [*usually*]   Is there someone here before 9:30 a.m.?
17 [*never*]   We have been to the Museum of Modern Art.
18 [*always*]   Why do you study your lessons with Georges?
19 [*ever*]   Does the foreman eat lunch with the other workmen?
20 [*usually*]   Are your English assignments difficult?
21 [*seldom*]   That store receives complaints from its customers.
22 [*always*]   Does that fellow do his share of the work?
23 [*often*]   Mr. Johnson dictates reports to his secretary.
24 [*never*]   That store closes before 5:30 p.m.
25 [*usually*]   Are you ready for breakfast by eight o'clock?
26 [*ever*]   Why don't you speak English with your friends?
27 [*often*]   Mr. Hanson rides to work with Mr. Anderson.
28 [*always*]   My former secretary did her work very promptly.
29 [*seldom*]   Miss Stewart is sick or absent from work.
30 [*never*]   Mr. Fox smokes cigars in the office during the day.
31 [*usually*]   We learn many new words in our English class.
32 [*always*]   They have tried to follow his instructions very carefully.

Copy each sentence and add the indicated word or words in the correct position. Do not add any other words.

1 [*too*]   Mr. Johnson bought a leather briefcase.
2 [*still*]   Are you studying English at the same school ?
3 [*usually*]   We use that word in a little different way.
4 [*ever*]   Have they visited that national park ?
5 [*yet*]   Are you accustomed to our climate ?
6 [*also*]   Our friends enjoy popular music.
7 [*to her*]   William mailed the letter several days ago.
8 [*always*]   Louis does his work at the last minute.
9 [*either*]   The police didn't notice anything unusual.
10 [*still*]   We don't have enough money to buy a new car.
11 [*him*]   We sent a very practical gift for his birthday.
12 [*never*]   They have visited the Scandinavian countries.
13 [*always*]   Is your teacher strict about your homework ?
14 [*yet*]   Has the carpenter repaired the hole in the roof ?
15 [*to us*]   Our friends returned the photographs yesterday.
16 [*already*]   Miss Peters has sent the letter, hasn't she ?
17 [*always*]   My secretary does her work very promptly.
18 [*still*]   Do you find the English language simple ?
19 [*either*]   We didn't go to the meeting last Friday night.
20 [*to us*]   Our teacher didn't explain the last assignment.
21 [*usually*]   Does that new employee do his part of the work ?
22 [*yet*]   They haven't found a solution to that problem.
23 [*seldom*]   Don and I go to that section of the city.
24 [*either*]   François didn't finish his work, did he ?
25 [*still*]   There are plenty of sandwiches on the table.
26 [*always*]   Have you been interested in that subject ?
27 [*already*]   You've done those two lessons, haven't you ?
28 [*to them*]   Has Miss Stewart sent that letter or not ?
29 [*too*]   There are many students in the second section.
30 [*still*]   The foreman hasn't spoken to Mr. Johnson about it.
31 [*often*]   Fred's brother stays with him over the weekend.
32 [*always*]   Is there a guard in this building during the night ?

Put the expressions within the parentheses into the correct order. Then put these expressions at the end of the sentence. Do not add or omit any words. Study the examples carefully. In connection with the second group, remember "duration" and "accompaniment" take the same position as "manner".

"PLACE" AND "TIME"

1 They're studying their lessons   (*right now -at the library*).
    They're studying their lessons at the library right now.
2 Frank met Mr. Wilson   (*on Thursday -at Mr. Hart's house*).
3 The boys ran   (*down the street -a few minutes ago*).
4 The students studied the lesson   (*yesterday -on page* 80).
5 Our friends flew   (*to Denmark -last summer*).
6 I had a very bad cold   (*two days ago -in my head*).
7 Roger and Marcel went   (*to a concert -on Wednesday night*).
8 That fellow studies with me   (*every afternoon -at the library*).

"PLACE" AND "MANNER"

1 That student always comes   (*on time -to this class*).
    That student always comes to this class on time.
2 Did Tom and you go   (*with your friends -to the movies*) ?
3 The angry customer looked   (*doubtfully -at the clerk*).
4 We are going to work   (*at the library -for three hours*).
5 Hélène usually walks   (*with her brother -to school*).
6 My friend and I ran   (*toward the train -with our baggage*).
7 That employee seldom gets   (*to the office -late*).
8 The secretary wrote the message   (*on the paper -hastily*).

"MANNER" AND "TIME"

1 The students are pronouncing the words   (*now -carefully*).
    The students are pronouncing the words carefully now.
2 The students know the irregular verbs   (*now -very well*).
3 Gilles studies his lessons   (*every night -for two hours*).
4 Our friends will arrive here   (*quite early -in the morning*).
5 Yvan did all of the work   (*alone -last Thursday*).
6 Everyone criticized the man   (*after the meeting -severely*).
7 Miss Foster described her vacation trip   (*in detail -last night*).
8 Frank and I watched television   (*last Saturday night -with Patrick*).

Put the expressions within the parentheses into the correct order. Then put these expressions at the end of the sentence. Do not add or omit any words. Study the example carefully and review Exercise 124. Remember that the direct object always follows the verb in English.

1 The students know (*very well -now -the irregular verbs*).
   The students know the irregular verbs very well now.
2 Jeanne studies   (*every evening -at home -her lessons*).
3 I pick up   (*at the office -my paycheck -every Friday*).
4 Mrs. Brown chose   (*without any difficulty -a dress -yesterday*).
5 Someone took   (*last night -from my desk -my dictionary*).
6 I drank   (*too much coffee -this morning -at breakfast*).
7 Their friend ate   (*after the meeting -with them -lunch*).
8 Mr. Wilson bought   (*an expensive camera -two days ago -there*).
9 Our team won   (*last year -the championship -in this region*).
10 Canada exports   (*to Japan -much timber -every year*).
11 We enjoyed   (*very much -on Saturday night -Mr. Moore's lecture*).
12 You seldom see   (*on the television -good programs -at this hour*).
13 We have studied   (*up to now -carefully -every lesson*).
14 Mr. Smith borrowed   (*two years ago -from a friend -the money*).

Follow the instructions given in Exercise 125. Also review Exercises 124 and 125.

1 My secretary sent   (*last week -to them -the letter*).
   My secretary sent the letter to them last week.
2 Miss Foster has described   (*several times -her trip -to me*).
3 Mr. Hilton often brings   (*after work -flowers -his wife*).
4 The teacher explains   (*in class -to the students -the lessons*).
5 The Taylors sent   (*a bracelet -their daughter -for her birthday*).
6 That girl showed   (*Mr. Moore -after class -her homework*).
7 Mr. Smith sold   (*to my friend -his old car -last week*).
8 Would you please lend   (*for a few minutes -your pencil -Antoine*).
9 Their uncle built   (*a year ago -a new house -for them*).
10 The customer gave   (*reluctantly -the clerk -the money*).
11 Mrs. Johnson read   (*a story -just before bedtime -her son*).
12 Fred showed   (*to all of his friends -proudly -the photographs*).
13 Anne's mother made   (*a lovely dress -her -for the party*).
14 The messenger handed   (*the two boxes -carefully -to Albert*).

2
ADVANCED SECTION

NORTH AMERICA

STANDARD TIME ZONES

Use the correct form of the verb in parentheses in each sentence. Choose only the simple present tense (example : *he writes*), the continuous present tense (example : *he is writing*), or the perfect present tense (example : *he has written*).

1 That student *(know)* all of the new words very well now.
2 Mr. Howell *(work)* for that company for nine years.
3 The two mechanics *(finish)* the work right now.
4 It *(rain)* very much in this region in the spring.
5 Hélène's friend, Anne-Marie, *(lose)* her French-English dictionary.
6 Jean's brother *(graduate, just)* from the University of Alberta.
7 The plumber *(repair)* the leak in the pipe now.
8 That student *(make)* much progress since September.
9 Listen! I *(hear)* someone at the front door.
10 We *(see)* his famous uncle many times.
11 The earth *(circle)* the sun once every 365 days.
12 At present, Professor Moore *(write)* another book.
13 Our present teacher *(live)* in this city all of his life.
14 Jean-Claude *(take)* a course in European history this semester.
15 I *(call)* Mr. Lucas about five times in the past hour.
16 Yes, I *(remember)* that other fellow's name now.
17 Our friends from Joliette *(enjoy)* everything here up to now.
18 Mr. Harris *(teach)* English from two o'clock to five o'clock.
19 That brown briefcase *(belong)* to Professor Cromwell.
20 Philippe *(live)* in Roxboro three years now.
21 We *(study)* the use of verbs in English at the moment.
22 It *(rain)* very hard almost every day this week.
23 Jules Lapointe *(work)* about forty hours a week.
24 My uncle *(be)* in New York more than two months.
25 Just a minute ! I *(look up)* that word in the dictionary.
26 Up to the present, we *(write)* almost every lesson in the book.
27 The sun *(get)* very hot during the afternoon.
28 I *(watch)* hockey every Saturday night.
29 I *(have)* very little trouble with these lessons so far.
30 Helen and I *(wait)* right here since four o'clock.
31 For the time being, the workmen *(use)* a different method.
32 My friends, Charles and Tom, *(need)* some money right away.

Use the correct form of the verb in parentheses in each sentence. Choose between the past tense (examples : *she saw, they worked*) and the perfect present tense (examples : *she has seen, they have worked*).

1 Mr. and Mrs. Slater (*sell*)   their house several days ago.

2 Bruce Lethbridge (*work*) for the Cardwell Company since 1968.

3 Our instructor (*explain*)   that lesson to us last time.

4 The weather (*be*)   terrible ever since last Saturday.

5 We (*spend*)   several weeks in Mexico City last year.

6 Many people in this class (*see, never*)   the prairies.

7 Our friends (*return*) from Newfoundland a week ago yesterday.

8 Michelle (*study*)   English at this school for six months now.

9 I (*speak*)   to Mr. Scott about that matter several times already.

10 Miss Ross (*be*)   in Vancouver until two months ago.

11 My wife and I (*travel*)   by air many times in the past.

12 My friend Roger (*see, never*)   that television program.

13 Marcel and Henri (*finish, not*)   their homework yet.

14 I (*have*)   a little trouble with my car last week.

15 However, I (*have*)   no trouble with it since that time.

16 John (*see*)   Percé Rock three times.

17 I (*read*)   187 pages of this new novel already.

18 From the time of his arrival until now, he (*avoid*)   that topic.

19 We (*study*)   practically every lesson in the book so far.

20 The mailman (*deliver*)   the letter just a few minutes ago.

21 That fellow (*work*)   here for the past three weeks.

22 Our teacher (*give*)   us more than four examinations this semester.

23 Formerly, Mr. Foster (*work*) for the Reading Supply Company.

24 We (*have*) more than the normal amount of rain so far this year.

25 Before his graduation, Peter's brother (*apply*) for a job with them.

26 Mr. and Mrs. Lemaire (*live*)   in Sorel from 1965 to 1971.

27 A little while ago, we (*hear*)   some very bad news.

28 Professor Moore, our English teacher, (*write*)   three textbooks.

29 I (*read*)   that book three or four times before.

30 The Smiths (*go*)   to Belgium during their vacation.

31 Pierre and Jean-Paul (*learn*)   a great deal of English since June.

32 Mr. and Mrs. Benson (*fly*)   to Calgary twice since last summer.

Use the continuous perfect present tense of the verb in parentheses in each sentence. Notice that the verbs in these sentences show continuous action from the past to the present moment. Study the example sentences carefully.

1 Mr. Johnson (*work*) for that company for ten years.
   Mr. Johnson has been working for that company for ten years.
2 I (*listen*) to the professor's comments very carefully.
   I have been listening to the professor's comments very carefully.
3 René and André (*work*) on their English lessons all evening.
4 Those two fellows (*study*) English for six months now.
5 Helen and I (*stand*) right on this corner since five-thirty.
6 The children (*watch*) television programs since dinnertime.
7 It (*rain*) steadily since two o'clock this afternoon.
8 We (*have*) a great deal of trouble with our car recently.
9 Our teacher (*avoid*) that subject for a long time.
10 I'm getting tired. I (*drive*) this car since 8:00 a.m.
11 Mr. Wilson (*consider*) that possibility for quite a while now.
12 We (*read*) an average of 20 pages a day for three months.

If possible, change the form of the italicized verb in each sentence to the continuous perfect present tense. In some cases, this is not possible because the action is not continuous.

1 The Harveys *have lived* in Hamilton for three years now.
   The Harveys have been living in Hamilton for three years now.
2 I *have studied* English in this class for seven months.
3 Our guests *have* never *seen* the Expo 67 site.
4 Father *has felt* very well ever since last winter.
5 Dorothy and I *have waited* for you for a whole hour.
6 *Have* you *received* a letter from that company yet ?
7 That woman *has* already *talked* on the phone for fifteen minutes.
8 Mr. and Mrs. Séguin *have been* here since the first of the year.
9 George Howell *has worked* for this company for nine years.
10 My friend *has* already *spoken* to Mr. Fox about the matter.
11 I *have worked* on my English assignment since eight o'clock.
12 We *haven't seen* Mr. and Mrs. Brown for a long time.
13 Our car *has used* too much gasoline and oil recently.

have – taken
have – been – taking

Write "adjective" or "adverb" above each italicized word.

1 *Careful* students write their exercises *carefully.*
2 I learned the *easy* words. I learned the words *easily.*
3 She sings songs *beautifully.* She sings *beautiful* songs.
4 He has *good* pronunciation. He pronounces words *well.*
5 She speaks *fast.* I don't understand *fast* speech.
6 Smith buys his newspaper *early.* He buys an *early* edition.
7 She *really* enjoys stories. She enjoys *real* stories.
8 We have *generally* agreed. We made a *general* agreement.
9 I heard *sudden* movements. *Suddenly,* I heard movements.
10 *Finally,* I told the truth. I hate *final* examinations.
11 William is an *awkward* boy. William is *very awkward.*
12 Luc is *usually correct.* He *usually* writes *correctly.*
13 That's *probable.* That's *right.* That's *probably* right.
14 Frank told us *good* jokes. Frank told the jokes *well.*
15 That work was *hard* for those men. Everyone worked *hard.*

Write the correct form (adjective or adverb) of the word in parentheses in each sentence. Do not change the position of the word.

1 My friend Stewart plays the piano   (*beautiful*).
2 Of course, all the children were   (*happy*)   about that.
3 Jacques and Georges write   (*good*)   compositions in class.
4 Mr. Desjardins (*usual*)   speaks English very   (*good*).
5 (*Rapid*)   conversation is   (*good*)   practice for all students.
6 Mrs. Johnson closed the front door   (*quiet*)   and   (*cautious*).
7 The youngsters saw   (*real*)   elephants at the circus yesterday.
8 The driver was injured   (*bad*)   in the accident last night.
9 Of course, all of my students try to use   (*careful*)   diction.
10 (*Actual*), Miss Smith didn't tell you the   (*complete*)   story.
11 Jean studies   (*hard*)   and learns everything   (*good*).
12 Mr. Brown   (*general*)   arrives at his office   (*early*).
13 That other fellow never does   (*careful*)   work in class.
14 "Be   (*quiet*)   now !" Mr. Brown shouted at the boys   (*angry*).
15 That lesson was   (*easy*). Don't give me   (*easy*)   assignments.

Write "adjective" or "adverb" above each italicized word.

1 The man was *angry*. He shouted *angrily*.
2 He looked *unhappy*. He looked at me *unhappily*.
3 She appeared *sleepy*. She seemed *anxious* about it.
4 I tasted the medicine *cautiously*. It tasted *sweet*.
5 She feld the cloth *carefully*. She felt very *healthy*.
6 He was *nervous* about it. He became *nervous suddenly*.
7 We became *thirsty*. We became *quite suspicious*.
8 They got *curious* about it. They got the money *easily*.
9 Bill gets *angry easily*. He gets *tired very quickly*.
10 He made the remark *angrily*. He made me *angry*.
11 I find this case *unusual*. I found the money *quickly*.
12 He wants his coffee *hot*. He wants the property *badly*.
13 Please have everything *ready*. Please keep your room *clean*.
14 I consider him *intelligent*. I considered the case *carefully*.
15 We bought something *unusual* for her. It is an *unusual* gift.

Write the correct form (adjective or adverb) of the word in parentheses in each sentence. Do not change the position of the word.

1 I felt the surface of the table   (*careful*). It felt   (*smooth*).
2 The results of the election made us very   (*happy*).
3 We told them the news   (*happy*). They took the news   (*calm*).
4 Her dress looked   (*beautiful*). She was   (*happy*)   about it.
5 We looked at the dresses   (*careful*). They were   (*expensive*).
6 Would you please have those things   (*ready*)   for us.
7 Have the members suggested anything   (*different*)   (*recent*)?
8 We began to get   (*hungry*)   (*early*)   in the afternoon.
9 People   (*usual*)   feel   (*lazy*)   during   (*hot*)   weather.
10 Those two workers did   (*difficult*)   jobs   (*efficient*).
11 We couldn't keep our cigarettes   (*dry*)   in the rain.
12 I will be   (*complete*)   satisfied with something   (*inexpensive*).
13 The man seemed   (*nervous*)   and   (*anxious*)   about something.
14 The police became   (*suspicious*)   of the man very   (*rapid*).
15 I consider his behavior on the occasion very   (*suspicious*).

Write the correct form (adjective or adverb) of the word in parentheses in each sentence. Do not change the position of the word.

1 Laurent learned English (*rapid*) and (*easy*).

2 They (*general*) give all applications (*careful*) consideration.

3 Look at that sentence (*careful*). It looks (*incorrect*).

4 Helen announced her decision to us (*dramatic*).

5 Some kinds of flowers grow (*rapid*) in dark places.

6 We are using this room for our English class (*temporary*).

7 Frank will (*definite*) be (*anxious*) to hear from you.

8 (*Violent*) waves beat (*steady*) against the pier.

9 The boys got (*tired*) (*fast*) from working so (*hard*).

10 "Be (*quiet*) !" the man hissed at us (*angry*).

11 Johnson (*usual*) makes (*thorough*) reports to the company.

12 (*Real*), I'll be (*complete*) satisfied with something (*different*).

13 Jeanne spoke Spanish (*awkward*) and (*incorrect*).

14 She speaks the language (*considerable*) better now.

15 Everyone felt very (*sad*) about the news.

16 (*Automatic*) dishwashers are (*safe*) and (*convenient*).

17 (*Actual*), that author doesn't write (*true*) stories.

18 The maid was (*careful*) to keep the room (*clean*).

19 She cleaned the room (*regular*) and made it (*neat*) for us.

20 We moved (*fast*) with the (*strong*) wind behind us.

21 Everyone feels (*uneasy*) (*difficult*) situations.

22 The man looked at the policeman very (*uneasy*).

23 The coffee is (*strong*). We always like our coffee (*strong*).

24 Marie speaks both English and Italian (*good*).

25 I don't like (*final*) examinations. I always do (*poor*) on them.

26 Examinations make me (*angry*). I always get (*nervous*).

27 The director of our office is a (*good*) educated man.

28 His knowledge of English grammar is quite (*good*).

29 (*Sudden*), we heard (*loud*) noises outside the house.

30 He'll have everything (*ready*). He agreed with us (*ready*).

31 Our last two assignments were (*unusual*) (*difficult*).

32 The youngster seemed (*sleepy*). He smiled at us (*sleepy*).

33 There are (*various*) methods of doing that job (*efficient*).

34 (*Efficient*) employees (*rare*) do (*careless*) work on their jobs.

Complete each sentence with *no* or *not* as required. In some cases, a contraction is necessary.

1 There were .... students in the audience.

2 There were .... any chairs in the other room.

3 He's finished the first half of it, has .... he ?

4 .... paper ! .... pencils ! I can .... do any work.

5 Our new instructor is .... difficult to understand.

6 Do you .... prefer this one ? — ...., I do ....

7 I have .... time to read magazines or newspapers.

8 Is .... Frank ready to leave ? — ...., ... yet.

9 There was .... much milk in the refrigerator.

10 Guy said it was his cousin, ... his brother.

11 He hears .... difference between those two sounds.

12 Have the students finished their compositions or .... ?

13 Let's .... do that now. I have .... ambition at all.

14 English is .... a difficult language. Do .... you agree ?

15 The tall man, ... the fat one, is Mr. Williams.

16 Are .... you ready for your dessert ? — .... right now.

17 Do .... bother about that. — Oh, it is .... trouble.

18 Please answer these questions with "yes" or "..............".

19 I usually see Mr. Wilson on Mondays, but .... always.

20 Can .... you come tomorrow ? — .... I'm afraid ....

21 Those two fellows speak Portuguese, ... Spanish.

22 There are .... newspapers or magazines around here.

23 There are .... any books on those two shelves.

24 I understood the first part, but .... the last part.

25 .... much time remains before the final examination !

26 .... students were invited to the committee meeting.

27 .... a person has said anything about that matter yet.

28 Is there .... way to do it ? — .... that I know of.

29 Do you live nearby ? — Well, ... far from here.

30 .... many rooms in this building have good ventilation.

31 .... well-informed person agrees with him about that.

32 .... everyone enjoys the same type of entertainment.

33 .... business can afford .... to advertise today.

34 Mr. Johnson suggested .... telling them about our plans.

Study the comparisons in sentences 1 to 10. In sentences 11 to 34, complete the comparison with the adjective in parentheses. Do not omit any words.

1 The last story was *as interesting as* the other one.
2 Mr. Slater's house is *bigger than* our house.
3 Your example is *better than* the one in the book.
4 That brown chair is *more comfortable than* this one.
5 That brown chair is *less comfortable than* this one.
6 Luc is *a more ambitious* student *than* his brother.
7 Ellen Drake is *the prettiest* of all the girls.
8 That was *the worst* part of the entire job.
9 That lesson is *the most difficult* of all the lessons.
10 That fellow is *the least ambitious* student in the class.
11 Mr. Johnson was *(tactful)* than the other fellow.
12 Everyone else was *(nervous)* as you were.
13 Mr. Kelly is *(popular)* man in that organization.
14 Our car is *(old)* than Mr. Kennedy's car.
15 That big fellow was *(clumsy)* of the five players.
16 The weather is *(warm)* today than it was yesterday.
17 Brazil exports *(much)* coffee of all South American countries.
18 Marie is certainly not *(intelligent)* as her sister is.
19 William is *(homely)* boy than his brother.
20 Rimouski is *(far)* from here than Rivière-du-Loup.
21 Miss Peters is *(friendly)* of all the girls in this office.
22 We've had *(little)* difficulty with this part than the other one.
23 Does your country have *(bad)* weather as this ?
24 *(Few)* members came to the meeting this week than last week.
25 New York has *(many)* tall buildings of any city in the world.
26 Commerce Court is *(tall)* building in Toronto.
27 Elizabeth is *(charming)* a woman as her mother.
28 *(Many)* people in Switzerland speak German than French.
29 Roger is *(talented)* musician in that group.
30 The Gilberts bought *(expensive)* car than we did.
31 I didn't have *(good)* luck with it as Frank did.
32 Mr. Jackson was *(sensible)* person at the meeting.
33 That sort of thing is *(common)* in Europe than here.
34 Jean-Guy did *(good)* work in that class than anyone else.

Use the words (a) *almost*, (b) *practically*, and (c) *just* with *as . . . as* in the following sentences. Study the example carefully.

1 That's as cheap as this. (a) *That's almost as cheap as this.* (b) *That's practically as cheap as this.* (c) *That's just as cheap as this.*
2 The exercise on this page is as easy as the last one.
3 The tall girl is as pretty as the dark girl.
4 The bedroom is as wide as the living room.
5 Everyone else was as nervous as you were.
6 That company has as many employees as this one.
7 Mr. Foster earns as much money as his brother.
8 Mr. Wilson has as many responsibilities as Mr. Johnson.

Add *much* or *many* in the blank space in each sentence.

1 The weather is .... better today than yesterday.
2 Ellen Drake is a .... prettier girl than her sister.
3 Andrea, however, has .... more friends than Ellen.
4 I had .... more trouble with that lesson than the last one.
5 Football is .... more popular than soccer in this country.
6 There are .... more tall buildings in New York than in Paris.
7 Pierre Tremblay is a .... more intelligent student than Robert Drouin.
8 .... more students in this school study English than German.
9 We got .... worse results with that method than with this one.

Complete these comparisons with the words *as*, *to*, or *from*.

1 That other car is the same model .... this one.
2 This exercise is different .... the last two exercises.
3 Your new pantsuit is similar .... mine.
4 The customs there aren't the same .... those in Turkey.
5 The design of that house is similar .... the design of this one.
6 Your example was quite different .... the one in the book.
7 Mr. Johnson's suit is the same color .... yours.
8 This motor is different .... any other motor on the market.
9 His answer to the problem wasn't quite the same .... mine.

Read the following conversation between two prospective house buyers. Study the use of the comparative and superlative forms carefully. Answer the questions at the end of the selection.

Mr. Kelly : What do you think about the three houses ? *Mrs. Kelly :* I like the red house the best of all. Which one do you like the best ? *Mr.* I haven't decided that yet, but I like the blue house more than the red one. Do you think the red house is as beautiful as the blue one ? *Mrs.* I think the red house is the most modern and the most beautiful of the three. The blue house is almost as beautiful as the red one, but not quite. Of course, the white house is the least modern of all. *Mr.* That's true, but the white house is cheaper and more practical than the blue house. There is more space in the white house than in the red house. It also has more rooms than the red one. *Mrs.* Yes, the white house is larger than the red one, but the red one costs the least of the three. *Mr.* Yes, it's the cheapest of all, but the red one is too modern for me. Besides, the blue house is the most comfortable of the three. *Mrs.* Well, I think the modern style is more practical than any other kind. Naturally, you're right about the size. The red house is the smallest of these houses. The blue house is the biggest. The white house isn't as big as the blue house, but it isn't as small as the red house. *Mr.* Don't you think the red house is too small for us ? *Mrs.* No, I think it's big enough. Don't forget there are more windows in the red house than in the white one. *Mr.* That's right, but the blue house has the most windows of all. In addition, the red house isn't as conventional as the blue house. Remember it's easier to sell a conventional house than a modern house. *Mrs.* Of course, the white house is the most conventional of all, but the price of the white house is higher than the price of the red one. The blue house is the most expensive of all. *Mr.* Well, let's consider the white house then. It's not as big as the blue one, and it doesn't have as large a basement as the blue one, but it is apparently the most practical. *Mrs.* Well, the white house isn't as modern as either of the other two houses, but maybe it's the best one for us. It's less expensive than the blue house. Of course, is has the prettiest fireplace of all, and it has the most garden space of the three. *Mr.* That's true. Maybe the white house is the best for us. It's smaller than the blue house, but it's bigger than the red house. It has fewer rooms than the blue house, but it has more rooms than the red one. *Mrs.* The kitchen in the red house is nicer than the kitchen in the blue house, but the white house has the nicest kitchen of all. *Mr.* We'll get the most for our money if we buy the white house. *Mrs.* Now I think it's the most beautiful of all. Let's buy it today !

QUESTIONS ABOUT "THE HOUSE BUYERS"

1   Is the white house bigger than the red house ?   2   Which house is the biggest of the three ?   3   Is the red house as expensive as the white house ?   4   Which house is the most expensive of all ?   5   Is the blue house more practical than the white house ?   6   Is the red house less practical than the white house ?   7   Which house is the least practical of all ?   8   Does the white house have more windows than the red house ?   9   Which house has the most windows ?   10   Is the kitchen in the blue house nicer than the kitchen of all ?   12   Is the white house more modern than the blue house ?   13   Which house is the most modern of all ?   14   Is the red house prettier than the white house ?   15   Is the blue house as pretty as the white house ?   16   Which house is the prettiest ?   17   Are the windows in the blue house more beautiful than the windows in the red house ?   18   Which house has the most beautiful windows ?   19   Does the red house have more garden space than the white one ?   20   Is the blue one cheaper than the white one ?   21   Which one of the three is the cheapest ?

Use the adverb in each sentence in the indicated form of comparison. Notice that there are two possibilities in a few cases. Study the first six examples.

1 You speak   *(quickly)*   as he.   *You speak as quickly as he.*
2 She speaks   *(fast)*   than you.   *She speaks faster than you.*
3 He speaks   *(well)*   than you.   *He speaks better than you.*

4 I speak   *(fluent)*   than he. $\Big\{$ *I speak more fluently than he.*
                                                I speak less fluently than he.

5 He speaks   *(well)*   of all.   *He speaks the best of all.*

6 I speak   *(rapidly)*   of all. $\Big\{$ *I speak the least rapidly of all.*
                                                I speak the most rapidly of all.

7 You can tell Harris about it just   *(easily)*   as I can.
8 Johnson attends those meetings   *(often)*   than I do.
9 Alice plays the piano *(well)* than the other two girls.
10 You didn't do this part   *(thoroughly)*   as the first part.
11 That tall fellow works much   *(rapidly)*   than the others.
12 Jean knows English grammar   *(well)*   of all the students.
13 Smith always drives   *(carelessly)*   than his wife.
14 We plan to get there   *(early)*   than the other guests.
15 Pierre understands English   *(little)*   of all the students.
16 He speaks English   *(badly)*   than Marcel and Carole.
17 The letter will probably arrive   *(soon)*   than you expect.
18 Brown explains things   *(clearly)*   of all our teachers.
19 He is able to talk about that subject   *(confidently)*   than I.
20 I certainly hope to finish the work   *(fast)*   than that !
21 Wilson never discusses the subject   *(calmly)*   as Johnson.
22 Yvan attends class   *(regularly)*   of all the students.
23 He works much   *(hard)*   on his lessons than the others.
24 He always analyzes things   *(thoroughly)*   than the others.
25 I usually enjoy movies   *(much)*   than television plays.
26 Frank plays tennis   *(badly)*   of all the players.
27 However, he can swim   *(well)*   than John or Bill.
28 I think that you acted   *(wisely)*   than he did.
29 Mr. Adams works   *(seriously)*   of all the employees.
30 My secretary seldom gets to work   *(early)*   as I do.
31 I usually get here much   *(early)*   than the others.
32 The wind blew   *(hard)*   yesterday than it did on Monday.

Study the first two examples. In the remainder of the sentences, complete the comparisons with the correct forms of the words in parentheses. Do not omit any words.

1 Alice always welcomes people (*sincere*) than Betty.
   Alice always welcomes people more sincerely than Betty.
2 Alice is actually (*sincere*) person than her friend.
   Alice is actually a more sincere person than her friend.
3 Mr. Harvey comes here (*regular*) of all the members.
4 Mr. Wilson wasn't (*calm*) as the others in that respect.
5 Mr. Shaw explained the lesson (*clear*) than you did.
6 His explanation of the lesson was (*clear*) than yours.
7 Mr. Linton was (*confident*) of all the lecturers.
8 Mr. Linton spoke (*confident*) of all the lecturers.
9 Irène does her English lessons (*careful*) than I do.
10 In general, Irène does (*careful*) work than I do.
11 Mr. Caldwell is undoubtedly (*wise*) of the three officials.
12 Mr. Caldwell acted (*wise*) of the three in that matter.
13 Louise worked (*hard*) on those lessons than you did.
14 That's true, but those lessons were (*hard*) than the others.

Use the correct form of the word in parentheses in each sentence.

1 Jacques speaks English (*fluent*) of all the students.
2 You look much (*happy*) today than you did yesterday.
3 Françoise's poem is (*romantic*) than René's.
4 (*beautiful*) house in the neighborhood is that one.
5 That house is certainly much (*ugly*) than the one next to it.
6 That tall woman is (*ambitious*) secretary in this office.
7 Jacqueline usually dresses just (*neat*) as her sister.
8 Our friends go to the theater (*often*) than we do.
9 This exercise doesn't seem quite (*easy*) as the last one.
10 Bill presented his point of view (*confident*) than I did.
11 Is Charles Ratelle (*good*) student than his brother ?
12 Peter Lawrence is (*friendly*) person in this factory.
13 Louis didn't study this lesson (*thorough*) as the last one.
14 Well, he had (*little*) time for this lesson than for the last one.

Change the verb to the active voice and rewrite the sentence. Be sure to keep the same tense. In some cases, it will be necessary to supply a subject (see the second example).

1 The books were taken by John. *John took the books.*
2 The boxes were mailed today.   *He mailed the boxes today.*
3 The two packages were opened by my secretary.
4 Our homework is corrected by our teacher.
5 Two buildings have been constructed by that company.
6 That room wasn't cleaned carefully yesterday.
7 The truck is being loaded by the men now.
8 Was that machine checked by the inspector ?
9 Will that report be written by the same committee ?
10 Has the news been announced by the prime minister ?
11 The mail is delivered to this office twice a day.
12 All of us were surprised by his frank attitude.
13 Was the repair work done by that mechanic ?
14 He wasn't very much respected by the employees.
15 Are many courses in English given during the summer ?

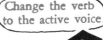

Change the verb to the active voice.

Change the verb to the passive voice and rewrite the sentence. Be sure to keep the same tense.

1 He *signed* the letter.   *The letter was signed by him.*
2 The secretary *opens* the mail every morning.
3 The committee *is considering* that proposal right now.
4 Pierre Desjardins *will complete* that project next year.
5 His boss *has transferred* him to another department.
6 *Will* the company *distribute* the announcements ?
7 An artist *wrote* that interesting article about Montreal.
8 Today a large number of people *speak* English.
9 *Didn't* they *return* those books to the library ?
10 The government *has* not *changed* that regulation yet.
11 Someone *stole* all her valuable jewelry last night.
12 Miss Peters *wrote* all of the reports for Mr. Johnson.
13 Bad weather *had delayed* Flight 202 from Dorval.
14 *Did* the court *divide* the money among the children ?
15 Many scholars *have translated* that famous Greek epic.

Use the correct voice (active or passive) and the correct tense of the verb in each sentence.

1 Everyone (*shock*) by the terrible news yesterday.
2 Almost everyone (*enjoy*) the lecture last night.
3 English (*teach*) in the schools of almost every nation.
4 That proposal (*consider*) by the members right now.
5 The accident (*happen*) right here at 6:30 last night.
6 Mr. Smith (*teach*) at the University of Manitoba since 1968.
7 Mr. Harris (*divide*) the class into two sections tomorrow.
8 Wilson (*borrow*) the money from Brown two weeks ago.
9 Not much (*say*) about the matter since that time.
10 My friend (*write*) to me about it several times now.
11 Corporal Davis (*promote*) to the rank of sergeant last week.
12 That event (*occur*) shortly after the meeting last week.
13 All the students (*bring*) guests to the party tomorrow night.
14 Less than half of the cans of paint (*use*) up to now.
15 More classes in English (*list*) for next fall.
16 Everything (*go*) well so far. There (*be*) no trouble yet.
17 That movie about Napoleon's life (*disappoint*) me greatly.
18 The mail (*deliver, always*) to this office before 10 a.m.
19 Who (*furnish*) the food for the picnic next weekend ?
20 At this time, much attention (*devote*) to that problem.
21 Think carefully. I'm sure you (*remember*) his name.
22 We (*treat*) very kindly by our hosts last Saturday.
23 Mr. Wilson (*make*) some interesting statements yesterday.
24 A new textbook (*publish*) by that company next year.
25 The noise from the trains (*annoy*) me terribly last night.
26 That old red house (*build*) in the year 1822.
27 The report (*examine, not*) by a committee of experts yet.
28 Cocktails (*serve*) to the guests about 10 minutes from now.
29 His sharp remarks (*embarrass*) everyone last night.
30 Fred (*introduce*) to the fellow by Mr. Brown yesterday.
31 Listen to this ! I think this news (*surprise*) you !
32 The Banbury Shoe Company (*employ*) 25 new men next month.
33 Only 45 new students (*admit*) into the department last year.
34 A second coat of paint (*spread*) over that surface tomorrow.

Use *can* with the verb in parentheses to express "ability" in the present or future. Write the sentence (a) in statement form, (b) in question form, and (c) in negative form. Study the example carefully.

1 Ed (*go*) downtown with us. (a) *Ed can go downtown with us.*
   (b) *Can Ed go downtown with us?* (c) *Ed can't go downtown with us.*
2 Mr. Lucas (*give*) you all the money tomorrow.
3 Antoine (*play*) the piano very well.
4 The students in that class (*speak*) English fluently.
5 You (*find*) many bargains in the stores after Christmas.
6 I (*use*) the same key for the front door and the back door.
7 That fellow (*speak*) to the director on Sunday morning.
8 Mr. Burke (*get*) someone to substitute for him tonight.
9 Roger (*borrow*) Mr. Kennedy's car for the party tomorrow.
10 Dr. Hanson (*usually, attend*) the Friday night meetings.
11 You (*buy*) all of those things at a hardware store.
12 Father (*read*) the newspaper without his glasses.
13 Harold and his friend (*meet*) us right after class today.

Change *can* (present and future) to *could* (past) in the following sentences. Study the first two examples carefully.

1 I can understand that part.   *I could understand that part.*
2 Can't you go with Mr. Fox?   *Couldn't you go with Mr. Fox?*
3 I can see a big difference between the two examples.
4 We can't find Dr. Hanson's address in the directory.
5 Can your friend help you with the difficult part of the work?
6 Can't Miss Cunningham find her hat and overcoat?
7 I can hear those men's voices from the next room.
8 Elizabeth can play the piano, but she can't sing.
9 Why can't you explain everything to your boss on Monday?
10 No one can predict the results of the conference.
11 Can't that other fellow take his vacation the following week?
12 Serge can't express his thoughts in English very well.
13 Why can't you ask Roger to help you with the work on Friday?
14 Not many of the students can spell all those words correctly.
15 Can't you postpone your trip to Boston until the following week?

Use *can* in place of *be able* in the following sentences. Study the examples.

1 Mr. Burke will be able to go.   *Mr. Burke can go.*
2 Carol wasn't able to find it.   *Carol couldn't find it.*
3 Fred will be able to return the money before Thursday.
4 Are you able to understand everything the teacher says ?
5 Miss Peters wasn't able to find her gloves in the drawer.
6 We won't be able to announce the change until next week.
7 Weren't your friends from Magog able to go to the party ?
8 I was able to finish only half of the lesson last night.
9 Which sections weren't you able to do by yourself ?
10 Are you able to get those two stations on your radio ?
11 Wasn't Maurice able to follow the instructions in the book ?
12 I'll be able to tell you much more about our plans next week.
13 Not many of these students are able to pronounce that sound.
14 Who will be able to deliver the message to Mr. Franklin ?
15 Won't you be able to attend the meeting tomorrow afternoon ?

Use *be able* in place of *can* in the following sentences. Study the examples.

1 They can understand me.   *They are able to understand me.*
2 We couldn't hear everything.   *We weren't able to hear everything.*
3 You can get that information from Miss Stewart tomorrow.
4 Mr. Harris can speak three or four foreign languages.
5 I could answer all of the questions in the lesson except one.
6 Can you finish all of the work for us by next Thursday ?
7 No one could explain the exact meaning of the word to me.
8 Unfortunately, I can't attend the meeting with you tomorrow.
9 I couldn't find Dr. Hanson's name or address in the directory.
10 Can't you help your friend with the difficult parts of the work ?
11 We can certainly pay back the money before that time.
12 Couldn't the students follow the teacher's instructions ?
13 Why can't Mr. Johnson do that work sometime next week ?
14 Could your friends see most of the parade from their window ?
15 Who can translate these two sentences into English for me ?

Use both *should* and *ought* with the verb in parentheses to express "advisability" or "obligation" in the present or future. Study the example carefully.

1 We (*invite*) the Browns to the party. (a) *We should invite the Browns to the party.* (b) *We ought to invite the Browns to the party.*
2 You (*return*) the money to Mr. Lucas as soon as possible.
3 Your friends (*leave*) now. It's getting quite late.
4 Everyone (*help*) his friends and neighbors whenever possible.
5 Robert (*speak*) to Mr. Kramer about that matter soon.
6 Mr. Burke (*try*) to find a better job with another company.
7 Students (*always, spend*) time on their lessons at home.
8 You (*be*) a little more careful about that in the future.
9 Dr. Hanson (*take*) a taxi home ; it's a very long walk.
10 We (*urge*) all of our friends to attend that meeting.
11 Drivers (*always, be*) courteous to pedestrians.
12 Lucien (*stay*) at home tonight and (*study*) his English lesson.
13 You (*go*) to parties more often and (*make*) new friends.
14 They (*write*) that letter to James and (*mail*) it right away.

Change the verb in each sentence to the past tense form. After each sentence, add another sentence to show that the action did not occur. Study the examples.

1 Mr. Kennedy should go to the meeting. *Mr. Kennedy should have gone to the meeting. However, he didn't go to the meeting.*
2 You ought to speak to the director. *You ought to have spoken to the director. However, you didn't speak to the director.*
3 You should tell your boss the truth about the accident.
4 Miss Irwin ought to sent the company a check immediately.
5 I should study very hard for the next examination.
6 We ought to eat our dinner at a convenient time.
7 Harold should take some courses in history.
8 Mr. Farrell should answer that telegram soon.
9 You ought to explain all of the details to me.
10 Mrs. Wilson ought to stay in bed and rest.
11 Everyone ought to do his share of the work.
12 You ought to call her and tell her the news.

Use the verb in parentheses in negative sentences with both *should* and *ought*. Use the correct tense. Study the first two examples carefully.

1 You (*help*) Fred tomorrow. (a) *You should not help Fred tomorrow.* (b) *You ought not to help Fred tomorrow.*

2 Bill (*go*) home last week. (a) *Bill should not have gone home last week.* (b) *Bill ought not to have gone home last week.*

3 Frank (*tell*) anyone about his plans until next summer.

4 Mr. Foster (*write*) to them about that matter last week.

5 You (*go*) to bed so late every night of the week.

6 Mr. Black (*speak*) so frankly in front of his boss yesterday.

7 Mr. Burke (*give*) that fellow any more money last week.

8 We (*delay*) any longer than next Wednesday in answering.

9 You (*drink*) so many cups of coffee last night.

10 They (*nominate*) Mr. Kennedy at the meeting tomorrow.

11 The janitor (*lock*) the two front doors yesterday morning.

12 You (*force*) Tom and Fred to come with us tomorrow night.

13 Smith and Green (*object*) to Brown's suggestion yesterday.

Use the verb in parentheses in question form with both *should* and *ought*. Use the correct tense. Study the two examples carefully.

1 We (*tell*) everyone tomorrow. (a) *Should we tell everyone tomorrow?* (b) *Ought we to tell everyone tomorrow?*

2 We (*speak*) to Bill yesterday. (a) *Should we have spoken to Bill yesterday?* (b) *Ought we to have spoken to Bill yesterday?*

3 You (*tell*) your boss about that problem next Monday.

4 We (*give*) the message to someone else when we called.

5 I (*ask*) Mr. Kennedy for his advice about that tomorrow night.

6 Roger (*send*) them a telegram before he leaves tonight.

7 Mr. Johnson (*submit*) his application before this week.

8 The students (*stay*) there and (*wait*) for Mr. Fox yesterday.

9 We (*invite*) Mr. and Mrs. Hill to the party next week.

10 My friend (*announce*) the news to them sooner than he did.

11 I (*wait*) until next week and (*make*) a decision then.

12 Jim (*persuade*) Mr. Lucas to ride with us tomorrow.

13 Mr. Johnson (*take*) the papers and (*give*) them to you yesterday.

Use both *must* and *have* with the verb in parentheses to express "necessity" in the present or future. Study the first two examples.

1 We (*finish*) that work before Friday. (a) *We must finish that work before Friday.* (b) *We have to finish that work before Friday.*
2 Henri (*return*) to Joliette tomorrow. (a) *Henri must return to Joliette tomorrow.* (b) *Henri has to return to Joliette tomorrow.*
3 Mr. Lafleur (*make out*) his income tax report next week.
4 You (*inform*) the police about that accident right away.
5 Everyone (*take*) the English examination.
6 All members of the club (*pay*) their dues before Friday.
7 I (*finish*) this work by tomorrow and (*give*) it to Mr. Wilson.
8 Jean-Claude (*work*) much harder in order to improve his marks.
9 It's late ! We (*walk*) very fast to get there on time.
10 I (*cash*) this check. Otherwise, I won't have any money.
11 Mr. Kennedy (*have*) your reply no later than next Tuesday.
12 We (*be*) at the airport thirty minutes before flight time.
13 You (*write*) to the company and (*explain*) everything carefully.

Change the verb in each sentence to the past tense form, and make any other necessary changes. Notice that there is no past tense of *must*. Study the first two examples carefully.

1 We have to leave right away.   *We had to leave right away.*
2 Mr. Adams must go to Montreal.   *Mr. Adams had to go to Montreal.*
3 I have to read the instructions carefully to understand them.
4 We must drive very fast to get there before eight o'clock.
5 Mr. Wilson has to get to the airport thirty minutes early.
6 I must stay at my office until six-thirty tonight.
7 Bill and I have to finish all of the work by tomorrow night.
8 We must call a plumber to fix those broken pipes.
9 All of the members have to attend the meeting tomorrow.
10 Harold must send a telegram to his friends right away.
11 Everyone has to do his share of the work next Wednesday.
12 I must return the money to Mr. Lucas before Wednesday.
13 We have to sign the contract and return it immediately.
14 Our teacher often has to explain the same lesson twice.
15 Smith has to fill out the papers and submit them by Saturday.

Change these sentences to questions. Study the first two examples.

1 Mr. Hart must leave now.   *Must Mr. Hart leave now ?*
2 We have to study that lesson. *Do we have to study that lesson ?*
3 The students have to turn in their papers tomorrow.
4 Everyone in the class must take the final examination.
5 Mrs. Béliveau has to go shopping this afternoon.
6 Her friend has to get ready to leave right now.
7 We have to return those books to the library tomorrow.
8 Frank had to explain everything to Mr. Moore carefully.
9 You must speak to Mr. Brink before the meeting tonight.
10 Mr. Lemieux has to leave for Calgary next Tuesday.
11 Louise had to leave home early to get there on time.
12 The students must also write the other two exercises.
13 We must wrap that package and mail it to Hélène today.
14 The students had to study the lesson and learn the new words.
15 The man must fill out the blank and give it to the secretary.

Practice these
question forms.

Change the verb in these sentences to the negative form and make any other
necessary changes. Also indicate the meaning of the sentence ("prohibition" or "lack
of necessity"). Study the first two examples carefully.

1 Carol must leave before eight o'clock.
   Carol must not leave before eight o'clock. (prohibition)
2 You have to write these two lessons.
   You don't have to write these two lessons. (lack of necessity)
3 Miss Peters has to cash that check right away.
4 We must say something to Mr. Adams about that matter.
5 Dave and I have to be there at a specific time tonight.
6 Your friend must reveal all of his plans to those people.
7 We always have to write the exercises for our teacher.
8 The students had to ask for permission in order to leave.
9 We must also give the other one to Mr. Wilson's secretary.
10 The men had to show some kind of identification.
11 You must help your two friends with their homework.
12 I have to pay Mr. Lucas some of the money this week.
13 You must tell your friends your plans for next year too.
14 The students had to answer all of the questions on the page.

Change the following statements and negatives to the question form.

1 He has to leave.   *Does he have to leave ?*
2 Tom can't do it.   *Can't Tom do it ?*
3 Dorothy will be able to meet us here tomorrow.
4 You must tell your boss about your change in plans.
5 Miss Cunningham couldn't find her purse and gloves.
6 We have to answer all the questions on the page.
7 We should invite Mr. and Mrs. Wilson to the party too.
8 I must wrap the package and mail it today.
9 Mr. Stewart won't be able to attend the meeting.
10 I should tell them the truth about the accident.
11 The students had to ask for permission to leave.
12 The students can understand their teacher very well.
13 I should not tell anyone about it until tomorrow.
14 He's not able to help the men with it right now.
15 You must speak to Mr. Henderson before the meeting.

Change the following statements and questions to the negative form.

1 You should call them.   *You shouldn't call them.*
2 Can Roger help us ?   *Can't Roger help us ?*
3 I must call Mr. Kennedy at his office today.
4 We could hear the man from the back of the room.
5 I have to get the money from Harold right away.
6 Bill will be able to lend us some money next week.
7 You should urge them to join that organization.
8 Can your friends go to the meeting with us tonight ?
9 They must tell their boss all of their plans.
10 Were you able to finish the entire job yesterday ?
11 We had to ask our boss for permission to leave early.
12 I can think of a few examples similar to that one.
13 You should have said something to Louise about it.
14 We must also show those people the other one.
15 The employees had to work on Saturday and Sunday.

Select the correct word or words from the parentheses in each sentence. Do not add any other word or words to the sentence.

1 Everyone (*must, has*) to take the examination tomorrow.
2 Students (*should, ought*) spend much time on their homework.
3 Bill (*can, will be able*) help us with the work next week.
4 We (*must, have*) leave for home in a few minutes.
5 She (*couldn't, wasn't able*) to find her silver bracelet.
6 You (*should, ought*) to write to them today or tomorrow.
7 Johnson (*must, has*) send out the report right away.
8 We (*should, ought*) invite the Browns to the party.
9 Who (*can, is able*) explain that sentence to us ?
10 The men (*must, have*) finish the job before Monday.
11 Everyone (*should, ought*) have tried to be more careful.
12 The students (*could, were able*) understand everything.
13 They (*must, have*) to have your answer immediately.
14 You (*should, ought*) not to smoke quite so much.
15 We (*can't, won't be able*) to visit you next weekend.

Use the correct form of the verb in parentheses in each sentence.

1 Which one of them should I (*buy*) ? I can't (*decide*).
2 Why do you have (*explain*) everything to your boss ?
3 How long can you (*be*) away from your office ?
4 When will Mr. Kennedy be able (*give*) us an answer ?
5 What should we (*say*) to the director about that yesterday ?
6 How long must we (*wait*) here for those people ?
7 Why weren't those men able (*finish*) the work right away ?
8 How many sentences did you have (*write*) for the teacher ?
9 How much can you (*afford*) to pay for an apartment ?
10 Why should we (*speak*) to him when we have just seen him ?
11 When must we (*return*) all of these books to the library ?
12 How many students could (*translate*) those two sentences ?
13 Why ought Bill (*give*) them the money before this week ?
14 How many members can (*come*) to the meeting tomorrow ?
15 How far must we (*walk*) in order to get to the hotel ?

Read this conversation carefully.
Notice the use of the auxiliaries *will, should,* etc.

Bill: Are you going to attend the meeting tonight? *Tom:* I should go. Unfortunately, I won't be able to go. *Bill:* Why should you go? *Tom:* The speaker will talk about job opportunities. I ought to know all about this subject. As you know, I will graduate from school next June. Then I will have to find a job. *Bill:* In that case, you ought to cancel your other plans and attend the meeting. You shouldn't miss this meeting. *Tom:* You're right. But I can't go. *Bill:* Why can't you? *Tom:* Don't you remember? We're going to have an examination in our class tomorrow. I have to study for the examination. *Bill:* Do you have to study? Is it a necessity? *Tom:* Well, I suppose the expression, "have to study", is too strong. No one is forcing me. But I really ought to study tonight. I should devote the time to a thorough review. Everyone ought to review before an exam. Don't you agree? *Bill:* Yes, I do. *Tom:* In that case, shouldn't you study too? *Bill:* I don't have to study. I studied last night, and I'm sure I can pass it. Besides that, I must attend the meeting. *Tom:* Why must you attend it? *Bill:* Have you forgotten? I have to introduce the speaker to the audience. *Tom:* Yes, That's right. Does Fred have to go too? *Bill:* Yes, he does. By the way, that reminds me of something. I must not forget to call him. *Tom:* Why mustn't you forget? *Bill:* I must remind him to bring the microphone. As a matter of fact, I ought to call him right now because it's getting late. *Tom:* I can remind him for you. I'll see him in half an hour. *Bill:* Good. That will help me a lot. *Tom:* Say, Bill, would you do a favor for me? *Bill:* Sure, I'd be glad to help you. What can I do for you? *Tom:* Would you please take notes during the lecture tonight? *Bill:* Of course. I can do that very easily because I have to keep a record of the meeting anyway. Should I ask Fred to take notes too? *Tom:* No, that won't be necessary. Well, I have to go now. I'll see you later. *Bill:* All right. So long and thanks. *Tom:* I won't forget your message for Fred.

REVIEW : SIMPLE QUESTION FORMS

Change the following statements and negatives to simple questions. Study the examples.

1 David knows that fellow.   *Does David know that fellow ?*
2 He won't be able to come.   *Won't he be able to come ?*
3 The students understood the instructions completely.
4 Irène does her homework at the library.
5 They had to check every one of the reports carefully.
6 I should have written to the Browns and explained it.
7 All of those students have their own dictionaries.
8 I cannot think of anything to tell you right now.
9 Richard has not received any letters from them yet.
10 I shouldn't lend that fellow the money to pay for it.
11 Mr. Bouchard flies to Regina twice a year.
12 It is always hot in Montreal at this time of the year.
13 He always has to repeat the instructions for the students.
14 Jean-Pierre studied at Laval last year.
15 Mr. Johnson has already been introduced to that fellow.

REVIEW : NEGATIVE FORMS

Change the following statements and questions to the negative form.

1 I went to the meeting.   *I didn't go to the meeting.*
2 Can they go with us tonight ? *Can't they go with us tonight ?*
3 The instructor explained that lesson to us yesterday.
4 You should call Mr. Johnson before nine o'clock.
5 Could your friends see the parade from their window ?
6 Hurry ! We have to have all those things right away.
7 The inside of the house has already been painted.
8 The Taylors planned to leave for the weekend too.
9 There have been some very bad storms recently.
10 I had an opportunity to speak to Mr. Smith yesterday.
11 We saw someone in the hall outside your office.
12 Those two carpenters did the work very quickly.
13 The students had to answer all the questions on the page.
14 I felt quite sick at eight o'clock this morning.
15 Will you be able to finish the work before next Friday ?

(1) GERUND SUBJECT (2) INFINITIVE AFTER "IT"

Rewrite each sentence. Replace the italicized words with *it* and use the full infinitive as indicated in the first two examples.

1 *Learning English* is really quite easy.
  It is really quite easy to learn English.
2 *Seeing our old friends again* was wonderful.
  It was wonderful to see our old friends again.
3 *Complaining about that matter now* is useless.
4 *Sitting in one place for so long* was very uncomfortable.
5 *Going to that party next week* will be a lot of fun.
6 *Finding examples of that* is almost impossible.
7 *Traveling to Italy by boat* will be interesting for us.
8 *Understanding that fellow* was very difficult for me.
9 *Meeting the president in person* was exciting.
10 *Writing good compositions in English* is not so easy.
11 *Driving from here to Jonquière* takes about five hours.
12 *Getting to school by bus* usually takes me forty minutes.
13 *Flying to Vancouver* took us only four hours.

THE INFINITIVE TO SHOW REASON OR PURPOSE

Write a complete answer to each question. In your answer, use the full infinitive to show the reason or purpose. Study the first two examples.

1 Why did you enroll in this course ?
  I enrolled in this course to improve my English.
2 What did you close the window for ?
  I closed the window to keep out the loud noises.
3 Why did Mr. and Mrs. Gilbert go to Noranda ?
4 What did Father go down to the basement for ?
5 Why did you have to go to the grocery store today ?
6 What did you go to the post office for ?
7 Why are those two boys running so fast ?
8 Why should we tell Mr. Johnson about that matter ?
9 What did the students have to do that for ?
10 What should we go to that lecture for ?
11 Why did the guests go home so early last night ?
12 Why must you and your wife return to New York ?
13 Why did Mr. Anderson go to the bank this morning ?

Complete the sentences with (1) a full infinitive and (2) any other necessary words. Study the first two examples carefully.

1 Everyone was sorry *to hear the bad news.*
2 Miss Williams was pleased *to receive such a nice gift.*
3 The students are anxious ....
4 All of the members were satisfied.................................
5 You were very fortunate ....
6 His parents were ashamed...
7 Don and Dorothy will be ready...................................
8 Everyone was disappointed ....
9 Bill Black was certainly lucky ....
10 In my opinion, that man is unfit................................
11 That fellow was very polite.......................................
12 Yes, I'm fully prepared ....
13 Your friends were considerate...................................
14 Professor Moore is certainly qualified ....
15 I think you will be surprised ....

Complete these sentences with (1) the word *too,* (2) a full infinitive, and (3) any other necessary words. Study the first two examples carefully.

1 The examination was *too* long *to finish in an hour.*
2 Mr. Johnson was *too* angry *to say anything at all.*
3 That dress is .... formal.................................
4 Fifty miles is .... far ....
5 Is that method .... dangerous...........................?
6 That matter was .... important.........................
7 The man was .... stupid ....
8 At that moment, I was .... confused...................
9 Will the director be .... busy ....?
10 That actor was .... nervous.............................
11 At the time, I was .... involved ....
12 That work is definitely .... difficult...................
13 Mr. Green was .... annoyed ....
14 René is .... careless in his work ....
15 The woman was .... upset about the news...........

113

Complete these sentences with (1) the preposition *for* and an object, (2) a full infinitive, and (3) any other necessary words. Study the first two examples.

1 The last two lessons were hard *for me to understand.*
2 Our friends were anxious *for us to return to Quebec City.*
3 These exercises are practical ....
4 Our instructor was ready...
5 Was that book too boring...?
6 It's interesting and unusual...
7 Things like that are easy ....
8 It's not very uncommon...
9 The box was much too heavy...
10 That subject is difficult...
11 Don't you think it was strange...?
12 That shirt is too dirty...
13 I think it's good...
14 That sport is too dangerous ....
15 Were the people in the audience eager ....?

Complete these sentences with (1) the gerund form or the full infinitive form of the verb in parentheses and (2) any other necessary words. Study the examples.

1 (*learn*) ....was a difficult job.
   Learning all of those new words in one day was a difficult job.
2 I must go to the library (*get*) ....
   I must go to the library today to get those two books for my friend.
3 Most of the students were prepared (*answer*) ....
4 (*write*) ....was the hardest thing for me.
5 I went to the grocery store this morning (*get*) ....
6 That fellow is not dependable enough (*trust*)...
7 (*find*) ....took quite a long time.
8 I'm sure they will be disappointed (*hear*) ....
9 You should cover the machine (*protect*) ....
10 (*satisfy*)...is just about impossible.
11 I had to call Mr. Wilson (*remind*) ....
12 Not everyone there was pleased (*hear*)..
13 (*listen*) ....required a lot of patience.

Supply the correct preposition in the blank space in each sentence. Use the gerund ("–ing") form of the verb in parentheses after the preposition.

1 He always depends .... (*get*) help from other students.

2 Why did those fellows insist .... (*do*) everything themselves ?

3 Did Mr. Johnson finally succeed .... (*sell*) his old car ?

4 You shouldn't rely .... (*get*) assistance from Frank.

5 Pierre constantly worries .... (*fail*) his exams.

6 Our boss objects .... (*use*) any different method.

7 Mr. Moore doesn't approve .... (*study*) late at night.

8 Mr. Wilson forgot .... (*do*) that until later in the afternoon.

9 You must not plan (*hear*) from us before Christmas.

10 The board spoke .... (*change*) the membership rules.

11 The bad weather prevented them .... (*leave*) last Friday.

12 We have never forgiven him .... (*make*) that sarcastic remark.

13 Did you pay that fellow .... (*take*) care of your garden ?

14 Mr. Foster is afraid .... (*lose*) his job with that company.

15 Were the Browns successful .... (*get*) a loan from the bank ?

16 She was proud .... (*finish*) the work in such a short time.

17 He's really quite capable .... (*complete*) the work by himself.

18 I'm sorry .... (*lose*) it. I'll be responsible .... (*replace*) it.

19 I'm particularly fond .... (*attend*) hockey games.

20 The witness was very anxious .... (*testify*) in a courtroom.

21 We're still hopeful .... (*see*) them before next Saturday.

22 Why is he so intent .... (*learn*) English in a short time ?

23 The police are interested .... (*know*) more about that man.

24 Are you accustomed .... (*hear*) those planes over your house ?

25 I'm tired .... (*listen*) to nothing but complaints all day.

26 My friend is excited .... (*go*) to Norway this summer.

27 The scientist found a new method .... (*solve*) the problem.

28 He won't tell us his reasons .... not (*help*) them with it.

29 There is very little possibility .... (*find*) a substitute now.

30 You can get a catalog .... (*write*) directly to the company.

31 I don't have any intention .... (*mention*) it to her at all.

32 You have a choice .... (*work*) harder or (*lose*) your job.

33 Mr. Wilson has made a lot of money .... (*invest*) in bonds.

34 There's really no excuse .... (*be*) absent from work so often.

115

Choose the correct form (full infinitive or gerund) of the verb in each sentence.
Check your work with the answers.

1 My friend promised (*return*) the book very soon.
   My friend promised to return the book very soon.
2 Most people enjoy (*write*) letters to their friends.
   Most people enjoy writing letters to their friends.
3 Luc avoids (*study*) his lessons for as long as possible.
4 Did you offer (*translate*) those letters for them ?
5 David finished (*write*) the report about four o'clock.
6 How soon do you expect (*leave*) for Banff ?
7 The minister refused (*eliminate*) any of the major problems.
8 Have you ever considered (*try*) something different ?
9 Are you going to suggest (*travel*) by train ?
10 Did they promise (*reserve*) some good seats for us ?
11 I would appreciate (*hear*) from you as soon as possible.
12 They should postpone (*leave*) for another week or so.
13 I'll need (*buy*) a new winter overcoat before long.
14 Did the students practice (*use*) the words in sentences ?
15 Would you mind (*wait*) for 15 or 20 minutes ?
16 We don't dare (*suggest*) that possibility to them.
17 Why do you always put off (*write*) to your friends ?
18 Michelle hopes (*receive*) a reply within a few days.
19 Those men deny (*know*) anything at all about it.
20 Our guests don't plan (*leave*) until the end of the week.
21 We couldn't resist (*tell*) them the whole story.
22 Keep on (*study*). I don't want (*interrupt*) your work.
23 I hesitate (*say*) anything to him about the mistake.
24 I don't recall (*see*) your briefcase beside that desk.
25 His secretary failed (*include*) several important items.
26 I can't stand (*listen*) to his complaints any longer.
27 I don't want (*risk*) (*lose*) those valuable papers.
28 Marc claims (*be*) an expert on that particular subject.
29 Please stop (*interrupt*) me in the middle of a sentence.
30 I will remember (*give*) Mr. Brown your message.
31 Did the man agree (*pay*) for everything in cash ?
32 That fellow really resents (*take*) orders from other people.

Choose the correct form (full infinitive or gerund) of the verb in each sentence.
Check your work with the answers.

| to see |
| seeing |
| to work |
| working |
| to buy |
| buying |

1 We hope (*visit*) my uncle on our next trip.

2 Serge avoided (*speak*) to the teacher about it.

3 Mr. Foster definitely needs (*buy*) an overcoat.

4 The Andersons enjoyed (*go*) to that play.

5 He demanded (*see*) the report immediately.

6 My friend says he plans (*study*) Italian next year.

7 Bill doesn't wish (*reveal*) his plans to us yet.

8 Have you finished (*read*) that new novel yet ?

9 Would you mind (*shut*) both of those windows.

10 Jean-Guy admitted (*know*) very little about that subject.

11 You shouldn't put off (*write*) your homework.

12 We would appreciate (*receive*) your answer promptly.

13 I expect (*receive*) an answer from the Browns soon.

14 Mr. Green suggested (*leave*) before the weekend.

15 I definitely recall (*put*) the envelope here on my desk.

16 Why did they refuse (*give*) you the information ?

17 I really can't postpone (*tell*) them any longer.

18 We wanted (*buy*) something a little less expensive.

19 How can anyone resist (*like*) that charming girl ?

20 We don't want (*risk*) (*lose*) our money that way.

21 I don't intend (*tell*) anyone about my plans yet.

22 For a while, we considered not (*go*) with them.

23 The children promised not (*do*) that any more.

24 I don't deny not (*understand*) that part of the lesson.

25 Why don't you offer (*help*) him with that work ?

26 I hesitate (*suggest*) any changes at this time.

27 George delayed (*write*) the letter as long as possible.

28 I don't advise (*study*) for very long periods of time.

29 He seems (*know*) a great deal about that subject.

30 I resolved (*do*) much better work in the future.

31 Did you forget (*give*) Mr. Simmons that message ?

32 She pretends (*understand*) everything very clearly.

33 Miss Williams tends (*exaggerate*) things a great deal.

34 The police failed (*notify*) the man's relatives of the accident.

Complete these sentences with an object and a full infinitive. Study the first four examples carefully.

1 The foreman advised *me to ask for a raise next month.*
2 I finally persuaded *my friend to stay for two more days.*
3 The students wanted *Mr. Brown to explain the lesson again.*
4 Everyone urged *Paul Savard to continue his education.*
5 Her mother allowed ....
6 Our friends asked ....
7 Everyone wanted ....
8 We have invited ....
9 They didn't permit ....
10 Do his friends expect ....?
11 The children begged ....
12 The director advised ....
13 The company hired ....
14 The manager instructed ....
15 We finally persuaded ....
16 Did you remind .... ?
17 They finally convinced ....
18 We actually had to force ....
19 Did you promise ....?
20 The captain ordered ....
21 Almost everyone told ....
22 Why don't you urge ....?
23 Did your teacher advise ....?
24 You can depend on ....
25 Can't you persuade ....?
26 Our friends invited ....
27 Did they ask ....?
28 I don't expect ....
29 Should we remind ....?
30 They won't permit ....
31 Why can't you hire ....?
32 The policeman forced ....
33 They should urge ....
34 We didn't want ....

Use the correct form (infinitive or gerund) of each verb in parentheses.

1 Why did they insist on (*leave*) so early last night ?
2 It takes about six hours (*get*) there from Val d'Or.
3 How long do you expect (*stay*) in Portage La Prairie ?
4 We went to the lecture (*hear*) that famous author.
5 (*Learn*) English quickly is not an easy thing.
6 She promised (*return*) it just as soon as possible.
7 We are looking forward to (*see*) our friends next week.
8 It's very easy (*criticize*) other people's work.
9 You ought to postpone (*leave*) until next Wednesday.
10 We invited them (*attend*) the meeting next week.
11 I took the cover off the machine (*show*) it to them.
12 Would you mind (*open*) both of those windows ?
13 (*Write*) good compositions is extremely difficult.
14 Foster didn't explain his reasons for (*quit*) his job.
15 Did you remind the man (*lock*) both of the doors ?
16 Our teacher encourages us (*think*) for ourselves.
17 It took us only two hours (*get*) there by plane.
18 He mentioned the possibility of (*buy*) a new one.
19 We came (*listen*) to the music, not (*discuss*) it.
20 They have offered (*show*) us how (*work*) the machine.
21 He wants (*teach*) the students (*speak*) English correctly.
22 (*Travel*) abroad increases one's (*understand*) of life.
23 I didn't think of (*say*) anything to him at the time.
24 We hope (*finish*) (*paint*) the house by Thursday.
25 It is impossible (*do*) that without any help from you.
26 I need (*get*) a new briefcase (*replace*) this one.
27 We're afraid of (*offend*) them by (*suggest*) that.
28 Those two examples are quite difficult (*understand*)
29 His boss refused (*consider*) (*give*) him the day off.
30 I forgot (*ask*) his brother (*tell*) him about it.
31 Most people save for a long time (*buy*) a house.
32 Mr. Moore advised me (*change*) my method of (*do*) it.
33 They aren't depending on (*get*) a loan (*buy*) the house.
34 The students are enjoying (*learn*) (*write*) English correctly.

Let's see now. Do I use the infinitive or the gerund?

Write the correct infinitive form of the verb in parentheses in each sentence. Study the first two examples carefully.

1   That work must   (*complete*)   before tomorrow night.

     That work must be completed before tomorrow night.

2   These machines ought   (*inspect*)   once a year.

     These machines ought to be inspected once a year.

3   All seats have   (*reserve*)   at least a week in advance.

4   That information can   (*obtain*)   at the information desk.

5   A different method should   (*try*)   in the future.

6   All accidents must   (*report*)   to the police immediately.

7   Much more atttention should   (*devote*)   to that problem.

8   That assignment doesn't have   (*complete*)   until next week.

9   The statistics in that report ought   (*check*)   very carefully.

10   The entire amount must   (*repay*)   within twelve months.

11   Examples of that sort can   (*find*)   almost everywhere.

12   Part of the work should   (*assign*)   to another department.

13   The final examination has   (*take*)   by all students.

14   That part of the job can   (*do*)   anytime before next Friday.

---

179   **INFINITIVE vs. GERUND (PASSIVE FORMS)**

Write the correct form (infinitive or gerund) of the verb in parentheses in each sentence. Study the first two examples carefully.

1   That fellow seems   (*trust*)   by everyone.

     That fellow seems to be trusted by everyone.

2   Don't you recall   (*tell*)   about that by Mr. Burke ?

     Don't you recall being told about that by Mr. Burke ?

3   Mr. Foster hopes   (*transfer*)   by his company.

4   No one enjoys   (*deceive*)   by another person.

5   I absolutely refuse   (*cheat*)   by them in that manner.

6   We would appreciate   (*inform*)   about the matter promptly.

7   Naturally, I would like   (*promote*)   to a higher position.

8   Mr. Anderson wishes   (*notify*)   just as soon as possible.

9   That author doesn't mind   (*criticize*)   by his friends.

10   The whole problem certainly needs   (*consider*)   very carefully.

11   The old lady couldn't avoid   (*splash*)   by the passing bus.

12   I really didn't expect   (*introduce*)   to the president.

13   Of course, we intend   (*pay*)   in full for all of our services.

Make short additions to these sentences with the proper verb and *too* or *either*. Study the first four examples carefully.

1	I like classical music.	Bill *does too.*
2	They are working right now.	We *are too.*
3	Mr. Brown didn't meet that man.	I *didn't either.*
4	Alice won't have enough time.	Betty *won't either.*
5	Louise wasn't at the party.	Marie-Anne ....
6	The Moores went to that concert.	We ....
7	I should study for the examination.	You ....
8	We don't have enough money.	They ....
9	We've already done that lesson.	He ....
10	I'm not going to go tomorrow.	Roger ....
11	Her brother can speak Spanish.	She ....
12	Yvan didn't know that word.	Jacques ....
13	Yvonne bought a new spring coat.	Françoise ....
14	You must make a decision soon.	I ....
15	Not many people enjoyed his speech.	We ....

Make short additions to these sentences with *so* or *neither* and the proper verb. Study the first four examples carefully.

1	Gary usually works on Saturday.	So *does* Frank.
2	They could understand everything.	So *could* we.
3	We won't be at that meeting.	Neither *will* Bruce
4	The girls didn't get there on time.	Neither *did* I.
5	I know Mr. Harris very well.	.... Tom.
6	They haven't had any trouble yet.	.... she.
7	You should leave for home early.	.... we.
8	We don't usually drive to the office.	.... they.
9	Mr. Howell can't come tomorrow.	.... Bob.
10	She's been there several times.	.... we.
11	I fell on those slippery steps.	.... she.
12	Those students weren't absent.	.... I.
13	André would like to learn German.	.... Philippe.
14	We didn't finish the work yesterday.	.... they.
15	I am going to write a letter to him.	.... we.

Make a contrary short addition to each sentence. Study the examples carefully.

1 Tom and I can go with you, but Charles *can't.*
2 Henri doesn't know that word, but Richard *does.*
3 My friend understands the lesson very well, but I *don't.*
4 My brother won't be at home tomorrow night, but I ....
5 Mr. Johnson has seen the annual report, but we ....
6 The other students didn't enjoy the trip yesterday, but I ....
7 Harold and I ride to work on the subway, but Mr. Green ....
8 Almost everyone had a good time last night, but Mary ....
9 Daniel can't work on Saturday morning, but Ralph ....
10 My friends are going to leave early today, but I ....
11 Mr. Fox wasn't at the meeting, but the other men ....
12 Marc has to stay home and study tonight, but we ....
13 Mary Peters comes to work on time, but no one else ....
14 François speaks English with his friends, but Antoine ....
15 I finished my work on time, but none of the other students ....

Avoid repeating words by shortening the additions to these sentences. Study the first two examples carefully. Notice that the word *to* is not omitted.

1 We should invite them, but we don't want to invite them.
  We should invite them, but we don't want to.
2 I can't go there now, but I plan to go there tomorrow.
  I can't go there now, but I plan to tomorrow.
3 My friends study every night, but I don't need to study every night.
4 I haven't written that letter yet, but I intend to write it tonight.
5 I'm not going to use this ticket. Would you like to use this ticket ?
6 No one else did that work, and I don't intend to do that work either.
7 He would like to finish it today, but he won't be able to finish it today.
8 Bill doesn't want to leave now, but he has to leave now.
9 They can't visit us tomorrow, but they hope to visit us next Friday.
10 Alice hasn't read that book yet, but she plans to read that book.
11 Why should I ask for permission ? I don't have to ask for permission.
12 I haven't spoken to my boss yet, but I ought to speak to him very soon.
13 We didn't sign it today, but we're going to sign it later this week.

Complete each question. Then supply the anticipated short answer.

	QUESTION	SHORT ANSWER
1	Virginia can come, *can't she ?*	*Yes, she can.*
2	Mr. Roi lives in Lévis, *doesn't he ?*	*Yes, he does.*
3	His car doesn't start easily, *does it ?*	*No, it doesn't.*
4	Tom and Bill aren't working,............?	*No,* ....
5	You can't speak Russian,..............?	*No,* ....
6	Frank saw Mr. Wilson,................?	*Yes,* ....
7	That lawyer will be there,..............?	....
8	Mr. Brown went home late,............?	....
9	You had a good time,................?	....
10	You haven't done that yet,............?	....
11	You had to leave early,..............?	....
12	There wasn't any coffee left,............?	....
13	Those are your cigarettes,............?	....
14	That is Jean's notebook,..............?	....
15	Students should study hard,............?	....
16	Danielle wasn't able to get it,..........?	....
17	The lock didn't work properly,..........?	....
18	That fellow won't be there,............?	....
19	The plane leaves at six o'clock,..........?	....
20	There aren't any people there,..........?	....
21	That car cost quite a bit,............?	....
22	The bus hasn't left yet,..............?	....
23	Georges can speak German,............?	....
24	Alice and Fred weren't ready,............?	....
25	You should write the Wilsons too,..........?	....
26	That seems to be correct,............?	
27	They didn't do the work,..............?	
28	This book has enough exercises,..........?	
29	I don't have to do it now,............?	
30	Bill put sugar in his coffee,............?	
31	It isn't raining now,................?	
32	The men have returned already,..........?	

Ask a question about the italicized part of each sentence. Use the interrogative words *where, why, how, how much,* etc.

1 Lucien lives *in Gaspé.*   *Where does Lucien live ?*
2 It is *fifteen feet* wide.   *How wide is it ?*
3 They are going to leave *on the twelfth of July.*
4 I must go to the bank *to cash this check.*
5 The bridge across the river is *near that factory.*
6 The whole trip takes about *an hour and a half.*
7 The four packages will be sent *by registered mail.*
8 Irène can borrow *Jacqueline's* bicycle tomorrow.
9 Mr. Séguin seems to feel *much better* this morning.
10 It's only *about forty miles* to Hamilton from there.
11 *The* one *in the middle* belongs to Mr. Wilson.
12 *Mr. Brown* dictated that letter to Miss Adams.
13 We should meet the Browns *at the hotel.*
14 The yearly report was prepared by *those two men.*
15 Those fellows are talking about *the announcement.*
16 Mrs. Ford had to go to the store *to get some sugar.*
17 Jeanne forgot *to bring her dictionary to class.*
18 They're going to stay in Finland *for two months.*
19 The word "crazy" means *"insane" or "psychotic".*
20 That is *Mr. Anderson's* new briefcase.
21 We can't go tonight *because we have to study.*
22 He should study English *to improve his pronunciation.*
23 The president sent his reply to *our secretary.*
24 Accidents must be reported to the police *immediately.*
25 My English class usually begins at *eight-thirty.*
26 I plan to shop for *a new summer suit and hat.*
27 We have to have your reply *before next Tuesday.*
28 You shouldn't say that because *it's not polite.*
29 Mr. Larose *frequently* goes to Montreal on business.
30 Examples of that can be found *almost everywhere.*
31 You have to register *tomorrow at ten o'clock.*
32 That is usually done *by a different method.*
33 Mrs. Anderson bought *a winter* coat for her trip.
34 They need *very little* help in order to finish the job.

(1) Indicate the subject and verb of the main clause. (2) Indicate the subject and verb of the italicized, dependent adjective clause.

1 The book *which I am reading* is very interesting.
2 Everyone *that I met at the party* congratulated me.
3 That was the best movie *that I've seen this year.*
4 Is this the letter *that you wanted me to mail ?*
5 The fellow *whom you recommended to us* was very reliable.
6 The house *which you liked so well* has already been sold.
7 I have lost the book *which I borrowed from Jean-Claude.*
8 The student *who is walking with Pierre* is in my class.
9 The police caught the thief *who had stolen the money.*
10 He didn't remember the man *whose name you mentioned.*
11 I said the first thing *which came to my mind.*
12 Is the river *that flows through that town* very large ?
13 The actor *that played that role* comes from England.
14 The program *that we listened to* wasn't very good.
15 Have you seen the house *which is being built next door ?*

Put brackets [ ] around the dependent, adjective clause. Study the first two examples.

1 The dress [which I liked the best] was too expensive.
2 Maurice lives in the house [that you saw on the corner].
3 The flowers which you gave me are in that vase.
4 The man who stole the money has been caught.
5 Did you mail the two letters that were on my desk ?
6 I tried to read every book that the teacher recommended.
7 They accepted every suggestion which we made.
8 The man whose wife you met teaches at that university.
9 That car which John bought is at least ten years old.
10 The story that he told me can't possibly be true.
11 That's the girl whom Fred and Tom were talking about.
12 Who are those students that are talking to Hélène ?
13 Here's the book which I mentioned to you yesterday.
14 The house that I live in is on Pine Avenue.
15 Mr. Wilson is the kind of person that gets results quickly.

Select *who, whom, whose,* or *which* for the blank space in each sentence. Then put brackets around the adjective clause.

1 The book .... we are reading now is very interesting.
   The book [*which* we are reading now] is very interesting.
2 The fellow .... is walking with Maurice is in my class.
3 The assignment .... we did yesterday was quite easy.
4 The man .... you just met is a very famous writer.
5 The rumor .... we heard yesterday is not true.
6 He's the kind of person .... gets results quickly.
7 We met a woman .... name was very unusual.
8 The police caught the man .... had stolen the jewels.
9 The new model,............... has just come out, is the best so far.
10 He's the man .... installed our electrical equipment.
11 The box in .... she put the gift was very attractive.
12 The house .... Mr. Provost lives in is located on this street.
13 The teacher about .... she spoke was my teacher last year.
14 The subject .... you wrote about interested everyone.
15 Miss Fox belongs to an organization .... assists hospitals.

Change the italicized word *that* to *who, whom* or *which.* Then put brackets around the adjective clause.

1 That is the package *that* came in the mail.
   That is the package [*which* came in the mail].
2 He said the first thing *that* occurred to him.
3 I admire a man *that* tries to maintain high ideals.
4 The book *that* I'm using belongs to the teacher.
5 The person *that told it to me* knows the mayor well.
6 Is this the package *that* you wanted me to take ?
7 It's a custom *that* is quite difficult to explain.
8 The doctor *that* he recommended was very competent.
9 The lesson *that* we're studying seems quite easy.
10 He said something *that* everyone should remember.
11 She doesn't know the person *that* they mentioned.
12 The part *that* is the most difficult for me is this one.
13 He is the man *that* will take care of the matter.
14 The dress *that* my sister Angela wants is brown and yellow.

Write a question about the italicized part of each sentence. Write the question in the two ways indicated in examples (a) and (b). Notice the position of the preposition.

1 Those two fellows are talking about *the election.*
   (a) *What are those two fellows talking about?*
   (b) *About what are those two fellows talking?*

2 The men spoke to Mr. Wilson yesterday morning.
   (a) *Whom did the men speak to yesterday morning?*
   (b) *To whom did the men speak yesterday morning?*

3 Thomas and Frank are waiting for *their friends.*
4 That young couple got the money from *their parents.*
5 Mr. Kennedy has invested his money in *stocks and bonds.*
6 That difficult exercise is on page *one hundred and sixty.*
7 The teacher talked about *clauses* in class this morning.
8 Philippe's friend devotes most of his time to *studying English.*
9 Gilles Bouchard was born in *Lachute.*
10 Mrs. Beaubien is shopping for *a spring coat.*
11 The four salesmen report to *Mr. Johnson* once a week.
12 Mr. Wilson's secretary put the letters in *the first* drawer.
13 The chairman objected to *our suggestions* at the conference.
14 Mr. Wood's son is studying medicine at *McGill.*
15 My secretary addressed the letter to *the Ringwood Company.*
16 The men should connect the rope to *the post in the middle.*
17 Mr. Gregory is employed by *the Windsor Supply Company.*
18 I keep my money in *The Royal Bank of Canada.*
19 Miss Stewart sent the memorandum to *Mr. Green's* office.
20 We stayed the longest time in *Prince Edward Island.*
21 Mr. Philipps insisted very strongly on *a change in methods.*
22 Everybody was very excited about *the president's announcement.*
23 You can cover the opening with *a piece of metal* to protect it.
24 I confused this word with *the word "imminent".*
25 The insurance agent should give the report to *Mr. Burke.*
26 The treasurer explained the plan to *the board of directors.*
27 The students had the most trouble with *the first* part of the lesson.
28 You should submit your application to *me* after the interview.
29 Those people complained to me about *the amount of noise.*
30 Mr. Smith and Mr. Wilson were arguing about *the annual report.*

Change *who, whom,* or *which* to *that.* Make any other necessary changes. Study the examples carefully. Notice the position of the preposition in the second example.

1 The house which the Slaters bought is very small.
   The house that the Slaters bought is very small.
2 The subject about which Professor Moore wrote is interesting.
   The subject that Professor Moore wrote about is interesting.
3 The movie which we saw last night wasn't very exciting.
4 That fellow is the mechanic who fixed Guy's car.
5 The speaker to whom we listened mentioned that matter.
6 The woman about whom you were talking is here now.
7 The car which Bill bought from Edward cost only $800.
8 The apartment in which we live is on the twelfth floor.
9 The man who called today left this message for you.
10 The paper with which you wrapped the gifts was very pretty.
11 The man about whom Anne spoke teaches English here.
12 The picture which Bob took last week turned out quite well.
13 The person to whom Mr. Green wrote answered his questions.

Re-write each sentence and eliminate, if possible, the words *who, whom, which,* or *that.* In some cases, the connecting word cannot be eliminated. Study the examples. Notice the position of the preposition in the second example.

1 The church which we visited last Sunday was beautiful.
   The church we visited last Sunday was beautiful.
2 The house in which Mr. Thompson lives is on the corner.
   The house Mr. Thompson lives in is on the corner.
3 The camera that Fred bought from Bill was expensive.
4 Have you read the postcard which the Browns sent us ?
5 Here's the book about which you and I were talking yesterday.
6 The part of the lesson that's the most difficult is this one.
7 The man who owns that store knows me very well.
8 The women whom you met at the party are all nurses.
9 The accident which Tom and I saw happened late last night.
10 The fellow that told us about the situation knows all the details.
11 The house that is being built next door will be quite large.
12 The teacher that I like the best of all is Professor Moore.
13 The people who are in the same groups with you will help you.

Combine sentences (a) and (b) as indicated in the first two examples. Use sentence (b) as an adjective clause.

1 (a) Those boys are brothers.
   (b) Those boys are walking together.
     Those boys who are walking together are brothers.

2 (a) The lesson wasn't easy.
   (b) We did the lesson yesterday.
     The lesson which we did yesterday wasn't easy.

3 (a) We know the man very well.
   (b) The man wrote that book.

4 (a) The car formerly belonged to me.
   (b) He is driving the car now.

5 (a) I spoke to the professor yesterday.
   (b) The professor teaches that subject.

6 (a) Is this the letter ?
   (b) You wanted me to deliver the letter.

7 (a) The students are all in this class.
   (b) He knows the students.

8 (a) He put the marker in the book.
   (b) He was reading the book.

9 (a) The mechanic found the difficulty.
   (b) We hired the mechanic.

10 (a) I handed the telegram to the man.
    (b) The telegram had just arrived.

11 (a) She tried to remember the rule.
    (b) She had learned the rule last week.

12 (a) The lady will give you a package.
    (b) The lady works in the book department.

13 (a) Did you buy that suit ?
    (b) You looked at that suit first.

14 (a) That fellow is a well-known poet.
    (b) You spoke to that fellow.

who
which whom
whose that

Add an adjective clause to each sentence at the indicated point.

1 The lesson *which*..was very difficult.

2 The man *who*..used to live next door to us.

3 Have you read the book *which*...yet?

4 That was the first thing *which*...................................at the meeting.

5 The principal speaker *whom*.................................was very brilliant.

6 The house *which*.................................has a very interesting history.

7 Everyone *who*.............................always speaks very highly of him.

8 The part *which*...was the third one.

9 Is that the same fellow *who*..?

10 The organization *which*.....................offers scholarships every year.

11 Did you read the magazine article *which*.......................................?

12 We didn't know the woman *whom*.............................or her friend.

13 The fellow *who*...............................returned from Boston yesterday.

14 The thing *which*...was his strange manners.

15 Mr. Burke is the kind of person *who*..

16 The excuse *which*..........................didn't seem very believable to us.

17 Frank Wilson, *who*................................., will be at the meeting too.

18 That book was one of the best *which*...

19 A man *who*...is seldom very popular.

20 Have you ever been employed by a company *which*.....................?

21 The only thing *that*..was a brown envelope.

22 Professor A. G. Moore, *who*................................, will be our guest

23 The gift *that*...was very unusual.

24 I seldom enjoy talking to people *that*... .

25 There was something about the situation *that*...............................

26 The photograph of her *which* ....was taken several years ago.

27 The fellow *that*..*to* is Mr. Howell's brother.

28 The message *that*.................................left him in a bad mood.

29 The girl *whom*............................*about* turned out to be an old friend.

30 The building *that*...................................*in* was built a long time ago.

31 The house *which* .... belongs to the man *that*................. .

32 The one *which* .... is the same one *which*........................ .

33 He's a fellow *who* .... and *whom*............................. .

34 That's the building *which*.................. *who*............................. .

Shorten the adjective clause to an adjective phrase. Study the first two examples carefully.

1 The man who is talking to Mr. Wilson is the accountant.
The man talking to Mr. Wilson is the accountant.
2 The book which was taken from that desk belonged to me.
The book taken from that desk belonged to me.
3 The fellow who is walking with Edward is his brother.
4 That's a book which is known by almost all children.
5 The answer that was given to this question was inadequate.
6 The message which was delivered by them solved the mystery.
7 Have you seen the house that is being built next to ours ?
8 A man who was recommended by the agency will come tomorrow.
9 They bought the house which was formerly owned by Mr. Brown.
10 The teacher who is substituting for Mr. Moore is from Hull.
11 The firm repaired the boats which were damaged during the storm.
12 Is this the book that was recommended to you by Mr. Harris ?
13 Did the man that was appointed by the committee accept the job ?

Use the correct participle form of the verb in parentheses in the blank space. Study the first two examples carefully.

1 (*follow*)   The students will study the *following* words.
2 (*break*)   The carpenter will repair the *broken* chair.
3 (*import*)   That company sells only .... merchandise.
4 (*run*)   The .... water flowed over the edge of the sink.
5 (*dance*)   Miss Peters attended a .... school last year.
6 (*assume*)   Many famous authors write books under .... names.
7 (*exist*)   The .... buildings will be torn down next year.
8 (*steal*)   The police recovered the .... jewelry yesterday.
9 (*swing*)   The carpenter installed .... doors in those rooms.
10 (*accuse*)   The judge and jury found the .... man guilty.
11 (*lead*)   The .... actor in that play is also a director.
12 (*tire*)   That was certainly .... work !
13 (*tire*)   The .... workers sat down to rest for a minute.
14 (*freeze*)   That big grocery store sells a lot of .... food.
15 (*freeze*)   The temperature went below the .... point last night.

(1) Indicate the subject and verb of the main clause. (2) Indicate the subject and verb of the dependent noun clause in italics.

1 His secretary said *that he was very busy.*
2 Do you think *that they will agree with us ?*
3 I don't suppose *that he intends to return until later.*
4 Do you realize *that nobody else agrees with you ?*
5 At that time, I believed *that I knew the answer.*
6 I guess *that he doesn't plan to go with his friends.*
7 He admitted *that he had enjoyed it a great deal.*
8 Did she mention *that she had already spoken to him ?*
9 He stated *that he would refuse their offer.*
10 Don't forget *that you have to leave before noon.*
11 Let's assume *that it's going to be expensive.*
12 We didn't tell them *that we couldn't go.*
13 I finally convinced him *that he was wrong.*
14 Please remind her *that she has an appointment.*
15 I had to promise Mr. Johnson *that I would help him.*

Put brackets [] around the dependent noun clause in each sentence. Then rewrite the sentence and omit the word *that* at the beginning of the dependent noun clause.

1 I don't think [that I can go tomorrow].
   I don't think I can go tomorrow.
2 My teacher says [that the test will be difficult].
   My teacher says the test will be difficult.
3 Everybody believes that Carole will be chosen.
4 I presume that you didn't like that movie.
5 Have you heard that Jacques has a new car ?
6 We didn't know that he had enough money.
7 I guess that she hasn't heard the news yet.
8 He hopes that they will accept his application.
9 The man denied that he had stolen the money.
10 He pretended that he had understood everything.
11 At the last moment, I decided that I couldn't go.
12 Remember that we have to leave by 10:00 p.m.
13 He didn't notice that his sleeve was torn.
14 Mr. Anderson thought that we didn't know about it.

Indicate (1) the subject and verb of the main clause and (2) the subject and verb of the italicized noun clause. Study the word order carefully.

1 René knows *what that word means.*
2 I tried to guess *what was in the packages.*
3 We didn't tell them *who had written the letter.*
4 Does Bill know *who gave him the birthday gift ?*
5 We asked Miss Brown *why she didn't like it.*
6 I can't understand *why Frank lied to them about it.*
7 The man finally found out *where the books were kept.*
8 Didn't your friend know *where everyone had gone ?*
9 We can't imagine *when the Hansons intend to return.*
10 Did you ask Réjean *when he's going to leave for Shawinigan ?*
11 I can't tell you *which books will be used next year.*
12 Have you decided *which one of them you want to buy ?*
13 They didn't mention *what countries they had visited.*
14 Mr. Fox doesn't know *who will be at the meeting tonight.*
15 Miss Peters didn't say *whether she had finished it or not.*

Put brackets [] around the dependent clause in each sentence. Identify the dependent clause as an adjective clause or a noun clause. Study the examples.

1 The hat [*that you bought*] is pretty. (adjective clause)
2 Alice said [*that it was too expensive.*] (noun clause)
3 Mr. Anderson knows who told you the news.
4 All the men who attended the class were doctors.
5 I enjoyed the novel which you lent me last week.
6 I can't remember what you told me about it.
7 Do you know the man who is walking with Mr. Brown ?
8 We didn't know who had suggested that plan to them.
9 I don't know the fellow that you mentioned last night.
10 I gave Anne-Marie the letters that I wanted her to mail.
11 I told her that she should mail them right away.
12 The postcard they sent us was mailed two weeks ago.
13 Have you seen the pictures Bill took several days ago ?
14 Mr. Kent's secretary said he had already left for Ottawa.
15 The part of the lesson that's most difficult for me is this one.

Choose *what* or *which* for the blank in each sentence.

(PART ONE)

1 Did you understand .... the teacher taught us today ?
2 Did you understand the part .... the teacher discussed ?
3 I don't recall the story .... you are talking about.
4 I don't recall .... you said about the story yesterday.
5 I always enjoy a story .... has a surprise ending.
6 Our friend didn't tell us .... Mr. Foster had said to her.
7 The used car .... Bill bought last week has a good engine.
8 Can you tell the students .... the population of Quebec is ?
9 That's the house .... the Millers were talking about.
10 I always read every book .... the teacher recommends.
11 Mr. Smith didn't reveal .... he had discussed with the director.
12 I gave Helen the boxes .... I wanted her to deliver for me.
13 I told her .... she should do with the two boxes.
14 Bernard repeated the same things .... you had already told me.
15 Did Jeanne buy the pantsuit .... she liked the best ?
16 She didn't mention .... the price of it was.

(PART TWO)

1 Please tell us .... you think about our suggestion.
2 This is .... I recommend for you to do.
3 I tried to do everything .... you wanted me to do.
4 Did Mr. Wilson tell you .... happened at the conference ?
5 I have several books .... I hope to read this week.
6 That's something .... we should all try to remember.
7 Betty forgot to ask Jim .... he had done the previous week.
8 I read the article .... you recommended to me.
9 The lesson .... we studied yesterday was quite difficult.
10 I can't remember .... Mr. Harris said about the lesson.
11 Do you know .... that man does for a living ?
12 It's very difficult to find the things .... you need there.
13 A man is judged by the books .... he reads. (proverb)
14 The teacher explained .... the words in the sentence meant.
15 There are few questions .... do not have an answer. (pro-
    verb)

134

Re-write each sentence, and omit, if possible, the word *that* at the beginning of the dependent clause. In some cases, the connecting word *that* cannot be omitted. Review Exercises 191 and 193.

1 Bill paid $800 for the car that he bought from Edward.
   Bill paid $800 for the car he bought from Edward.
2 Howard told us that the car was in perfect condition.
3 I can't afford a second-hand car that costs more than $650.
4 Please remember that we must get to the office before noon.
5 No one was hurt in the accident that John and I saw today.
6 The accident that happened at the corner was quite unusual.
7 The police have assumed that the other driver was at fault.
8 Don and I enjoyed the program that we listened to last night.
9 How did you like the actor that played the leading role ?
10 Doesn't Alice realize that we don't agree with her ?
11 I didn't know that Mr. and Mrs. Miller owned that house.
12 Do you know the fellow that owns the house next to theirs ?
13 Mr. Miller admitted that he had never met his neighbor.
14 Did you notice the typewriter that they bought for the office ?
15 Yes. I also noticed that the typewriter made very little noise.

CLAUSES WITHOUT CONNECTING WORDS (2) 203

Re-write each sentence, and, if possible, omit the italicized connecting word. Make any other necessary changes. In some cases, the connecting word cannot be omitted. Study the three examples carefully.

1 The lesson *which* was studied in class today was difficult.
   The lesson we studied in class today was difficult.
2 The man to *whom* you should speak is Mr. Kennedy.
   The man you should speak to is Mr. Kennedy.
3 Did your friend mention *what* his father had said to him ?
   (The connecting word *what* cannot be omitted.)
4 We tried to follow the instructions *which* Tom had given us.
5 They have already decided *which* one they're going to buy.
6 The doctor to *whom* I went last week is a surgeon.
7 Try to remember *what* your teacher said about this exercise.
8 The lawyer *who* handles our legal problems mentioned that.
9 The part with *which* I had the most difficulty is that one.
10 Would you please explain *why* you didn't finish all of the work.
11 What's the name of the song *which* those girls are singing ?
12 No one here knew the man *who* delivered those packages.

Add connecting words (*which, who, that,* etc.) to these sentences only if necessary.

1 The man is sitting by the door takes care of requests for catalogs.

2 The gloves I lost at school yesterday were not my best ones.

3 Lots of students don't know the Island of Majorca is located.

4 I asked the clerk about the price of the camera in the window.

5 Please try to remember you did with my books and notes.

6 No one knew Mr. Hart had already accepted the director's offer.

7 The butcher sold me these steaks usually has very good meat.

8 We assured the man we weren't going to bother him in the least.

9 I wonder books and papers these are. Are they Philippe's ?

10 The girl you see at the rear door of the office is Miss Peters.

11 Can you suggest someone can give me some advice in this matter ?

12 At the last moment, I found I would be unable to help the men.

13 Walter Burns, spoke to you last night, would like to join the club.

14 Professor Moore, our English teacher, has written two textbooks.

15 Almost everyone believed the election would be won by Mr. Dupuis.

16 The fellow you spoke to at the convention is a good friend of mine.

17 The letter the mailman delivered today was from Mrs. Anderson.

18 Have you heard is coming to stay with us for a week or two ?

19 They're coming to visit us. We don't know they are coming.

20 The student wrote these two papers made a lot of mistakes.

21 Without any hesitation, the man denied the policeman's accusation.

22 The evening newspaper reported it would be quite cold tomorrow.

23 Hockey, is Canada's most popular sport, attracts many spectators.

24 Charles Dickens, lived in the nineteenth century, wrote many novels.

25 Can you tell me the janitor locked all of the doors so early ?

26 That tall fellow reminds me of someone I knew a long time ago.

27 I didn't mention anything at all to my boss about my plans.

28 The report Mr. Johnson is writing must be finished before Friday.

29 I can't imagine they're going to invite to the reception party.

30 The instructor teaches that class teaches another section at night.

31 I think the man is talking to Mr. Gilbert works for the Luton Company.

32 The Luton Company, exports metal products, employs 92 people.

33 This company, a branch of EXCO, Inc., was founded in 1946.

34 The student lent you his book speaks both Italian and Spanish.

Read question (a) carefully. Then put the subject and auxiliary verb in the correct order in the answer (b). Notice that the question word in each answer (b) is also the connecting word for a dependent noun clause.

1 (a) Where *is William* working now ?
  (b) I don't know where *William is* working now.
2 (a) When *will the guests* arrive ?
  (b) I don't know when *the guests will* arrive.
3 (a) Where is Frank going to eat lunch ?
  (b) I don't know where .... going to eat lunch.
4 (a) When should we tell them the news ?
  (b) I don't know when .... tell them the news.
5 (a) What are they laughing about ?
  (b) I don't know what .... laughing about.
6 (a) Where will you spend your vacation ?
  (b) I don't know where .... spend my vacation.
7 (a) What town is Pierre from ?
  (b) I don't know what town .... from.

Carefully read the question (a). Then, eliminate the auxiliary verb *do, does,* or *did* and use the simple present or simple past form of the verb in the answer (b). Notice the difference between the form of the verb in the question and in the dependent noun clause in the answer.

1 (a) Where *does* Mr. Anderson *live ?*
  (b) I don't know where Mr. Anderson *lives.*
2 (a) When *did* Louise *write* that letter ?
  (b) I don't know when Louise *wrote* that letter.
3 (a) Where does George usually eat his lunch ?
  (b) I don't know where George usually .... his lunch.
4 (a) How much does that typewriter cost ?
  (b) I don't know how much that typewriter ....
5 (a) Where did Mary go during her vacation ?
  (b) I don't know where Mary .... during her vacation.
6 (a) What does Mr. Smith do for a living ?
  (b) I don't know what Mr. Smith .... for a living.
7 (a) When did the mailman deliver the letter ?
  (b) I don't know when the mailman .... the letter.

Finish the sentence at the right with a noun clause based on the preceding direct question. Study examples 1 through 4. Keep the same tense throughout.

1	Where will he be ?	Let's ask him *where he will be.*
2	Why did she leave ?	Do you know *why she left ?*
3	Who is that man ?	I don't know *who that man is.*
4	When did Tom return ?	Please tell me *when Tom returned.*
5	Where is Charles going ?	I don't know ....
6	Where does Fred live ?	Do you remember ....?
7	When did they arrive ?	I can't tell you ....
8	When are they leaving ?	Let's ask them...........................
9	Why were you absent ?	Please explain...........................
10	Why didn't you return ?	I can't understand ....
11	Why did you buy it ?	Please tell me...........................
12	Who is that tall fellow ?	Can you find out.....................?
13	Who is doing the work ?	I don't know ....
14	Who wrote this paper ?	Can you tell me ....?
15	Whom did they invite ?	I can't imagine...........................
16	Whom should I speak to ?	I would like to know....................
17	Whose house is that ?	Can't you ask somebody ....?
18	Whose book did he use ?	I wonder...................................
19	What happened to you ?	Won't you tell me...................?
20	What is he talking about ?	Can you guess ....?
21	What does the word mean ?	Can you tell me ....?
22	What do you call that ?	I really don't know......................
23	What did she ask them ?	Do you remember ....?
24	What town is he from ?	Let's ask Henri ....
25	What cities did you visit ?	Please tell us...........................
26	Which one is Brown's ?	Don't you know ....?
27	Which one does he want ?	I don't remember ....
28	Which do you prefer ?	Please tell the clerk......................
29	How does it work ?	The man will explain....................
30	How old is Mr. Wilson ?	Can you guess ....?
31	How much does it cost ?	Ask the manager ....
32	How much did it cost ?	He doesn't remember ....
33	How do you say this ?	Can you tell me ....?

Change the italicized verb in each sentence to the simple past tense (example : *he says* to *he said*). Then change the following verb to the simple past tense or the continuous past tense (example : *he is talking* to *he talked* or *he was talking*). Make any other necessary changes. Study the first two sentences carefully.

1 I *think* Robert needs some money right away.
I thought Robert needed some money right away.

2 Tom *says* Frank is writing letters to his friends.
Tom said Frank was writing letters to his friends.

3 I *know* that they always study their lessons very carefully.

4 My friend *believes* there is absolutely nothing to worry about.

5 The newspaper article *says* that the professor teaches at Loyola.

6 Jean-Guy *thinks* the students are talking to the teacher.

7 He *says* the members are discussing that matter now.

8 That article *says* it rains a great deal in that country.

9 I *think* Marie is working on her English assignment.

10 Mr. Jackson *says* he usually works thirty-five hours a week.

11 I *think* that Professor Duncan is writing another book this year.

Change the italicized verb in each sentence to the simple past tense (example : *she reports* to *she reported*). Then change the following verb to the perfect past tense (first example : *she has written* to *she had written* ; second example : *she forgot* to *she had forgotten*). Study the first two sentences carefully.

1 Mr. Kirby *claims* that he spoke to those people.
Mr. Kirby claimed that he had spoken to those people.

2 The foreman *says* the men have done the work already.
The foreman said the men had done the work already.

3 I *think* that Serge has never been to Europe.

4 François *says* he forgot to buy a new dictionary last week.

5 Their boss *reports* that they have had no trouble with the machine.

6 I *assume* that you had no difficulty with that lesson yesterday.

7 The newspaper *reports* that there have been several bad storms.

8 I *hear* that your friend fell on some steps and broke his arm.

9 I *remember* that the wind blew very hard the week before last.

10 We *suspect* that Dr. Gray has heard the news already.

11 Walter *says* that he won twenty-five dollars on that election bet.

12 I *know* my friends haven't received any letters from Robert.

13 Our neighbors *say* the water in their pond froze very quickly.

Change the italicized verb to the simple past tense. Then change the following verb in order to keep the same time relationship between the two verbs. Study the first five examples carefully.

1 Dr. Gray *says* he will return next Monday or Tuesday.
   Dr. Gray said he would return next Monday or Tuesday.
2 We *regret* that we can stay only fifteen minutes longer.
   We regretted that we could stay only fifteen minutes longer.
3 Mr. Thompson *thinks* we should go to the meeting tomorrow.
   Mr. Thompson thought we should go to the meeting tomorrow.
4 My teacher *says* I ought to work harder in future.
   My teacher said I ought to work harder in future.
5 Miss Adams *says* she must leave early tomorrow morning.
   Miss Adams said she had to leave early tomorrow morning.
6 Harold *thinks* he can go to the movies with us tonight.
7 His secretary *says* he will return on the sixteenth of May.
8 My friend *thinks* we should ask Mr. Fox about it tonight.
9 Mr. Blanc *says* he can help us now but not tomorrow.
10 I *suppose* Marc will finish the work before next Friday.
11 John *says* you ought to send the letter today or tomorrow.
12 The message *indicates* he will be back from Calgary next week.
13 Mr. Harris *says* we must write two compositions for tomorrow.
14 My friend *says* she can't come along with us this afternoon.
15 I *regret* that we must drive so fast to get there on time.
16 I *think* they will be able to return it before next Thursday.
17 His letter *implies* that you should tell him the truth about it.
18 Mr. Wood *says* he can pay back all of the money before that time
19 Jeanne *thinks* we ought to invite them to the party tomorrow.
20 I *presume* that we'll have to show the men how to use the machine
21 Everyone *anticipates* that we won't succeed in getting permission.
22 *Do* you *recall* who has to stay in the office next Friday evening ?
23 Of course, I *regret* that I can't help my friend financially.
24 The evening paper *says* the weather will be cloudy tomorrow.
25 Mr. Simmons *says* I should ask my boss for a day off.
26 I *think* that I will have plenty of time to finish all of the work.
27 No one *believes* that you can persuade him to leave before Friday.
28 The policeman *says* we must appear in court next Monday morning.

Select the correct word or words from the parentheses in each sentence.

 1 Helen regretted that she (*can, could*) not go with us.
 2 André says that he (*has, had*) forgotten the name of the book.
 3 Did the man tell you when he (*is, was*) going to leave ?
 4 We assumed that the meeting (*will, would*) be over by that time.
 5 Yvan hopes that they (*will, would*) accept his application.
 6 I didn't know that Tom (*has, had*) enough money to buy a car.
 7 Janet didn't recall what I (*told, had told*) her the day before.
 8 I guess that our friends (*haven't, hadn't*) heard the good news yet.
 9 They didn't know that we (*must, had to*) leave before ten o'clock.
10 We had to promise Charles that we (*will, would*) help him.
11 The senator claimed that he (*agrees, agreed*) with the others.
12 The man admits he (*has, had*) had little experience in that field.
13 We assume that the man (*can, could*) help us with the work.
14 Our friends asked us why we (*came, had come*) there so early.
15 He thought we (*should send , should have sent*) the wire next week.

Change the italicized verb to the simple past tense. Then change the following verb in order to keep the same time relationship between the two verbs.

 1 I *wonder* what Mr. Fox is going to say to George.
   I wondered what Mr. Fox was going to say to George.
 2 The newspaper *says* it will be cloudy and cold tomorrow.
 3 I *know* that there were very few requests for that catalog.
 4 James *says* he has to leave for home just as soon as possible.
 5 Mr. Shaw *believes* that he tore his sleeve on a sharp nail.
 6 My friend Antoine *says* that he enjoys studying grammar.
 7 Marcel *thinks* he can find someone to explain everything to us.
 8 *Does* Frank *recall* who is taking care of that matter ?
 9 I *can't remember* what my teacher said about that sentence.
10 Everyone *assumes* that the work will be finished very soon.
11 We *suspect* that Mr. Kelly has already spoken to the director.
12 No one *can anticipate* exactly what the director will do.
13 The teacher *says* that we must study hard for the test.
14 Elizabeth *wants* to know when Mr. and Mrs. Miller arrived.

(1) Add a dependent clause after the adjective or participle in each sentence. Then (2) change the principal verb to the simple past tense, and change the verb in the dependent clause in accordance with the rule for sequence of tenses. Study the first three examples carefully. Review Exercise 169 before writing this exercise.

1   We are happy *(that)* *Charles can come with us after all.*
    We were happy *(that)* *Charles could come with us after all.*

2   I'm delighted *(that)* *the guests have had a good time up to now.*
    I was delighted *(that)* *the guests had had a good time up to then.*

3   It is strange *(that)* *that fellow doesn't try to find a good job.*
    It was strange *(that)* *that fellow didn't try to find a good job.*

4   Bill and I are sure *(that)*...

5   Everyone is sorry *(that)*...

6   It is very interesting *(that)*...

7   The boys are ashamed *(that)* ....

8   We are very happy *(that)*...

9   It is wonderful *(that)* ....

10 Of course, I am disappointed *(that)*...

11 No one in the group is aware *(that)*..

12 Bob's friends are surprised *(that)* ....

Complete each sentence with an appropriate clause. Follow the rule for tense relationships carefully. The parentheses indicate that the use of the connecting word is optional.

1   My boss always says *(that)*..

2   Can you tell me *why*...

3   Everyone was positive *(that)*...

4   My friends all think *(that)*...

5   I really didn't know *what*..

6   Isn't it quite peculiar *(that)*..

7   The teacher suspected *(that)*...

8   All the students assume *(that)* ....

9   Have you forgotten *who*..

10 Don couldn't remember *which* ....

11 It's quite probable *(that)*...

12 Didn't anyone believe *what*...

13 I really can't imagine *why*...

14 Of course, we were pleased *(that)*...

Complete the sentence at the right with a noun clause based on the preceding direct question. Change the tense of the verb in the clause in accordance with the rule for sequence of tenses. Add the correct punctuation (period or question mark) at the end of each sentence. Study the first four examples carefully.

1	Where will he be ?	I didn't know *where he would be.*
2	When did she go ?	Did you ask Ed *when she had gone ?*
3	Why isn't it ready ?	He explained *why it wasn't ready.*
4	Who is that man ?	I wondered *who that man was.*
5	When are they leaving ?	Bill asked them ....
6	What did he find ?	I couldn't imagine ....
7	Whose book is that ?	He didn't know...........................
8	Who will help us ?	Didn't he tell you ....
9	When can they come ?	I didn't ask them ....
10	Why was he absent ?	Did he explain...........................
11	What does she want ?	Didn't she mention...........................
12	Which one is hers ?	I couldn't remember ....
13	When should we leave ?	Laurent didn't say ....
14	How much does it cost ?	Did she ask him...........................
15	How far is it ?	I forgot to ask Ed...........................
16	Whom should I call ?	I couldn't decide...........................
17	When did she arrive ?	Did she mention ....
18	What are they doing ?	We wondered...........................
19	How will he do it ?	Everyone asked him...........................
20	Where is he from ?	Couldn't she guess...........................
21	What did Henri tell her ?	I didn't recall ....
22	Why didn't he return ?	No one knew...........................
23	Where can I get it ?	Jean told me...........................
24	Who wrote that article ?	Did she remember...........................
25	Where does she live ?	They didn't know ....
26	What does it mean ?	He asked the teacher...........................
27	Who is that tall man ?	Did she mention ....
28	What has happened ?	They couldn't tell us ....
29	Where will he buy it ?	We didn't ask him...........................
30	Who is doing the work ?	Didn't Harry know...........................
31	Whose book did she use ?	Hélène didn't mention...........................
32	What countries did he visit ?	Mr. Brown told us ....
33	Whom should we speak to ?	Did you ask him...........................

Write the correct form of *say* or *tell* in each blank space. Study the use of *say* and *tell* in the first four examples.

1 Mr. Brown *said* that he had been too busy to leave his office.
2 Mr. Brown *said* to his wife, "I have to go to that meeting."
3 Mr. Brown *told* his wife that he had to leave right away.
4 "I will return in an hour or two," Mr. Brown *said.*
5 Mr. Gagnon .... that he would describe his trip to us.
6 Mr. Gagnon is .... the boys about his trip to France now.
7 He .... that he had enjoyed the trip to France a great deal.
8 My friend .... me that he was planning to leave right away.
9 John .... to me, "I will meet you at the train station."
10 "I think we should choose a better place to meet," I ....
11 Bill .... his friend had .... him about the announcement.
12 Did you .... everyone what his friend had .... about it ?
13 Bill's friend .... us that his friend would .... everyone else.
14 We couldn't .... the man exactly what Bill's friend had ....
15 Yesterday we .... that Alice shouldn't have .... them any-
    thing.
16 "I really should have .... the truth," Alice .... later.
17 "Alice .... a lie about that matter last week," Ian ....
18 Don't .... anything about what Ian has just .... you.
19 I .... them that I hadn't .... a word about it to anyone.
20 I.............. quickly, "Don't worry. I haven't...........anything at all. "
21 Ian didn't .... why he had already .... his own friends.
22 "I'll .... you a secret about that," Ian .... to his friends.
23 Ian's friend ...., "I have something to .... to you too."
24 Ian .... you that, didn't he ?" Alice .... with a smile.
25 Actually, I didn't .... Ian had already .... me the news.
26 ".......... something in English," Betty .... to Jules.
27 "You didn't .... the word correctly," Betty .... frankly.
28 Tom .... the children had asked Mary to .... a story.
29 Mary .... to me unhappily, "I'll never .... that story
    again !"
30 "Don't just stand there," I .... angrily. ".......... something !"
31 I .... him that it was not nice to .... things like that.
32 Ed didn't .... when he intended to .... us about his plans.
33 Ed didn't .... us what he intended to .... about his plans
34 Ed .... to us, "I can't .... anything to you about my plans."

Change the direct speech in each sentence to indirect speech. In changing to indirect speech, apply the rule for sequence of tenses carefully (refer to Exercises 211 and 212). Notice the use of the verbs *say* and *tell* in the examples. Also notice the use of the comma, the period, and quotation marks.

1 "I have written that letter already," my friend said.
   My friend said (that) he had written that letter already.
2 Yvonne said to me, "I will ask Mr. Harris about that word."
   Yvonne told me (that) she would ask Mr. Harris about that word.
3 I said, "I can't understand those two lessons at all."
4 "I know those two girls quite well," Catherine said.
5 Charles said to me, "I have to leave the office before 3:00 p.m."
6 "My secretary didn't finish the work," Mr. Johnson said.
7 George remarked, "I can't possibly finish the work by that time."
8 Mr. Anderson said, "I have been smoking too much recently."
9 "Our entire trip cost us two thousand dollars," Mr. Brown added.
10 "Your health will improve very quickly," the doctor said to me.
11 "It has not been possible to do that so far," the man repeated.
12 "You must study hard for the test," the teacher informed us.

Change the direct speech in each sentence to indirect speech. Notice the use of the verb *ask* in place of the verb *say* in the second example. Study the use of the question mark carefully.

1 "Where did you put my hat and gloves ?" Jacqueline asked me.
   Jacqueline asked me where I had put her hat and gloves.
2 Mr. Farrell said, "How soon can you pay back the money ?"
   Mr. Farrell asked us how soon we could pay back the money.
3 "How well does Carole play the piano ?" her aunt asked.
4 The agent said, "When do you plan to leave for Portugal ?"
5 The woman asked me, "Where can I find the director's office ?"
6 Antoine said to me, "What will you offer me for this camera ?"
7 "When must I turn in this report ?" the treasurer asked.
8 Mr. Johnson asked Mary, "How soon can you finish the letters ?"
9 "What kind of suit did you buy ?" my friend asked me.
10 Irène said, "Why should I reveal my plans to the other girls ?"
11 "How long ago did you make the reservation ?" the clerk asked us.
12 Father asked, "Who gave you all of the money to pay for it ?"
13 The student said to the teacher, " What does the word, *outfit*, mean ? "

Change the direct speech in each sentence to indirect speech. Use both forms given in the examples. Study Exercises 215 and 216 before doing the exercise.

1 Roger asked us, "Have you seen that movie yet ?"
   Roger asked us if we had seen that movie.
   * *Roger asked us whether or not we had seen that movie.*
2 I said to her, "Do you understand that lesson ?"
   I asked her if she understood that lesson.
   I asked her whether or not she understood that lesson.
3 My friend asked me, "Do you enjoy your English class ?"
4 "Will everyone be ready to leave by ten ? the driver asked.
5 Frank said to me, "Did you give the letters to Mr. Watson ?"
6 "Are you going to join that organization ?" Howard asked me.
7 Anne-Marie said, "Do you like my new summer dress ?"
8 "Can you go to the meeting with me tonight ?" Bill asked us.
9 Mr. Moore said, "Have you taken the other two courses yet ?"
10 "Do I have to lock both of the doors ?" the janitor asked.

* Other commonly used variations are : (a) *Roger asked us if we had seen that movie or not.* (b) *Roger asked us whether we had seen that movie or not.* (c) *Roger asked us whether we had seen that movie.*

Change the direct speech in each sentence to indirect speech. Study the examples carefully. Before doing this exercise, review Exercise 176.

1 "Show me your driver's license !" the policeman ordered.
   The policeman ordered me to show him my driver's license.
2 The clerk said to us, "Don't come back before one o'clock."
   The clerk told us not to come back before one o'clock.
3 The teacher said to us, "Write the next two exercises."
4 "Turn left at the corner and drive two blocks," the man directed.
5 My friend said, "Show me all of the photographs."
6 "Don't leave your coat on the chair," Mr. Lane's wife said to him.
7 I said to the waitress, "Bring me a cup of black coffee, please."
8 "Be careful ! Watch out for reckless drivers !" Frank urged.
9 The speaker exclaimed, "Don't forget to vote for Pierre Blanc !"
10 "Stop now and give me your papers," the teacher ordered.
11 I said to Miss Peters, "Come here and show me your notes."
12 "Don't forget to lock all the doors," the janitor said to the boys.

Change the direct speech in each sentence to indirect speech. Review Exercises 215 through 218 before doing this exercise.

1 I asked Bill, "What will you say to your friends afterwards ?"
   I asked Bill what he would say to his friends afterwards.
2 The announcer said, "It's difficult to make a prediction so soon."
3 Michelle said, "Has your brother ever taken an English course ?"
4 Réjean said to me, "Why did those people leave so early ?"
5 Dorothy said to Don, "Turn the lights on in the living room."
6 "Can you go to the party with me tomorrow ?" Arthur asked us.
7 "Go to the stoplight and then turn left," the policemen directed me.
9 "When do you plan to leave for Sudbury ?" my secretary asked.
10 Miss Peters said to us, "You can't speak to him until tomorrow."
11 "Will you have enough money to pay for everything ?" my boss asked.
12 Dr. Davis said, "How long will you stay in Alberta ?"
13 "Don't forget about your appointment," John's friend reminded him.
14 "I told the police the truth about the accident," the man repeated.
15 Mr. Shaw asked the students, "Did you enjoy your trip yesterday ?"
16 Where are those two fellows going ?" the man said to me.
17 "Turn in your term papers tomorrow," the teacher reminded us.
18 "Have you had a good time so far " Uncle Robert asked me.
19 I said to my friend, "When did you buy your new car ?"
20 My aunt said to me, "Put your hat and coat in the front closet."
21 "Must I finish these reports before Friday ?" the secretary asked.
22 "Where will you wait for me after work ?" Miss Stewart asked us.
23 Father said to us, "I'm going to tell you a big secret about that."
24 The manager said, "Don't deliver the box to anybody but Mr. Lucas."
25 Paul said to me, "How can I find out that girl's name and address ?"
26 The teacher said to the students, "Do all of you understand this ?"
27 "Who is going to help me with the work ?" Tom asked the men.
28 "Be sure to read the instructions carefully," the clerk advised us.
29 "Your strength will increase quite rapidly," the doctor said to me.
30 "Do we have to turn in our homework today ?" I said to Mr. Shaw.
31 The student asked, "When should Lucien and I come to your office ?"
32 My friends said to me, "We have known about that for a long time."
33 "Get away from those wires !" the watchman shouted at the boy.

Supply an appropriate verb in the dependent clause in each sentence. Use only the subjunctive form of each verb (examples : *I come, you come, he come, she come ; I be, you be, he be, etc.*). Study the examples carefully. Notice which verbs introduce clauses with a verb in the subjunctive form. Also notice that the subjunctive form is used after these verbs regardless of their tense.

1 I recommend that the student *speak* to the director.
2 I will recommend that the student *speak* to the director.
3 Our boss insists that we *be* careful with that machine.
4 Our boss insisted that we *be* careful with that machine.
5 I will propose that the president .... the report next week.
6 Tom suggests that we .... ready before ten o'clock.
7 The policeman demanded that the man .... him his permit.
8 I would prefer that Alice .... to Mr. Wilson herself.
9 Mary's boss insists that she .... on time every morning.
10 The members proposed that the treasurer .... the money.
11 I will suggest that everyone .... a letter to his M.P.
12 The teacher demands that we .... prompt with our homework.
13 He preferred that Miss Peters .... the packages by messenger.

Complete each sentence by adding an appropriate dependent clause. The parentheses indicate that the use of the connecting word is optional. Add the correct punctuation (period or question mark).

1 Almost everyone thinks (*that*) ....
2 Do you recall *where*...
3 Of course, I'm happy (*that*)..
4 The teacher recommended (*that*)...
5 My brother doesn't know *what*...
7 I would suggest (*that*)..
8 My friend didn't mention *when*...
9 Everyone was disappointed (*that*)..
10 Didn't your teacher tell you *what*...
11 Donald couldn't understand *why* ....
12 Mr. Provost's boss demanded (*that*)...
13 Do you still regret (*that*) ....
14 I can't remember *who*..

Read this conversation carefully. Study the use of clauses in the sentences.

Bill : This is the car that John bought from Mr. Smith. *Tom :* I didn't even know that he had bought a new car. When did he tell you that he had bought it? *Bill :* He told me yesterday that he had bought it two days earlier. *Tom :* Do you know how much he paid for the car? *Bill :* Well, he said he paid $800 for it. Of course, I assume that he had to pay sales tax also. *Tom :* I wonder why he bought Mr. Smith's old car. I didn't think that he needed a car. *Bill :* Well, I suppose he will use it for his new job. Haven't you heard that he was hired as a salesman by the Burwell Company? *Tom :* Oh, in that case, I can understand why he wants to have a car. Do you think the car is in good condition? *Bill :* He told me the car was in perfect condition. The tires that Mr. Smith bought for it are practically new. The new generator that was put in works perfectly. Also, John knows the mechanic who fixed the motor. Frankly, I think that it was a good bargain. *Tom :* I believe you're right. I hope that he doesn't have any trouble with it. I guess he won't have any trouble after all those repairs. *Bill :* Mr. Smith promised John that he would pay for any necessary repairs in the next two months. Mr. Smith is a man who sticks to his promises too. *Tom :* Now I'm convinced that John got a real bargain. A man who's as honest as Mr. Smith is very rare. I don't know anyone who has gotten a guarantee like that. *Bill :* I didn't mention that the car has been driven only 25,000 miles. Also, the covers which are on the front seat are brand new. They're made of material that can be washed. *Tom :* Of course, performance is the thing that's the most important of all. Now I want to see how well the car really runs. *Bill :* O.K. Let's ask John when he's going to take us for a ride. Then we can see whether or not the car runs well. *Tom :* Do you know if John is going to come back here soon? I think he went to the store at the end of the block. *Bill :* Yes, I'm sure he'll be back right away. Do you want to walk to the store and meet him? *Tom :* No, I suggest we be patient and wait for him right here. By the way, can you tell me where John is keeping his car? *Bill :* He's using the garage that belongs to the people that live next door.

In the following sentences, indicate (1) the subject and verb of the main clause and (2) the subject and verb of the dependent adverb clause in italics. Notice how these clauses are used to show "result", "place", "time", etc.

"REASON" OR "PURPOSE"

1 Rogatien left for home early *because he had to study.*
2 *Since Mr. Fox was sick,* he had to cancel the appointment.
3 I sent the letter airmail *so (that) he would get it sooner.*

"RESULT"

4 I couldn't hear the speaker, *so I moved to the first row.*
5 The man spoke so rapidly *(that) I couldn't understand him.*
6 I had such a wonderful time *(that) I didn't want to go home.*

"OPPOSITION"

7 Ralph bought that used car *although we advised him against it.*
8 *Although he's 65 years old,* Mr. Cole is still an active man.

"COMPARISON"

9 The weather is better today *than it was yesterday.*
10 There are as many students in this class *as there are in that one.*

"PLACE"

11 Would you please put the book *where it belongs.*
12 Our dog Kim usually goes *wherever he wishes to go.*
13 *Wherever we went,* we seemed to see very interesting things.

"TIME"

14 The Browns saw the Eiffel Tower *when they were in Paris.*
15 *When I visited Rome,* I saw the famous Coliseum.
16 George and I will wait right here *until you get back.*
17 *Before the secretary leaves,* she will put the letters on your desk.

"CONDITION"

18 I will give Mr. Anderson your message *if I see him tomorrow.*
19 *If I had had enough time,* I would have gone to the meeting with you.

Choose *because, since,* or *so (that)* as the connecting word for the dependent clause in each sentence. Study the first five examples carefully.

> The word *that* is optional.

1 Bill needs some money *so (that)* he can buy a new suit.
2 Bill needs some money *because* he wants to buy a new suit.
3 I moved to the front row *so (that)* I could hear the speaker.
4 I moved to the front row *because* I couldn't hear the speaker.
5 *Since* I couldn't hear the speaker, I moved to the front row.
6 I borrowed ten dollars from Ed .... I could pay for my books.
7 I borrowed the money from him .... I had to pay for my books.
8 Dorothy gave Don a list .... he wouldn't forget anything.
9 .... Don often forgets things, his wife usually gives him a list.
10 You should call Mr. Slater .... he wants to talk to you.
11 You should call Mr. Slater .... you can get the information.
12 .... you have changed your plans, you should call Mr. Slater.
13 We should leave for home early .... we won't be tired tomorrow.
14 We should leave for home early .... Mother will be waiting for us.
15 .... we must go to work tomorrow, we should leave for home early.

WRITING CLAUSES OF REASON OR PURPOSE   227

Complete these sentences with appropriate clauses of reason or purpose.

1 I let Françoise my dictionary *so that*..
2 We stayed at home last night *because*..
3 *Since*.., I left the message with his secretary.
4 I can't write to Jean-Paul *because*..
5 I wrote the sentence on the blackboard *so*......................................
6 *Since*..., would you like some coffee instead ?
7 Please open both of the windows *so that*..
8 He's studying Economics at the University of Montreal *because*.....
    ....
9 I'm going to borrow some money from Tom *so*................................
10 *Since*........................., I wasn't able to help Maurice with the lesson.
11 I took all the books off my desk *so that*..
12 I got up at 6:30 this morning *because*..
13 *Since*........................., you should spend more time on your lessons.
14 I will put the package right here..
15 I won't be able to go with you tomorrow..
16 I gave John the keys to my car *so that*..

Choose *so* or *such* for the blank space in each sentence. Study the examples carefully.

1   Mr. Anderson wasn't at home, *so* I called him at his office.
2   Mr. Anderson was *so* busy that he couldn't meet me.
3   He is *such* a busy man that he really needs a secretary.
4   Dr. Davis has *so* much work to do that he can't come tonight.
5   Dr. Davis has *so* many patients that he's always busy.
6   We saw a nice house for sale, ... we stopped to look at it.
7   The house was .... beautiful that I took a picture of it.
8   It was .... a beautiful house that we decided to buy it.
9   This coffee is .... strong that I really can't drink it.
10   That was .... strong coffee that I really didn't care for it.
11   The coffee was too strong for me, ... I didn't drink it.
12   The lesson was .... hard that I asked Charles for some help.
13   We have .... hard homework that I always need help.
14   I didn't understand the explanation, ... I had to ask for help.
15   There was .... much food that everyone ate too much.
16   There were .... many guests that there wasn't enough food.

Complete each sentence with an appropriate clause of result.

1   It was such a hot day *that*...
2   I couldn't find a seat, *so*...
3   That lesson was so difficult *that*..
4   Mr. Moore is such a good teacher *that*...
5   The food was so good *that*..
6   Mr. Wilson was so busy today *that*...
7   Guy didn't hear the instructions, *so*..
8   It's so far across Canada *that*..
9   I have a lot of work to do, *so*..
10   We enjoyed the music so much *that*..
11   I ate so many sandwiches *that*...
12   Steve can't bring his car tonight, *so*...
13   Mr. Houle speaks so rapidly *that*..
14   I didn't have enough money, *so*..

Change the italicized phrase in each sentence to a dependent adverb clause of opposition introduced by the word *although*. Study the first two examples carefully.

1 *Despite the slippery roads,* he drove his car today.
   Although the roads were slippery, he drove his car today.
2 I bought that used car *in spite of John's advice.*
   I bought that used car *although John had advised against it.*
3 Mr. Watkins is surprisingly active *despite his age.*
4 *In spite of the rain,* we went for a walk in the park.
5 *Despite his lack of education,* that man has a good position.
6 Our team won the hockey game *in spite of injuries to key players.*
7 *Despite the narrow streets in that city,* many people drive cars.
8 *In spite of your objections,* I'm going to mention my plan.
9 Mr. Anderson went to work yesterday *despite his bad cold.*
10 *In spite of his laziness,* that fellow always does good work.
11 *Despite the high cost of living here,* there are many advantages.
12 *In spite of all the noise outside,* I went to sleep immediately.
13 Virginia told all of her friends the secret *despite her promise.*

Practice completing these sentences.

1 Although many people attended the meeting, ...
2 I didn't tell my friends the news although...
3 Although Jeanne doesn't speak English well,.....................................
4 Frank won't be able to come with us although.................................
5 Although no one helped Mr. Lucas yesterday,.....................................
6 My roommate lent me some money although.....................................
7 Although she has never complained about the noise, ...
8 I seldom go to the movies during the week although.......................
9 Although Father didn't promise to come along, ...
10 Some people enjoy operas and concerts although ....
11 Although we don't have very much free time, ...
12 We won't be able to meet you tonight although.............................
13 Although I can't help you tomorrow morning,.............................
14 Mr. Simmons didn't tell me about it although.............................
15 Although Mr. Shaw teaches only twelve hours a week, ...

Complete each sentence with an appropriate adverb clause of comparison introduced by *as* or *than*. Remember that a clause always includes a subject and a verb. Review Exercise 182 before writing this exercise. Use question marks where necessary.

1   The weather is much better today *than it was yesterday.*
2   My friend, Serge, works just as hard *as the other students do.*
3   Mr. Shaw's speech was more interesting...
4   You speak English just as well...
5   Do you always drive as carefully ....
6   There are more students in this class ....
7   You look very much happier today ....
8   That brown cotton dress is less expensive...................................
9   Are you studying harder this semester ....
10 Frank doesn't seem to be as nervous..
11 I hear less difference between those two words............................
12 Mr. Wilson has much more money ....
13 Does Mr. Moore have as many students this year ....
14 I usually enjoy television programs more ....
15 My secretary usually gets to the office earlier.............................

Complete each of these sentences with a dependent adverb clause of place. Study the first two examples carefully.

1   Would you please put those books back *where they belong.*
2   *Everywhere we went,* we saw very unusual things.
3   Please don't sit *where*..
4   Just put your coat and hat *wherever* ....
5   *Wherever*...you will also find much poverty.
6   We saw examples of neglect *everywhere.*....................................
7   *Every place*........................., we stopped and asked for information.
8   You can park your car *wherever*...
9   Unfortunately, there's another car right *where*............................
10 *Everywhere*.., someone or other objected.
11 That police station is located *where*...
12 There are usually police stations *wherever*.................................
13 *Every place*................................., the people stared at us strangely.
14 This road is very dangerous *where*...
15 Roads are very dangerous *wherever*..

Complete each sentence with an appropriate clause.

1 You should write to Mr. Lane *because*..

2 I put the money in my wallet *so*...

3 We didn't discuss the matter *although*..

4 My teacher gave me so much homework *that*...................................

5 You should not park your car *where*..

6 I made too many mistakes, *so*...

7 That fellow works much harder *than*..

8 It was such a difficult examination *that*...

9 Just put your hat and coat *wherever*..

10 I didn't go to the meeting with Bill *because*.................................

11 Mary couldn't find her umbrella, *so*...

12 Please leave everything right *where*..

13 Mr. Shelton didn't accept our offer *although*...............................

14 I have to leave a message *so that*...

15 My friend can't help us tomorrow *because*....................................

16 The wind was blowing so hard yesterday *that*...............................

Put brackets [] around the dependent adverb clause of time in each sentence. Study the use of the different tenses in these clauses of time.

1 Our friends will wait for us here until we get back.
   Our friends will wait for us here [*until we get back*].

2 Mrs. Howell cut her finger while she was slicing the bread.

3 After I had asked the girl twice, she finally told me her name.

4 The maid is going to clean up the house before the guests arrive.

5 When I left for work this morning, it was raining very hard.

6 Please don't say anything to them until we're sure about that.

7 Since I last spoke to you, I have had a lot of trouble with my car.

8 As we were getting out of the car, the car started moving forward.

9 While you are getting ready, I'm going to make a telephone call.

10 I'm going to ask the teacher a question after the class is over.

11 Before Marc graduated in June, he had already been offered a job.

12 I'll be waiting right here when you come out of the building.

13 Until I had actually seen it myself, I could hardly believe it.

14 We haven't received one letter from him since he left a month ago.

Use only the continuous past tense of the verb in parentheses in each sentence. Study the two example sentences carefully.

1 The truck (*go*) very fast when it hit our car.
   The truck was going very fast when it hit our car.
2 The Andersons (*eat*) their dinner when we arrived.
   The Andersons were eating their dinner when we arrived.
3 When I left the house this morning, it (*rain*) very hard.
4 The handle broke just as they (*move*) the heavy box into place.
5 As we (*cross*) the street, the policeman shouted at us.
6 The students (*write, still*) their papers when the bell rang.
7 When we arrived at the meeting, everyone (*discuss*) the plan.
8 I read the newspaper while David (*get*) ready to leave.
9 While I (*walk*) around the park, I saw two different accidents.
10 Jean-Pierre (*argue*) with Georges when we walked into their office.
11 When the Pronovosts' son, Albert, got married in 1968, they (*live*) in Lachine.
12 I mailed the letters while Edward (*talk*) on the phone.
13 The man motioned to us just as we (*get*) ready to leave the store.
14 Howard (*sit*) in the cafeteria with Isabel when we saw him.
15 While the man (*write*) the check, I glanced at the contract again.

237　　　　THE SIMPLE PAST vs. THE CONTINUOUS PAST (1)

Write the correct form of each verb in parentheses. Use only the simple past tense (example : *he spoke*) or the continuous past tense (example : *he was speaking*).

1 Mr. Lemieux (*talk*) to another man when I (*see*) him today.
2 As I (*cross*) the street, two cars (*race*) by me at full speed.
3 When we (*meet*) the Vachons in 1970, they (*live*) in Pierrefonds.
4 Our English teacher (*give*) us an examination yesterday.
5 The boy (*fall*) and (*hurt*) himself while he (*ride*) his bicycle.
6 Bill (*have*) breakfast when I (*stop*) at his home this morning.
7 When I (*leave*) my office last night, it (*rain, still*) very hard.
8 Mr. Brown (*borrow*) the money from Mr. Wilson two weeks ago.
9 That tourist (*lose*) his camera while he (*walk*) around the city.
10 The two men (*argue*) about the plan when I (*come*) into the office.
11 Our hosts at the party last Saturday night (*treat*) us very kindly.
12 The telephone (*ring*) while I (*take*) my shower this morning.
13 At the beginning of the semester, this class (*seem*) quite easy.
14 The teacher (*interrupt*) us just as we (*finish*) the last page.
15 Dorothy and I (*leave, just*) the house when the telephone (*ring*).

Use only the simple past tense of each verb in parentheses. Note that both verbs in each sentence express momentary (not continuous) action. Study the first example carefully.

1 When the alarm (*ring*), Frank (*jump*) out of bed quickly.
   When the alarm rang, Frank jumped out of bed quickly.
2 The moment I (*notice*) the man's injury, I (*call*) an ambulance.
3 When the teacher (*open*) the door, the students (*stop*) talking.
4 The minute we (*hear*) the news, we (*send*) them a telegram.
5 When I (*hear*) the loud crash outside, I (*run*) to the window.
6 When Donald (*say*) that, Dorothy (*wink*) at me secretly.
7 The moment I (*get*) out of the plane, I (*see*) them at the gate.
8 When the elevator (*stop*) at the tenth floor, everyone (*get*) out.
9 When I (*see*) the fire trucks, I (*put on*) my brakes immediately.
10 Mr. Kelly (*tell*) the manager about it the next time it (*happen*).
11 The next time Mary (*see*) Harold, she (*give*) him the message.
12 When I first (*arrive*) here, the amount of traffic (*surprise*) me.
13 Every time the doorbell (*ring*), Susanne (*run*) to the door quickly.
14 When the man (*snap*) his fingers, the dog (*jump up*) immediately.

THE SIMPLE PAST vs. THE CONTINUOUS PAST (2)   239

Write the correct form of each verb in parentheses. Use only the simple past tense (example : *she worked*) or the continuous past tense (example : *she was working*).

1 Charles (*talk*) to Professor Moore when I (*see*) him.
2 When the students (*hear*) the bell, they (*get up*) and (*leave*).
3 My friend Louise (*buy*) a new spring coat last week.
4 We (*eat, still*) our dinner when Mr. and Mrs. Drapeau (*arrive*).
5 Mr. Harvey (*ask*) me about my plans the next time he (*see*) me.
6 Just as I (*leave*) for home, a student (*stop*) me in the hall.
7 The train for Saint John (*leave*) at five o'clock.
8 The moment Georges (*hear*) the news, he (*phone*) me.
9 Since you (*leave*) last year, many unusual things have happened.
10 I (*see*) a bad accident while I (*wait*) for you on this corner.
11 The two men (*discuss*) the election when we (*interrupt*) them.
12 The agent (*sell*) Mr. Lane a house in Longueuil at a low price.
13 I haven't seen Roger at all since he (*move*) to his new apartment.
14 Catherine (*wave*) at us happily as soon as she (*see*) us there.
15 When Mr. Shaw (*stop*) us, we (*work, still*) on the last section.

Use only the perfect past tense of the verb in parentheses in each sentence.

1 Almost everyone (*leave*) for home by the time we arrived.
Almost everyone had left for home by the time we arrived.

2 I (*see, never*) the Louvre before I visited Paris last year.
I had never seen the Louvre before I visited Paris last year.

3 We (*walk*) no more than two blocks when we met Frank.

4 After Jim (*read*) the message carefully, he wrote a reply.

5 Mr. Smith (*leave*) about five minutes before I called his office.

6 The manager (*close, just*) the store a moment before I got there.

7 The men left the office after they (*receive*) their instructions.

8 Harold couldn't leave for home until he (*complete*) everything.

9 By the time Bill and I got there, the meeting (*start, already*).

10 When I saw David in July, he (*finish, almost*) his new garage.

11 I called Mr. Fox just as soon as I (*check*) the report carefully.

12 Before you mentioned that author, I (*hear, never*) of him.

13 The man wouldn't leave until he (*receive*) a definite answer.

Write the correct form of each verb in parentheses. Use only the simple past tense (example : *he ate*) or the perfect past tense (example : *he had eaten*). Review Exercises 233 and 235 before writing this exercise.

1 The pharmacist (*leave, already*) for home when we (*get*) to the store.

2 The Andersons (*move*) into their new apartment last week.

3 The next time I (*see*) George, he (*have*) a different car.

4 Dorothy (*sign*) the check and (*give*) it to Dr. Davis yesterday.

5 When John and I (*get*) to the theater, the movie (*start, already*).

6 Whenever it (*rain*), Mr. Gilbert (*take out*) his old umbrella.

7 When I (*see*) Arthur in May, he (*write*) 280 pages of his novel.

8 After Pierre (*graduate*), he (*go*) on a fishing trip in the Yukon.

9 Everyone (*eat*) dinner by the time we (*get*) to the dining room.

10 When the policeman (*shout*) at me, I (*stop*) the car immediately.

11 Since I (*speak, last*) to you, I have had no trouble with my car.

12 We (*turn off, just*) the lights when we (*hear*) someone at the door.

13 Our friends (*arrive*) in Charlottetown on the first of May.

14 The same day Bill (*arrive*), I (*receive*) a wire from his father.

15 When Father (*return*) from downtown, I (*prepare, already*) dinner.

Express future action by using only the simple present tense of the verb in parentheses in each sentence. Note that the simple present tense ʟ used after the conjunctions *when, until, before, after,* etc. Study the example sentence carefully.

1 Harold will give Catherine your message when he (*see*) her.
   Harold will give Catherine your message when he sees her.
2 I'll be ready to leave for home when my friend (*arrive*).
3 When we (*get*) the photographs, we'll show them to you.
4 Virginia and I will wait right here until Ralph (*get*) back.
5 Before Mr. Fox (*leave*) for Rouyn, he'll explain that to you.
6 After the play (*be*) over, we'll meet you in front of the theater.
7 Miss Irwin will help you as soon as she (*finish*) that letter.
8 The two drivers must not leave until the police (*get*) here.
9 The next time I (*see*) the Gilberts, I'll ask them about it.
10 We'll pay for the materials when the company (*deliver*) them.
11 You should ask the boss about it before you (*make*) any changes.
12 When Mr. Wilson (*return*) from Truro, we're going to tell him.
13 I want to speak to Professor Moore as soon as he (*be*) free.
14 After the class (*be*) over, ask the teacher about that sentence.

THE SIMPLE PRESENT vs. THE FUTURE   243

Write the correct form of each verb in parentheses. Use only the simple present tense (example : *he leaves*) or the future with *will* or *go* (example : *he will leave* or *he is going to leave*).

1 We (*send*) you a telegram as soon as we (*arrive*) in Amsterdam.
2 When George (*come*) this afternoon, he (*bring*) his friends.
3 Mr. Green (*leave, not*) the office until you (*call*) him.
4 I (*speak*) to you about that matter after the meeting tonight.
5 As soon as our guests (*arrive*) tonight, we (*serve*) dinner.
6 You (*have*) less to say about your rights when you (*be*) thirty-one.
7 I (*help*) you with your homework as soon as I (*finish*) this letter.
8 We (*send*) the company a check when we (*receive*) a bill.
9 The company (*deliver*) the materials to you next Wednesday.
10 Alice and I (*wait*) at that corner until you (*come*) with the car.
11 The next time I (*go*) to the library, I (*get*) that book for you.
12 Our friends (*be, still*) here, when Louise (*return*) from school.
13 Don't worry ! We (*start, not*) dinner until everyone (*get*) here.
14 When Miss Stewart (*come*) back from lunch, give her the message.

Use only the continuous future tense of the verb in parentheses in each sentence. Study the two example sentences carefully.

1 We (*wait*) for you when you get back tomorrow.
   We will be waiting for you when you get back tomorrow.
2 I (*work*) on the report when you arrive this afternoon.
   I will be working on the report when you arrive this afternoon.
3 When he receives his diploma, his family (*sit*) in the audience.
4 I (*wait*) for you right here when you come out of the building.
5 It's too early. Our friends (*eat*) dinner when we arrive.
6 By the time you receive this letter, we (*travel*) through Spain.
7 We (*live*) in our new house by the time Christmas comes.
8 When you return with the car, I (*pack, still*) my suitcases.
9 The sky is dark. It (*rain*) by the time we're ready to leave.
10 When you come to Room 410, I (*work*) at the desk in the rear.
11 Don't call me at 2:30. I (*interview*) job applicants at that time.
12 Just about that time, Mr. Fox (*dictate*) letters to his secretary.
13 Frank (*wait*) here for your telephone call at eleven o'clock.
14 At this time tomorrow, we (*drive*) through the Gaspé.
15 André (*live*) in St. Anne de Bellevue this time next year.

245   THE SIMPLE FUTURE vs. THE CONTINUOUS FUTURE

Write the correct form of each verb in parentheses. Choose between the simple future tense (example : *he will write*) and the continuous future tense (example : *he will be writing*).

1 I (*give*) Mr. Harris your message when I see him tomorrow.
2 Mr. Brink (*cross*) the Atlantic by the time the news reaches him.
3 When you go into the office, Mrs. Roland (*sit*) at the front desk.
4 Our English teacher (*explain*) that lesson to us tomorrow.
5 Mr. and Mrs. Taylor (*live*) in their new house by next spring.
6 I (*try*) to explain it to the students when they ask me about it.
7 We (*wait*) for you right here when you return at 5:30 p.m.
8 The Grégoires (*travel*) through Saskatchewan this time tomorrow.
9 When we see Mr. Johnson tomorrow, we (*remind*) him of that.
10 When you come today, I (*work*) at my desk in Room 12.
11 Don't take so many books. Your suitcase (*weigh*) too much.
12 It's too early. Our friends (*eat*) their dinner when we get there.
13 Marie (*give*) us the information after she has spoken to Antoine.
14 Jack says he (*return*) the money to you at two o'clock tomorrow.

Supply the correct form of the verb in parentheses.

At the time I first (*meet*) Mr. Dubois in 1968, he (*consider*) the possibility of (*study*) foreign languages again. He said that he (*forget*) everything that he (*learn*) about English in high school. However, the language he (*want*) (*learn*) at that time (*be*) German. I suggested that he (*study*) German at a language school in Montreal. Soon afterwards, he (*enroll*) in an intensive course for one year.

After my friend (*finish*) (*study*) in the spring of 1970, he (*decide*) (*go*) straightaway to Germany for a year. He (*travel*) extensively. Since he (*be, never*) there before, he (*enjoy*) (*visit*) such famous cities as Munich, Heidleberg, Bonn, and Hamburg. He liked Munich so much, in fact, that he (*consider*) (*stay*) there much longer. He even thought that he (*enjoy*) (*live*) there for the rest of his life. However, he (*spend, finally*) all of his money and (*force*) (*return*) to Canada.

Now my friend, Mr. Dubois, (*plan*) (*visit*) England next year. He (*leave*) by boat from New York on May 15th. Naturally, all his friends (*try*) (*be*) there (*say*) "goodbye" when his boat (*leave*) for Southampton. When he (*start*) his first letter to us on May 17th, he (*cross, still*) the Atlantic Ocean. Mr. Dubois said he (*visit, also*) Belgium, Holland, and Denmark on the same trip. I know that he (*have, always*) a great deal of curiosity about those countries. Therefore, he (*appreciate*) (*visit*) all the famous places which he (*read*) about so many times in the past.

Mr. Dubois realizes that he must (*relearn*) English before he (*go*). At the moment, he (*take*) an advanced course in English in preparation for the trip. He (*think*) it is quite easy. Of course, he (*be, never*) to England up to now, so he (*have*) little opportunity (*hear*) English (*speak*) by the natives. He (*find*) that there (*be*) many different accents too. I'm sure that he (*have*) no language problem in the other countries when he (*get*) there. Many people in those countries (*understand*) English and/or French.

Use only the simple present tense of the verb in parentheses in each sentence to indicate a possible or anticipated future action. Study the first two examples carefully.

1 The teacher will explain that part to you if you (*ask*) him.
   The teacher will explain that part to you if you ask him.
2 If Harry (*invite*) me, I will probably go to the party.
   If Harry invites me, I will probably go to the party.
3 You will have enough time to eat lunch if you (*get*) here early.
4 If Tom (*see*) Miss Irwin, he'll give her your message.
5 We are going to leave tomorrow if the weather (*be*) good.
6 If Betty (*like, not*) this sweater, can she exchange it at the store ?
7 Will you lend me the money if you (*get*) your check tomorrow ?
8 If I (*decide*) to join the club, I will fill out this application form.
9 We will get there before midnight if the train (*arrive*) on time.
10 If Mr. Burton (*need*) any assistance, I will tell you right away.
11 Father will surely get wet today if he (*take, not*) his umbrella.
12 If you (*be, not*) more careful in the future, you'll have an accident.
13 The teacher will get angry at me if I (*make*) that mistake again.
14 If anyone (*ask*) for you, I will tell him to call back later today.

Practice completing the following conditional sentences.

1 Professor Moore will help you if ....
2 If Edith goes to the post office, ...
3 I will explain everything to Harold if ....
4 If I see Mr. Miller at the meeting, ...
5 I am going to buy Mr. Smith's car if ....
6 If you have any trouble with that lesson, ...
7 Bill and I will wait for you right here if ....
8 If the weather is bad tomorrow, ...
9 What will you do if ....
10 If I find your purse and gloves, ...
11 Daniel will not understand you if ....
12 If you study these lessons carefully, ...
13 We're going to go on a picnic if ....
14 If no one answers the telephone, ...
15 What will you say to Mr. Cole if ....

Complete these conditional sentences of instruction following the pattern of the two example sentences. Note that (1) the simple present tense is used in the "*if*" clause to express a future possibility and (2) the following instructions are expressed by use of the imperative form.

1 If you find any mistakes on the paper, show them to the teacher.
2 If you get lost in this city, don't hesitate to ask a policeman for help.
3 If you.., give him both of the packages.
4 If anyone asks for me today, ...
5 If Mr. Smith ...., don't say anything to him about it.
6 If you have any trouble with the machine,..
7 If the mailman, ...please call me right away.
8 If the students don't understand you,..
9 If anyone ...., ask him to leave a message.
10 If you see Mr. Johnson today,..
11 If you...................................., look up the words in your dictionary.
12 If the plumber comes this afternoon, ...
13 If the dog.., just talk to him calmly.
14 If you don't have enough time to finish,..

Use only the simple present tense of the verbs in parentheses in each sentence. Note that each sentence describes a conditional general truth.

1 If I (*make*) a mistake, the teacher (*find, always*) it.
   If I make a mistake, the teacher always finds it.
2 My dog (*bark, always*) if he (*hear*) any strange sounds.
   My dog always barks if he hears any strange sounds.
3 If a policeman (*see*) anything unusual, he (*report, usually*) it.
4 Mary (*call, always*) Mr. Green if anyone (*ask*) for information.
5 If I (*know, not*) the answer, I (*admit, always*) it right away.
6 A teacher (*be, always*) happy if his students (*study*) hard.
7 If the train (*get*) to my station late, I (*get*) to my office late.
8 Luc (*get, usually*) angry if we (*say*) anything about his accent.
9 If the newspaper (*predict*) rain, he (*carry, always*) his umbrella.
10 The stockholders (*get*) dividends if the company (*make*) a profit.
11 If there (*be*) any doubt about a case, the jury (*be, usually*) lenient.
12 Mr. Nelson (*drive, seldom*) to work if the weather (*be*) bad.
13 If we (*understand, not*) Mr. Shaw, he (*speak*) more slowly.
14 Farmers (*complain, always*) if it (*rain, not*) enough in the summer.

Use the simple past tense of the verb in parentheses in each sentence to indicate (1) a future action which is unlikely or improbable or (2) an action which is unreal or contrary to the truth at the present time. For the past tense of *be*, only the subjunctive form (*were*) is used after *if*. Note that the past future tense is used in the main clause.

1   If I (*have*) the day off tomorrow, I would go to the beach.
    If I had the day off tomorrow, I would go to the beach.

2   If I (*have*) a million dollars right now, I would retire.
    If I had a million dollars right now, I would retire.

3   If I (*be*) the mayor of this city, I would change certain things.
    If I were the mayor of this city, I would change certain things.

4   If that man (*work*) harder, he could earn more money.

5   I would gladly tell you the answer if I only (*know*) it myself.

6   If Don and I (*have*) enough money, we would buy a house.

7   If the weather (*be*) better right now, we could go for a walk.

8   That student would get much higher marks if he (*study*) harder.

9   If Mr. Smith (*call*) me, I would explain everything to him.

10   Mr. Moore would give up teaching if he (*enjoy, not*) it so much.

11   If I (*be*) in your place, I would accept Mr. Anderson's offer.

12   People would understand you better if you (*speak*) more carefully.

Practice completing the following conditional sentences.

1   If the weather were better today, ...

2   I would be a millionaire if...

3   If we had a different English teacher, ...

4   We could play a game of cards if...

5   If everybody dressed the same way, ...

6   I wouldn't do that if...

7   If I had more free time, ...

8   No one would be happy if...

9   If I spoke Dutch fluently, ...

10   Your suit would look better if...

11   If I knew all of the details, ...

12   Almost anyone would be frightened if...

13   If I had the day off tomorrow, ...

14   The world would be a better place if ....

15   If Alice were a little more careful, ...

Use the perfect past tense of the verb in parentheses in each sentence to indicate an action which was unreal or contrary to the truth in the past. Note that the perfect past future form (*would have spoken, could have spoken*) is used in the main clause. Study the two example sentences carefully.

1   If George (*have*) the money, he would have lent it to me.
    If George had had the money, he would have lent it to me.
2   I would have spoken to Frank if I (*see*) him yesterday.
    I would have spoken to Frank if I had seen him yesterday.
3   If the weather (*be*) better, we would have left Friday morning.
4   Alice would have told you the truth if you (ask) her about it.
5   If you (*study*) a little harder, you would have passed the test.
6   I could have lent you some money if I (*spend, not*) everything.
7   If there (*be*) any complaints, we would have heard about them.
8   We would have gone with Fred last Friday if he (*invite*) us.
9   If you (*ask, only*) me, I could easily have given you the answer.
10   Bill would have taken more photographs if he (*had*) more film.
11   If Tom (*be*) here yesterday, he would have been able to advise us.
12   We would have bought that house if the price (*be*) a little lower.
13   If they (*need*) any help with the work, they would have called us.

WRITING CONDITIONAL SENTENCES   254

Practice completing the following conditional sentences.

1   If you had taken my advice,...
2   I would have had less trouble if ....
3   If anyone had asked me about it,.....................................
4   Our dog Pop would have barked if.................................
5   If I had been in your place,..
6   Bill wouldn't have said anything if................................
7   If you had followed my instructions,.............................
8   You wouldn't have lost your money if...........................
9   If John had taken better care of his car,.......................
10   We couldn't have gone on our trip if.............................
11   If you had only left your house earlier, ...
12   It would have been much better if ....
13   If my watch hadn't been five minutes slow, ...
14   Things would have been different if................................
15   If I had been born a century ago,...................................

Substitute the word *unless* for *if... not* or *if...no* in the following sentences. Study the example sentences carefully.

1 If you don't leave immediately, I will call a policeman.
   Unless you leave immediately, I will call a policeman.
2 Serge wouldn't do that if he didn't have your permission.
   Serge wouldn't do that unless he had your permission.
3 I won't bother to call you if I don't hear from Mr. Brown.
4 If you didn't agree with him, Charles wouldn't even suggest it.
5 We can't write to Mr. Girouard if he doesn't send us his address.
6 If you don't study harder, you're going to fail the examination.
7 I wouldn't have believed it if I hadn't seen it with my own eyes.
8 If she doesn't start the letter now, she'll have to do it tomorrow.
9 The lawyer wouldn't say that if he didn't have strong evidence.
10 If you don't invest your money wisely, you will lose all of it.
11 I won't say anything if Maurice doesn't bring it up himself.
12 If no more guests come, there will be enough food for everyone.
13 Our dog wouldn't have barked if he hadn't heard a strange noise.
14 If no one complains, we'll leave everything just the way it is now.

Write the correct form of the verb in parentheses in each sentence. Notice the forms of the verbs which are used in clauses after the verb *wish* to indicate future (examples : *he would be, they would write*), present *(he were, they wrote)*, and past *(he had been, they had written)*. Study the examples carefully.

1 I wish you (*write*) more carefully in the future.
   I wish you would write more carefully in the future.
2 I wish my uncle (*be*) here now to give us some advice.
   I wish my uncle were here now to give us some advice.
3 I wish I (*know*) all about this matter several weeks ago.
   I wish I had known all about this matter several weeks ago.
4 I wish I (*have*) more time now to help you with your lesson.
5 I wish I (*study*) psychology when I was a college student.
6 I wish someone (*offer*) to help me with that work tomorrow.
7 I wish it (*be*) possible for me to help you with it yesterday.
8 I wish it (*be*) a little warmer in this room. I feel very cold.
9 I wish it (*rain*) tomorrow in order to cool the air a little.
10 I wish I (*pay*) attention to the teacher's explanation yesterday.
11 I wish our teacher (*explain*) that lesson to us again tomorrow.

Supply the correct form of the verb or verbs in parentheses in each sentence.

1 If we (*receive*) the news sooner, we'd have written to George.
2 I'm sure they (*give*) Ellen the information if they had it.
3 If a policeman (*see*) an accident, he (*take*) the drivers' names.
4 We would have gone sailing if Mr. Drouin (*bring*) his boat.
5 What would you do tomorrow if you (*be*) a millionaire ?
6 If you (*go*) downtown, take these letters to the post office.
7 I don't think you (*believe*) me even if I told you the truth about it.
8 If Henri (*be, not*) so careless, he wouldn't have lost his good job.
9 Please (*leave*) a message if anyone (*call*) while I (*be*) away.
10 I (*accept, certainly*) Mr. Lane's offer if I (*be*) in your place.
11 The accident (*happen, never*) if the driver (*see*) the stop sign.
12 If a large number of guests (*come*), they'll use the other room.
13 I know Louise (*tell*) you if she (*go*) to the party last night.
14 If you (*understand, not*) the instructions, read them again.
15 I wouldn't accept that job even if the manager (*offer*) it to me.

Practice completing these conditoinal sentences.

1 Many people would be in accidents if ....
2 If my friend had taken my advice, ...
3 Can I return this dress to the store if...
4 Unless I get the money before tomorrow,..
5 My brother would have written to me if...
6 What would you say to your boss if ....
7 I'm sure Doris wouldn't do that unless ....
8 If I hadn't spent my money so foolishly,..
9 My grandfather always gets mad if ....
10 If everyone agreed with you completely, ...
11 Things would have been quite different if...
12 If you find anything you don't understand, ...
13 That fellow won't give you the money unless.......................................
14 If you had been a little more ambitious,...
15 Almost everyone could afford a new house if ....

Write the correct form of the verb or verbs in each sentence.

1 At present, my friend André (*write*) a book about Quebec.
2 I think it (*become*) a "best seller" when it (*publish*) next year.
3 André got the original idea for the book while he (*go*) to college.
4 When I saw André last June, he (*write*) about 125 pages of the book.
5 André is quite prolific. He (*write*) four books and 43 articles.
6 Many of these articles (*be*) about French Canada.
7 Although André enjoys writing, he (*like*) to be a history teacher.
8 We would prefer that Mr. Lemieux (*speak*) to Mr. Gagnon himself.
9 I strongly suspected, however, that Mr. Lemieux (*speak, already*) to Mr. Gagnon.
10 Mr. Wood will speak to Mr. Howell before he (*leave*) the office.
11 Mr. Howell, our director, (*work*) for this company for nine years.
12 Mr. Hill interrupted Mr. Wood while he (*speak*) to Mr. Howell.
13 Don't you think that the subways (*run*) behind schedule lately ?
14 Yes, but at this time, much attention (*devote*) to that problem.
15 I wish that I (*know*) more about that particular problem than I do.
16 When you have read today's paper, you (*understand*) everything.
17 The earth (*move*) around the sun once every 365 days.
18 This fact (*prove*) by scientists more than 300 years ago.
19 We'll meet Alice at the corner. She (*wait*) when we (*arrive*).
20 As I (*go*) to work today, I saw Alice on her way downtown.
21 Whenever I meet Alice on the street, she (*wear*) something new.
22 It (*rain*) very much in this part of the country every spring.
23 When I (*leave*) my office last night, it (*rain, still*) very hard.
24 The radio announcer said that it (*be*) cloudy and cold tomorrow.
25 Ever since Jim (*win*) that $60,000 contest, he (*refuse*) to work.
26 Jim will never look for a job unless someone (*force*) him to do it.
27 If Jim (*win, not*) that contest, he (*resign, not*) from his good job.
28 When I discovered my camera (*steal*), I called the police at once.
29 The police think that the camera (*take*) sometime during the day.
30 If I (*take*) the camera with me yesterday, all of this (*happen, not*).

After each number, there are two sentences, (a) and (b), representing two speakers. Use the emphatic forms of the simple present or past tense (examples : *I do work, he does write, they did see,* etc.) of an appropriate verb in the blank space in sentence (b). Study examples 1 and 2 carefully.

1 (a) Mr. Smith said John didn't write the letter.
  (b) But John *did write* the letter ! I saw the letter.

2 (a) Did Jean write the report you assigned to him ?
  (b) He didn't do all of it, but he *did do* the first part.

3 (a) Of course this seems difficult. You didn't study it.
  (b) That's not true, I .... it ! Look at my notes !

4 (a) I've heard that Guy doesn't attend class regularly.
  (b) But Guy .... class regularly ! I'm sure of that.

5 (a) I thought that you were going to finish the report yesterday.
  (b) Well, I .... it. It's on your desk now. Take a look.

6 (a) The man said that you didn't give him the money.
  (b) He's wrong. I .... it to him ! Here's the receipt.

7 (a) Since you don't ever wear this suit, let's give it away.
  (b) I certainly .... it ! Don't give it away.

8 (a) Did you speak to the director about that problem ?
  (b) No, I didn't speak to him, but I .... to his secretary.

9 (a) Did his secretary call up the men to tell them about it ?
  (b) She didn't call John, but she .... Fred and Edward.

10 (a) Does that fellow like football or basketball ?
   (b) Well, he doesn't like those sports, but he .... baseball.

11 (a) I don't think I know that tall fellow. What's his name ?
   (b) But you .... him ! You met him just last week.

12 (a) Did Eleanor buy a new spring hat yesterday ?
   (b) No, she didn't buy a hat, but she .... a new purse.

13 (a) Your English teacher speaks Dutch doesn't she ?
   (b) No, she doesn't speak Dutch but she .... German.

14 (a) You probably didn't read the instructions in the book carefully.
   (b) But I .... them carefully ! I even copied them !

Express habitual action in the past with the verb *used* and the full infinitive of the verb in parentheses in each sentence (examples : *I used to work, he used to work,* etc.). Remember : this form implies that a contrary condition exists at the present.

1 Mr. Smith (*smoke*) cigars, but he doesn't any more.
   Mr. Smith used to smoke cigars, but he doesn't any more.
2 Bill (*work, not*) very hard, but he does now.
   Bill didn't use to work very hard, but he does now.
3 I (*enjoy*) "detective stories," but I don't any more.
4 Mr. Shaw (*teach*) in the morning, but now he teaches at night.
5 Many years ago, people (*travel*) by horse and buggy.
6 Mary (*get, not*) to work on time, but she does nowadays.
7 Mrs. Nelson (*walk*) downtown, but now she takes the bus.
8 What has happened ? Thomas never (*do*) his work poorly.
9 John (*attend*) the meetings regularly, but he doesn't any more.
10 When I was a child, I (*read*) the "comics" every Saturday.
11 We never (*like*) that kind of food, but we often serve it now.
12 I (*play*) the piano, but I haven't even tried it for years now.
13 I (*enjoy, not*) classical music, but I listen to it regularly now.

Use the expression *be used (to)* in place of *be accustomed (to)* in the following sentences to show acceptance of a condition or situation (or to show familiarization with it).

1 We are accustomed to the noise of the planes now.
   We are used to the noise of the planes now.
2 I am accustomed to working at night. It doesn't bother me.
   I am used to working at night. It doesn't bother me.
3 We are accustomed to the hot weather in this city now.
4 He writes poorly, but I'm accustomed to his writing by now.
5 Are you accustomed to living in a small apartment yet ?
6 Mr. Ratelle is accustomed to living in the suburbs now.
7 Is your friend accustomed to traveling by subway yet ?
8 We're not accustomed to hearing so much English every day.
9 Canadians are accustomed to cold weather.
10 Anne-Marie is not accustomed to having a baby brother yet.
11 I'm not accustomed to seeing so many cars and trucks.
12 Mr. Moore is accustomed to hearing many different accents.

Use both *get accustomed (to)* and *get used (to)* in place of *become accustomed (to)* in the following sentences. Study the examples carefully.

1 I shall never become accustomed to all these violent movies.
    I shall never get accustomed to all these violent movies.
    I shall never get used to all these violent movies.
2 You will become accustomed to hearing English every day.
    You will get accustomed to hearing English every day.
    You will get used to hearing English every day.
3 I am becoming accustomed to not having a car.
4 You will soon become accustomed to traveling by bus.
5 We soon became accustomed to the constant noise of the traffic.
6 They will become accustomed to the food here after a while.
7 I can't become accustomed to this method of learning English.
8 Marc soon became accustomed to writing everything in English.
9 I couldn't become accustomed to the confusion in that office.
10 You'll become accustomed to your new working hours very soon.

Use the correct form of *be supposed* with the full infinitive (example : *I am supposed to go, he was supposed to work,* etc.) to show action which is (or was) anticipated because of a duty or because of an appointment, schedule, plan, etc. Remember : the use of the past tense form implies that the action did not occur.

1 Dean Brown (*return*) before next Thursday.
    Dean Brown is supposed to return before next Thursday.
2 The work (*finish*) yesterday afternoon.
    The work was supposed to be finished yesterday afternoon.
3 Mr. Johnson (*get*) back to the office before three o'clock.
4 When he returns, Mr. Harris (*go*) to Dean Brown's office.
5 We (*meet*) our friends here yesterday, but we didn't.
6 You (*be*) ready to leave at eight o'clock tonight.
7 The plane from Toronto (*get*) here ten minutes from now.
8 I (*mail*) this letter to Mr. Fox yesterday, but I forgot to.
9 You (*sign*) your name on the last line of the contract.
10 Everyone in this office (*work*) from nine to five everyday.
11 These packages (*deliver*) to the Ashby Company tomorrow.

Express "expectancy" by using *should* or *should have* with the correct form of the verb in parentheses in each sentence. Remember: the use of the past tense form (*should have been, should have arrived*) implies that the action did not occur.

1 Our friend (*arrive*) from Victoriaville tomorrow morning.
   Our friend should arrive from Victoriaville tomorrow morning.

2 We (*receive*) a telegram from Mr. Cole last night.
   We should have received a telegram from Mr. Cole last night.

3 You (*hear*) from the committee today or tomorrow.

4 The plane from Boston (*arrive*) more than an hour ago.

5 The committee (*approve*) the plan at the meeting tomorrow.

6 Those men (*finish*) that work two or three hours ago.

7 Wait right here. We (*be*) back within 10 or 15 minutes.

8 That regulation (*cause, not*) you any trouble in the future.

9 The next exercise (*be*) very easy for you to understand.

10 The last exercise (*be*) very easy for everyone in the class.

11 You (*have*) no problems with the lesson for tomorrow.

12 You (*have, not*) any difficulty with your homework for today.

Read the following sentences carefully. Indicate the meaning ("advisability" or "expectancy") of the italicized verb in each sentence. Review Exercises 152-155.

1 You *should work* harder. advisability

2 They *should arrive* soon. expectancy

3 You *should read* that book. It's funny.

4 That work *shouldn't take* you very long.

5 I *should write* a letter to Mr. Jackson.

6 Fred *should have arrived* by this time.

7 I *shouldn't have borrowed* that money.

8 The Taylors' trip to France and Italy *should be* very interesting.

9 Miss Williams *should take* a taxi. It's too far to walk tonight.

10 We *should have heard* from our friends long before this time.

11 You *shouldn't have said* anything to your boss about that matter.

12 Mr. and Mrs. Anderson *should be here* within a few minutes.

13 I think that you *should have stayed* there and *waited* for the girls.

14 We *should receive* a reply from the company today or tomorrow.

Use both *have* and the full infinitive (*I have to go, he has to work*) and the informal expression *have got* and the full infinitive (*I have got to go, he has got to go*) in place of *must* in the following sentences. Remember : in using *have got*, the word *have* or *has* is usually contracted (*I've got to go, he's got to go*). Study the examples carefully.

1 You must go to the dean's office right away.
   You have to go to the dean's office right away.
   You've got to go to the dean's office right away.

You've got to do it!

2 Philippe must finish all of the work by noon tomorrow.
   Philippe has to finish all of the work by noon tomorrow.
   Philippe's got to finish all of the work by noon tomorrow.

3 We must give our boss a good reason for leaving early.
4 If you want to earn more money, you must work harder.
5 George says he must return the map to them tomorrow.
6 We must write the next two lessons for tomorrow.
7 Mr. Shaw says everyone must take the final examination.
8 I must go to the bank right away in order to cash this check.
9 If you plan to go with us, you must get ready right now.
10 Miss Elliot knows she must finish that work before two-thirty.

Use the verb *had* with the full infinitive (*I had to leave, she had to leave*) as the past tense form of the italicized verb in each of the following sentences. If necessary, change the expression of time (change *tomorrow* to *yesterday*, etc.).

1 Dr. Davis must leave for home before two o'clock.
   Dr. Davis had to leave for home before two o'clock.

2 The messenger has to deliver those two packages today.
   The messenger had to deliver those two packages today.

3 We've got to return René's dictionary to him tomorrow.
   We had to return René's dictionary to him yesterday.

4 The director must finish that report by 4:00 p.m. today.
5 Mr. Bouchard has to make a trip to Thetford Mines next week.
6 They've got to fill out the application before next Thursday.
7 We have to send a telegram to the main office of that company.
8 Everyone must do his share of the work this afternoon.
9 Miss Stewart's got to leave the office early tomorrow afternoon.
10 René says we must return the dictionary before Wednesday.
11 When Mr. Brown returns, we've got to explain everything to him.

Indicate "assumption" in each of the following sentences by using *must* or *must have* with the proper form of the verb in parentheses. Study the examples carefully.

1 Mr. Foster isn't here. He (*be*) in the other room.
   Mr. Foster isn't here. He must be in the other room.
2 The secretary wasn't there. She (*go*) home already.
   The secretary wasn't there. She must have gone home already.
3 I hear someone at the front door. It (*be*) the mailman.
4 I don't see the package. John (*mail*) it yesterday.
5 By this time, your friend Gilles (*speak*) English very well.
6 Mr. Johnson looks tired. He (*work*) very hard today.
7 I've seen the boys there several times. They (*go*) regularly.
8 The ground is quite wet today. It (*rain*) very hard last night.
9 Mr. Fox didn't say anything, so he (*think*) that we are right.
10 When I met the Slaters, it (*be*) at least seven or eight o'clock.
11 You (*think*) I don't have a job because I'm at home so often.
12 I can't get either of these doors open. They (*lock*).
13 George (*assume*) that we had already taken care of the matter.

Read the following sentences carefully. Indicate the meaning ("necessity" or "assumption") of the italicized verb in each sentence. Review Exercises 156-159.

1 We *must leave* for home right away.   [necessity]
2 Mr. Foster *must be* in the other room.   [assumption]
3 It's very late now. I *must go* home and study my lessons.
4 I've never seen Mr. Miller on the bus. He *must drive* to work.
5 When you see Mr. Moore, you *must tell* him about this.
6 Since you play tennis so often, you *must* really *enjoy* it.
7 You look healthy. You *must have rested* during your vacation.
8 You *must explain* that part again. I didn't understand it at all.
9 Mr. Vocat *must have gone* home. I don't see his briefcase.
10 Virginia *must believe* that we're angry about her remarks.
11 I *must complete* that report for my boss before next Friday.
12 When the man brings the groceries, you *must pay* him.
13 When our friends left, it *must have been* well after midnight.
14 You *must be* ready to leave when Charles and Frank get here.
15 That car is certainly beautiful, but it *must be* very expensive.

Rewrite these sentences using the auxiliary verb *may* to show "permission" or "possibility".* Study the first three examples carefully.

1 Perhaps your friends will return tomorrow night.
   Your friends may return tomorrow night. [possibility]
2 It's possible that Mr. Johnson won't arrive on time.
   Mr. Johnson may not arrive on time. [possibility]
3 You have my permission to tell everyone the news.
   You may tell everyone the news. [permission]
4 Possibly Mary will know the answer to your question.
5 You have our permission to leave whenever you're ready.
6 It is possible that Mr. Kennedy will do that for you.
7 Perhaps Mr. Howell, the director, won't agree with you.
8 You have my permission to try that method if you wish to.
9 If you ask the men politely, possibly they will help you with it.
10 Maybe the work will be a lot easier than you expect it to be.
11 It's possible that there will not be enough food for everyone.

*Notes : *Might* (the past tense sequence form of *may*) is frequently used in place of *may* to indicate "possibility". *Can* is frequently used in place of *may* to indicate "permission".

Use the informal expression *had better* (with the short infinitive) in place of *should* and *ought* in the following sentences to express "advisability". Remember : in using *had better*, the word *had* is usually contracted (*I'd better go, you'd better ask*). Study the examples carefully. Notice the negative forms.

1 It's getting quite late. We ought to go home very soon.
   It's getting quite late. We'd better go home very soon.
2 You should not say anything to Mr. Wilson about the matter.
   You'd better not say anything to Mr. Wilson about the matter.
3 Shouldn't we explain exactly what happened to Mr. Wilson ?
   Hadn't we better explain exactly what happened to Mr. Wilson ?
4 You ought to buy yourself a new suit and overcoat.
5 It's much too far to walk. Miss Stewart should call a taxi.
6 Shouldn't the children wear something very warm today ?
7 You shouldn't leave the building until you get permission.
8 I think we ought to send a telegram to Mr. Pronovost right away.
9 Shouldn't we tell them that we won't be able to meet them ?
10 You shouldn't leave your car in front of Mr. Kelly's garage.

Make a polite or unemphatic statement with *would* and the verb in parentheses in each of the following sentences. Study the examples carefully. Review Exercise 222 for practice in using the general form after the verbs *suggest, prefer,* etc. For practice with polite requests with *would,* review Exercise 23.

1 I (*like*) to eat dinner earlier than usual tonight.
   I would like to eat dinner earlier than usual tonight.

2 I (*appreciate*) receiving a prompt reply to my letter.
   I would appreciate receiving a prompt reply to my letter.

3 I know I (*enjoy*) visiting the Scandinavian countries.

4 I (*suggest*) that you speak to Dean Brown as soon as possible.

5 I think that I (*prefer*) to stay at home and read a book tonight.

6 I (*hesitate*) to say anything to the director about that matter.

7 I am sure Alice (*like*) to go shopping with us tomorrow.

8 I (*advise*) you to investigate carefully before doing anything.

9 I (*suggest, definitely*) trying a different method next time.

10 I (*recommend*) that you ask Mr. Anderson for his advice.

11 I (*prefer*) seeing a movie to watching television tonight.

12 I (*appreciate*) hearing from you regarding this problem.

13 I (*enjoy, really*) having a chance to meet all of your friends.

Practice making statements, questions, and negatives which indicate "preference" with *would rather* and the verb in parentheses in each sentence. In this usage, *would* is often contracted (*I'd rather go, he'd rather work*). Study the example sentences carefully. Notice the negative forms.

1 I (*walk*) downtown this afternoon.
   I would (I'd) rather walk downtown this afternoon.
   Would you rather walk downtown this afternoon ?
   Wouldn't you rather walk downtown this afternoon ?
   I would (I'd) rather not walk downtown this afternoon.

2 I (*stay*) at home over the Christmas holiday.

3 I (*live*) in Lachine than in Roxboro.

4 I (*sit*) in the first row of seats than in this one.

5 I (*tell*) Mr. Anderson about the problem myself.

6 I (*eat*) my lunch now than later in the day.

7 I (*meet*) you in the lobby of the building than on the corner.

8 I (*work*) for a very large company than for a small one.

9 I (*stay*) at home tonight and write my English lesson.

10 I (*watch*) a television program than go to the movies.

Analyze the use of auxiliaries in these sentences ("advisability", "necessity", "permission", etc.).

1 May we smoke in this room ? 2 You'd better wear an overcoat. Otherwise, you may catch a cold. 3 This lesson is very easy. It shouldn't take much of your time. 4 My friend couldn't tell me who would be at the party. 5 I've got to complete all of this work before tomorrow night. 6 You ought to have paid more attention to your guests than you did. 7 Yvonne said she would rather live here than in Dorval. 8 Edward must have been disappointed when you told him the news. 9 Would you please slow down; I can't walk quite so fast. 10 If you can't control your temper, you shouldn't get into arguments. 11 You must not say a word about this to anyone. 12 Fortunately, we don't have to pay the money back right away. 13 Our guests should arrive almost any moment now. 14 You ought to have been more attentive in class this morning. 15 We couldn't get used to their way of doing things. 16 I'd rather not go with you tonight ; I have a great deal of work which I should do. 17 I tried to convince him, but he wouldn't listen to me. 18 It must be quite late because everyone has already gone home. 19 You may use my car anytime you want to. 20 I couldn't understand the lesson, so Luc had to help me with it. 21 Do you want some coffee ? — Yes, I would like some. 22 Don't you think that you should see a doctor right away ? 23 Even though it rained, I should have gone to the cottage yesterday. 24 Our teacher said we didn't have to answer all of the questions. 25 We must not forget to ask the teacher about that matter. 26 Hadn't you better wait until tomorrow and make your decision then ? 27 I would suggest that you try a different method next time. 28 I suppose I could do that kind of work if I had to. 29 Frankly, I would prefer to stay at home and read tonight. 30 I wish that you could stay with us for a few more days. 31 Must we turn in our homework tomorrow morning ? 32 You should have called your friends and told them the news. 33 I didn't do the first part of the lesson, but I did do the last half. 34 Would you mind speaking a little more softly. 35 Anne must have finished the report yesterday. 36 Do you have to return ? Can't you stay a while longer ?

Complete these sentences with an object and an infinitive. Remember : the short infinitive is used after the object if the principal verb is *feel, have, hear, help, make, see, let,* or *watch.* Review Exercise 176 before writing this exercise. Put the correct punctuation at the end of each sentence. Study the first four examples carefully.

1 Did the foreman permit the men *to leave* before five o'clock ?
2 Yes, the foreman let the men *leave* before five o'clock.
3 Does the girl's mother force her *to study* every night ?
4 No, the girl's mother doesn't make her *study* every night.
5 My boss advised...
6 Did your friend help ....
7 Shouldn't we remind ....
8 I think I hear...
9 Almost everyone expects..
10 Why don't you make ....
11 Our teacher won't let...
12 The boy's parents wanted ....
13 We really saw...
14 I think we should watch...
15 We finally had to ask ....

Review these sentences. Put the italicized object after the verb *get* or *have,* and use the past participle (*moved, taken,* etc.) in place of the infinitive (*to move,* or *move, to take* or *take,* etc.). Study the first two examples carefully.

1 Mr. Wilson had the man take *the telephone* out of that office.
   Mr. Wilson had the telephone taken out of that office.
2 I got the man to deliver *all of the packages* yesterday.
   I got all of the packages delivered yesterday.
3 We had the janitor repair *that old chair* several days ago.
4 Georges finally got a mechanic to fix *his car.*
5 I'll have a carpenter cover *the holes in that wall* tomorrow.
6 Mrs. Kelly got the butcher to cut *the meat* into small pieces.
7 We usually have that man wash *our car* once a week.
8 I'm going to get him to check *those reports* very carefully.
9 You'd better have someone paint *your house* very soon.
10 Why don't we get the electrician to put *the light* on this wall ?
11 We really ought to have someone take *that junk* away.
12 John said he'd get someone to mail *the letters* tomorrow.

From the list of words at the top of the page, select the correct synonym for each of the italicized two-word verbs in the following sentences. Rewrite the sentences using the synonyms.

appear	discover	omit	resemble
cancel	discuss	postpone	return
consider	display	prepare	stop
continue	erect	reduce	select
delay	examine	reject	review
delete	execute	represent	submit
demolish	occupy	require	tolerate

1 You will have to *cut down* your living expenses a little.
2 I must *think* that matter *over* carefully before I answer you.
3 That company is going to *put up* a new building on this corner.
4 First of all, the company will have to *tear* this building *down*.
5 The two girls *take after* their mother very much in appearance.
6 *Look* each sentence *over* carefully. *Cross out* the incorrect words.
7 Mr. Foster's new job seems to *take up* all of his spare time.
8 We had to *call off* the picnic because of the bad weather.
9 I think that problem will *call for* some very careful planning.
10 Those books are overdue. When are you going to *take* them *back* ?
11 When you *make up* that list for me, don't *leave* any names *out*.
12 Everyone must *turn in* his income tax report before April thirtieth.
13 That woman certainly tried very hard to *show off* her new jewelry.
14 When I was *looking through* my papers, I *came across* this picture.
15 I suggest that you *talk* the matter *over* with your boss first of all.
16 Did the men *carry out* the foreman's instructions carefully ?
17 Is the committee going to *turn down* Ed's application for admission ?
18 Should we *go over* the lesson now or *put* it *off* until later tonight ?
19 How many people do you expect to *show up* at the meeting tonight ?
20 I think this storm will *hold up* the flight to St. John's.
21 There are some nice ties here. Why don't you *pick out* one or two ?
22 I tried to interrupt the two men, but they *went on* arguing anyway.
23 *Cut* it *out* right this minute ! You're making too much noise !
24 Those three letters are an abbreviation. They *stand for* something.
25 Our teacher is strict. He won't *stand for* any nonsense in class.

In the two blank spaces in each sentence, complete the two-word verb with the correct particle (*up, out, on*, etc.). Remember : if the two-word verb is "separable", the object pronoun must precede the particle (see the first example).

1   If you find any unnecessary things on the list, cross *them out.*
2   I'd like to see the Coles' new house. Why don't we call *on them* ?
3   I submitted an application, but the committee turned ....

Look it up !

4   We didn't arrive there until late because the bad weather held ....
5   You can't act that way here. No one in this group will stand ....
6   I don't know Mr. Nelson's address, but I can find .... easily. I can look .... in the telephone book.

7   I missed two assignments. I must make .... before Monday.
8   I think this blouse is your size. Why don't you try .... ?
9   He feels bad about his failure now, but he'll get .... soon.
10 Here's an application form for you. Fill .... carefully.
11 I hate new shoes because it's so hard to break ....
12 Don't offer Mr. Green any coffee. He doesn't care .... at all.
13 If you don't understand it now, you'll probably figure .... late
14 I wrote the lesson last night and handed .... this morning.
15 Mrs. Kelly had a good job, but she gave .... to get married.
16 This coat is much too warm. I am going to take ....
17 You should do things on time. Don't put .... until later.
18 If you go to the second counter, the clerk there will wait ....
19 Bill bought some paper last week, but he's used .... already.
20 If that word is incorrect, why don't you cross .... ?
21 Since Jean-Pierre couldn't find his mistakes, I pointed .... to him.
22 You can ride to work with me. I'll call .... at eight o'clock.
23 Your question was embarrassing. Why did you bring .... ?
24 If you keep on wearing that suit every day, you'll wear ....
25 Whenever you don't know a word, look .... in your dictionary
26 If Pierre doesn't understand that lesson, I'll go .... with him.
27 I can't find the papers now, but I'm sure I'll run .... later.
28 Ed is dependable. You can always count .... to help you.

Supply the correct preposition in the blank space in each sentence.

1 Everyone laughed at Ed's joke, but I didn't catch on .... it.
2 I don't have a book today. May I look on .... you, please ?
3 George really goes in .... tennis. It's his favorite sport.
4 Before they hire anyone, they check up .... his background.
5 I don't see how you can put up .... such bad working conditions.
6 When I was a child, I once tried to run away .... home.
7 The Coles are probably home tonight. Let's drop in .... them.
8 You should always do your best to get along .... other people.
9 We like to get away .... the city during the hot summer months.
10 If you walk fast, you can catch up .... them in the next block.
11 Our car won't start. We have run out .... gas !
12 When did you get back .... your vacation in France and Italy ?
13 Are you anxious to get back .... work after your vacation ?
14 Do you and Irène plan to go back .... Europe again next year ?
15 People often look back .... their childhood as a very happy time.
16 It's impossible to do away .... classroom discipline completely.
17 What time did you get through .... your assignment last night ?
18 Mr. Kennedy said that he was going to go ahead .... his plan.
19 Why don't we get together .... him in order to discuss the plan ?
20 You'll have to work hard to make up .... the time you've lost.
21 I'd prefer not to play golf today. I really don't feel up .... it.
22 You should try to keep up .... the other students in your class.
23 Be careful ! Watch out .... cars whenever you cross the street.
24 If they insist on it, I suppose we'll have to give in .... them.
25 I don't think I can get out .... going to that meeting tomorrow.
26 How is Marcel getting along .... his classwork these days ?
27 Hang on .... that end of the box very tightly. Don't let go of it !
28 That fellow violated the rules, but he apparently got away .... it.
29 I don't want to break in .... their conversation. I'll wait here.
30 Get away .... that fence ! Keep away .... those electrical wires !
31 I just can't go on .... this work any longer. I'm too discouraged.

In most cases, the words and expressions within the brackets are not in the correct order. Put the sentence elements which are within the brackets into their normal order. Do not add or eliminate any words or expressions.

1 Donald bought a [green -little] jewelry box for his wife.
2 The man made a [plastic -square] cover for the box.
3 Fred was given that [unusual -modern] pocket watch.
4 That museum has [ancient -Egyptian -valuable] vases.
5 My father always used a [fishing -long -bamboo] pole.
6 My [sons -friend's -three] were all at the meeting.
7 The girl returned [to the library -promptly -those books].
8 The wind takes [in the fall -the leaves -from the trees].
9 You can see [good programs -at night -on television].
10 Alain studies [carefully -his lessons -every night].
11 That firm exports [to India -much machinery -every year].
12 The professor dictates [in class -to us -short sentences].
13 Mr. Beliveau sold [to Gilles Grégoire -his old car -last week].
14 The man gave [the money -reluctantly -the bill collector].
15 Michelle had to go [to school -on a bus -with boys].
16 The Taylors were [in the Yukon -last year -for two months].
17 That employee gets [to the office -every morning -late].
18 Jacques worked [in St. Boniface -for one summer -in a factory].
19 Those people can't conceal [forever -the truth -from us].
20 The man asked [for the rent -in advance -the tenants].
21 I wanted to take [with my friend -the train -to Ottawa].
22 He allowed himself [two years -completely -to finish it].
23 I hope [my English quickly -to improve] by studying hard.
24 Georges said it was [yesterday -downtown -quite cool].
25 Hockey is [in Canada -everywhere -very popular].
26 These things seemed [at first -to me -quite unimportant].
27 It is difficult [to speak -correctly -for me -English].
28 I don't know why [didn't -say -the man] anything to me.
29 What [will -say -your friends] about this change in plans ?
30 Mr. Cunningham doesn't know whose [that -is -car].
31 When [were -they -in Paris], they visited the Louvre.
32 Where [have -gone -all of the students] since last week ?

In most cases, the words and expressions within the brackets are not in the correct order. Put the sentence elements which are within the brackets into their normal order. Do not add or eliminate any words or expressions.

1 Henri said he liked [than television -better -movies].
2 Our dog likes to play with a [rubber -soft] ball.
3 I'm sure it [has -been -tried -never] before this time.
4 How [can -believe -you] such a peculiar excuse ?
5 No one here seems to know whose [is -bicycle -that].
6 When [did -arrive -your visitors] at the train station ?
7 I'm sure that [will -be -always] a source of difficulty.
8 I asked her when [had -finished -her husband] the work.
9 She explained [again -the part -to me -about verbs].
10 [haven't -been -ever -you] inside that famous building ?
11 When [have -done -you] that part, show it to Mr. Shaw.
12 The owner charged us his [usual -high] price for it.
13 I think that you are [that shelf -to reach -enough -tall].
14 She inherited [from him -of money -a large sum -in 1969].
15 I can't think [to improve -your plan -of any way at all].
16 That author was [in Canada -unknown -until a year ago].
17 Judge Parker introduced a [legal -new] concept in that case.
18 How [could -know -possibly -they] about it so soon ?
19 I can't imagine how [could -know -possibly -they] about it.
20 You can inquire [by the door -at the desk -about that].
21 The city has [well-organized -bus -two] companies.
22 I'll ask my friend, Maurice, what [lesson -today's -is].
23 When [had -finished -Alice] her speech, she sat down.
24 When [can -expect -we] to hear from you regarding this ?
25 He said it was a [square -wrapped in cloth -object -hard].
26 Who [can -explain -that part] for the rest of the students ?
27 She's a person in whom [will -have -you] much confidence.
28 The [along the edge -ornaments -small] were removed.
29 I didn't ask how much [them -had cost -their trip -to Calgary].
30 He mentioned [known by everyone -a poet -Shakespeare].
31 The Wilsons live in that [big -brick] mansion on the hill.
32 Wives work, but [all the responsibilities -husbands -have].

183

The words and expressions in the following sentences are not in the correct order. Put these separated sentence elements into their correct positions. Do not add or eliminate any words or expressions. Capitalize the first word in each sentence, and add the proper punctuation at the end of the sentence.

1 every day -at the school cafeteria -our lunch -we don't eat
   We don't eat our lunch at the school cafeteria every day.
2 those fellows -will -remain -how long -in Washington, D.C.
3 an official -about this rule -a question -the two men asked

is following -the man -the dog

4 who is a famous writer -Remarque -lived -at that time -in Switzerland

5 the flowers -to see -it's wonderful -in the spring -come to life

6 are mine -the purse -and -the coat -with the red collar -with the handle

7 this fine sport -don't -enjoy -why -you -please tell me

8 only in the winter -lives -in this part of the country -that bird
9 to their daughter -for her birthday -a bracelet -they sent
10 television -watches -seldom -during the afternoon -my wife
11 for some artists -is -Montreal -a very good place
12 those letters -yesterday -to Mr. Fox -delivered -the postman
13 the car -to the country -drove -last weekend -the two men
14 is very interesting -on the table -of the glass bowl -the shape
15 today -cold -is it -enough -for a heavy winter overcoat
16 was -to me -the whole idea -new and unusual -something
17 the large red house -is -Mr. Anderson's -next to ours
18 were finished -more than 50 units -the manager said -in two days
19 the two suitcases -moved -the man -to his wife -closer
20 the examinations -so far -have -taken -how many students
21 to anyone's face -adds -a warm smile -always -charm
22 to understand -was -for me -the last lesson -very difficult
23 two times -they have visited -in the past week -that museum
24 to improve -the student -he'd have to study harder -realized
25 a very easy decision -that's certainly not -to make -for anyone
26 cars -at very high speeds -is extremely dangerous -driving
27 what Mr. Shaw had said -the students -confused -for a while

Copy each sentence and add the italicized word to the sentence in its correct position. Do not add or eliminate any other words.

 1 [*almost*]   My friend Albert got lost on his way over here.
 2 [*all*]   Love, hate, and fear are abstract words.
 3 [*possibly*]   How can you consider such a peculiar suggestion ?
 4 [*rarely*]   We attend the school programs on Tuesday night.
 5 [*still*]   There is a strike on at that factory.
 6 [*only*]   I am trying to help you with your English lesson.
 7 [*always*]   Does their teacher ask them difficult questions ?
 8 [*later*]   We expect to visit Switzerland in the summer.
 9 [*really*]   Do the students in the class believe what he said ?
10 [*even*]   I think he wrote about that subject before Flaubert.
11 [*never*]   Those students used to complain about their work.
12 [*not*]   I had to ask them to smoke in the other room.
13 [*seldom*]   Ordinary people have that kind of opportunity.
14 [*yet*]   Have you heard anything from Mr. and Mrs. Fox ?
15 [*hardly*]   It was so dark that we could see the lake.
16 [*always*]   Plan your composition carefully before you begin.
17 [*better*]   We will be able to understand our own customs.
18 [*still*]   I don't agree with Mr. Harris on that subject.
19 [*both*]   I'm sure they contain exactly the same material.
20 [*just*]   There is one more thing I must tell you about.
21 [*long*]   Thérèse and Marie have not been in Florida.
22 [*always*]   The teacher has to explain everything carefully.
23 [*daily*]   I had to study English grammar, and I hated it.
24 [*not*]   Many people had sufficient interest in the subject.
25 [*never*]   That possibility has been considered carefully.
26 [*twice*]   They have visited Laurentides Provincial Park.
27 [*often*]   Lucien does his homework at the public library.
28 [*either*]   Doris couldn't find her purse, and I couldn't.
29 [*a little*]   I think you'd better change that last statement.
30 [*always*]   Why is that part so difficult for you ?
31 [*the most*]   The girl's hair was what attracted my attention.
32 [*detailed*]   Green submitted a report to his boss at once.
33 [*not*]   Do you think that Howard did a very good job ?
34 [*more*]   Has the teacher said anything to you about that ?

Add the definite article *the* in the blank spaces if necessary.

There is no part of .....world which I have not visited. I have traveled through .....thickest jungles of .....Africa and .....upper regions of .....Amazon. I have been through .....Taj Mahal, ...Vatican, and .....Leaning Tower of .....Pisa. I have even gone to .....Seven Wonders of .....World. I wonder if you can tell me .....names of .....seven great structures in this group ?

I have been over .....Cuba, ...Philippine Islands, ...England, and .....Soviet Union. I have touched ..... top of ..... Empire State Building, ... peak of ..... Mount Everest, and ..... whole range of ..... Rocky Mountains. I have drifted on ..... Rhine, ... Atlantic Ocean, ... Lake Superior, ... Caribbean, and ..... Gulf of ..... Mexico. I have been through ..... streets of ..... New York, ... Berlin, and ..... Singapore. I have wandered through .... Balkans, ... Near East, and .... Scandinavian Peninsula. How many of these things have you done ?

I have passed through ..... Houses of ..... Parliament in ..... Ottawa, through ..... White House in ..... Washington, and through ..... Kremlin in ... Moscow. I have been to .... Coliseum in .... Rome, ... Acropolis in ..... Athens, ... Louvre in ..... Paris, ... Lenin's Tomb in ..... Russia, and ..... Statue of Liberty in ..... New York Harbor. I have been in ..... Saskatchewan in ..... Western Canada, in ..... Venezuela, ... northermost country of ..... South America, and in ..... Republic of ..... Panama, split by ..... Panama Canal. Do you think that you could locate all these places on your map ?

I have been through ..... Orient, over ..... length of ..... Long Island, and down ..... Park Avenue. I have traveled down ..... St. Lawrence River, over ..... Island of ..... Formosa, and around ..... entire Australian Continent. I have gone through ..... United Nations Building and ..... Imperial Japanese Palace. I have been through all ..... countries in ..... North and South America, in all ..... cities in ..... Europe, and from ..... one end of ..... British Commonwealth to ..... other.

Although I have gone to ..... Columbia University and ..... M.I.T., ... Saint Andrews, ... Oxford, and ..... Sorbonne, ... University of British Columbia, and ..... McGill, I didn't learn geography or any other subject at these schools. Now can you guess who I am ?

Choose *the, a,* or *an* for each blank in the following story.

I live .....small house in .....country. There is .....small city ....few miles away. Going to .....city is no problem unless you are in .....hurry. There is .....bus which stops at .....little gas station opposite our house, but .....driver of .....bus never carries .....watch or pays any attention to .....printed schedule which he distributes regularly. Therefore, when I have .....appointment or .....important engagement, I never depend on .....Weston Transportation Company (.....name of .....bus line). .....week ago, I wanted to go into .....city to buy .....suit. However, I was expecting .....guest to come to spend .....evening with us, so I wanted to get back to .....house early. In order not to lose any time, I drove to .....city. I parked in front of .....one-hour parking meter. When I returned with .....suit, ...policeman was standing there. .....meter indicated .....violation. I had been away more than .....hour. .....policeman was putting .....parking ticket on .....car. I tried to persuade him to tear up .....ticket. I soon realized this was .....waste of time. When I went to .... Court House .... day later, I found out ....fine for ....violation was **five** dollars.

Choose *the, a,* or *an* for each blank space in the following story.

In .....middle of .....summer last year, my wife and I were out for .....Sunday drive. Since it was .....beautiful day, we drove almost to .... border, ... distance of 60 or 70 miles. On ....way back, we stopped in ....small village. We had ....sandwich and ....cup of coffee in ....only restaurant in ....village. As we were leaving, we noticed ....roadside stand managed by ....old Indian. There was ....tiny painted sign above ....stand. Of course, we went over to see ....merchandise he was selling. .... proprietor's name was Barking Fox. ....old Indian was reading ....book. ....name of ....book was *Modern Advertising.* He said that it was ....important book. ....book had taught him ....importance of advertising. He then told us that he was going to modernize ....stand. He had ordered ....new neon sign to replace ....tiny painted one. After we had left, I told my wife that ....little knowledge could be ....dangerous thing.

Add *the, a,* or *an* in the blank spaces if necessary.

.....man has to be .....combination of .....carpenter, ...plumber, ...electrician, and .....architect these days. When .....leak develops in .....pipe or .....faucet, ...head of .....family is expected to repair .....leak. If there is .....need for .....new addition to .....house, his wife, ...children, and .....neighbors all expect him to do .....work himself. If .....electrical wiring needs .....attention, ...jack of all trades (Father) is called by .....other members of .....family. One of .....main reasons for this is .....high cost of .....services of .....carpenters, ...plumbers, etc. On .....other hand, ...men take .....pride in having .....ability or ....."know-how" to do these things.

Add *the, a,* or *an,* in the blank spaces if necessary.

.....person can have .....interesting life after .....age of 65. Of course, this depends on .....person and .....attitude which he has toward .....life. Here is .....example. .....man who had been in .....large company before retiring started .....community center devoted to .....interests of .....people over 65. He later started .....company for .....members of .....community center. .....company was successful. It is now one of .....largest distributors of .....automobile parts in .....country. At .....age of 70, ...same man learned .....foreign language, built .....house, and wrote .....book titled .....*Benefits of* .....*Old Age.*

Add *the, a,* or *and* in the blank spaces if necessary.

When .....hunters visit .....southwestern part of .....United States, they often find .....large cat-like tracks along .....ground. These tracks are made by .....spotted jaguar, ...greatest hunter of all .....North American animals and .....largest member of .....cat family on .....American Continent. .....most animals have .....favorite food. .....favorite food of .....jaguar is .....wild pig. .....wild pigs move in .....bands of fifteen to twenty. They have .....great courage and .....strength in .....group. I once read .....story about .....courage and .....strength of these wild pigs. .....story pointed out that these pigs sometimes even attack .....human hunters. As .....result, ...jaguar tries to find .....wild pig which has been separated from .....pack and then attacks .....wild pig.

The articles *the, a,* and *an* have been omitted from the three following passages. Supply the correct article wherever necessary.

SUGAR

Sugar is one of most important plant products. Word *sugar* applies to more than 100 distinctive substances, each with scientific name. Sugar most commonly obtained from plants is sucrose. When it has been refined, sugar is colorless and odorless. However, sugar obtained from sap of maple tree tastes different from sugar derived from juice of sugar beet. Impurities account for difference in taste of two forms of sugar. Sugar is produced in Europe, Asia, Africa, Australia, and Americas.

WATER

Water is necessity for sustaining life in plants and animals. Men have always been interested in nature of water. At one time, water was considered to be element. Most water is derived from ocean directly or indirectly. Water which city dwellers use comes from large reservoirs. Water in these reservoirs is purified. However, absolutely pure water is probably unknown. Lake water is relatively pure, especially in mountainous regions. Most people think spring water is pure. However, water which comes from springs sometimes contains large amounts of salt. Therefore, water in your springs should be analyzed.

DUST

Dust is great inconvenience to housewives. It is difficult problem. Dust causes housewife hours and hours of housework week. To make things worse, dust always seems to settle in most inconceivable places. Dust which comes from chimneys seems to spread everywhere. Coal dust is one of worst types of dust to wipe up. In neighborhood where we live, dust from factory in next block causes us trouble. Edges of our windows are covered with dust in less than day. Dust on surfaces of tables in our apartment is not quite so difficult to remove. I know characteristics of dust very well because my wife frequently asks me to wipe up dust on desks and bookcases in our apartment.

The articles *the, a,* and *an* have been omitted from the following passage. Supply the necessary articles.

Flag is more than just brightly-colored piece of cloth. It is symbol, or sign, that stands for idea, cause, or purpose. Each country in world has flag of its own. Such flag has special meaning for people who live in that country. Country's flag can stir people to joy and sadness, to courage and sacrifice. It is important duty of every citizen to honor his country's flag. Flag floating in breeze is beautiful and stirring sight. For hundreds of years, flags have been used as symbol to follow and defend. Colors and designs tell ideals, goals, and history for which different flags stand. Some historians say that Egyptians flew first emblems that looked like flags. However, first flags which hung from vertical staff were probably used by Saracens in eighth century.

The articles *the, a,* and *an* have been omitted from the following quotations. Supply the necessary articles.

1 Advice is sought to confirm position already taken. — *Sir William Osler* 2 Goodness is only investment that never fails. — *Henry David Thoreau* 3 Election is like horse-race ; you can tell more about it next day. — *Sir J.A. Macdonald* 4 Sharp tongue is only edged tool that grows keener with constant use. — *Washington Irving* 5 Hope is pleasant acquaintance, but unsafe friend. — *Thomas C. Haliburton* 6 Great difficulty in education is to get experience out of ideas. — *George Santayana* 7 As pen is mightier than sword, so are brains mightier than muscles. — *Robert L. Borden* 8 Life is great bundle of little things. *Oliver Wendell Holmes* 9 I am great believer in luck, and I find harder I work, more I have of it. — *Stephen B. Leacock* 10 Not one student in thousand breaks down from overwork. — *William Neilson* 11 Doubt is beginning, not end of wisdom. — *George Iles.*

Use the word *some* in the blank spaces wherever possible. If the addition of *some* changes the meaning of the sentence, explain the difference in meaning carefully.

1 This book describes the lives of .... famous historical figures.
2 .... famous historical figures are less interesting than others.
3 .... students actually enjoy cheating on examinations.
4 .... students usually have to take examinations in their courses.
5 I had .... coffee around ten o'clock this morning.
6 Canada imports .... furniture from Denmark.
7 Afterwards, the teacher made .... comments about our mistakes.
8 .... apartments in that new building rent for $500 a month.
9 He has written .... articles for .... magazines for thirty years.
10 That store in Place Ville-Marie sells .... inexpensive clothes.
11 All of the children in that family have .... unusual names.
12 Our English instructor wrote .... examples on the blackboard.

In each section, choose one of the indicated forms of *other* for each sentence.

ANOTHER, THE OTHER, ANY OTHER, SOME OTHER

1 That building is taller than .... in Montreal.
2 Yes, those two examples are correct. Can you give me .... one ?
3 I received .... letter from my friend in Magog .... day.
4 Are there .... questions before we start the next lesson ?
5 Your composition is much too short. Write .... page or two.
6 I really can't go now. I'll have to go with you .... day.
7 Then we'll have to go on Monday. I don't have the time .... day.

ANOTHER, THE OTHER, THE OTHERS, OTHER

8 I had two copies of it originally, but I can't find .... one now.
9 Children should be taught how to get along with .... people.
10 Can you think of .... example of the same thing ?
11 Here are four boxes, but I can carry only two. Please bring ....
12 A student has much less liberty there than in .... countries.
13 He corrected a few papers, but he had no time to do ....
14 There are two reasons for this. You know the first. I'll tell you ....

Select the correct preposition for the blank or blanks in each sentence. If there are two possibilities, give both and explain the difference. Use only the following prepositions :

IN, ON, AT, BY, FOR, TO, FROM, UNTIL, SINCE, DURING

1 He said that the boat would be leaving the dock .... 25 minutes.
2 My friend, André Savard, married his sweetheart .... July first.
3 Mr. and Mrs. Laporte have been in Rimouski .... last August.
4 Those men have been working on the engine .... three hours now.
5 The contractor hopes to finish the entire job .... April or May.
6 The messenger won't get back here .... later this afternoon.
7 That student has been here .... the beginning of the semester.
8 We think the thief broke into the house sometime .... the night.
9 She said that she was going to return to Edmonton .... the tenth of December.
10 All of the guests had finished eating dinner .... ten o'clock.
11 The Andersons lived in Manitoba .... two or three years.
12 Pierre made his first trip to the United States .... October, 1971.
13 The train will leave Central Station .... twelve minutes.
14 Wait right here for me. I'll only be away .... fifteen minutes.
15 Our friend Bob is arriving here a week .... next Saturday.
16 Mr. Johnson said that the meeting would begin .... 8:30 sharp.
17 .... yesterday, I thought that the man had really told us the truth.
18 I told my boss that I would be there .... an hour or more.
19 Do you know if Helen's parents plan to stay there .... October 15 ?
20 We haven't seen our friends, the Moores, ... March.
21 Mr. Foster worked there .... quite late .... the evening.
22 .... the time Uncle Robert gets your letter, it will be too late.
23 Dr. Westman's office hours are .... 10 a.m. .... 3 p.m.
24 The two children stayed awake .... eleven o'clock last night.
25 The director has never said a word about the matter .... that time.
26 You returned .... July, 1970. I was in Nova Scotia .... that time.
27 The clerk said that he would try to have everything ready .... then.
28 .... a long time, everyone wondered if that method could be used.
29 Most Canadian literature has been written .... the turn of this century.
30 Mr. Paquette has worked for this company .... the war.
31 Dean and Mrs. Brown will be in Northern Ontario .... June .... September.

Select the correct preposition for the blank or blanks in each sentence. If there are two possibilities, give both and explain the difference. Use only the following prepositions :

IN, ON, AT, BY, FOR, TO, FROM, UNTIL, SINCE, DURING

1 The doctor was busy with another patient .... the time.
2 My wife and I go to the cottage .... time .... time.
3 .... no time .... all, he had learned to speak English fluently.
4 Just .... that moment, we heard a loud crash outside the house.
5 Once .... a while, I enjoy eating at a restaurant.
6 Philippe's command of English is improving day .... day.
7 I don't think Mr. Pépin plans to stay in New Brunswick .... very long.
8 The captain ordered Sergeant Hardy to leave .... once.
9 Howard drank three or four cups of coffee .... succession.
10 We got there just .... time to see the end of the program.
11 We had taken a taxi in order to get to the meeting .... time.
12 The director has decided to do something about that .... last.
13 .... the beginning, everything seemed to be difficult for us.
14 I drove downtown. .... the meantime, Dorothy prepared dinner.
15 .... occasion, we enjoy seeing a good play.
16 Both of the men were trying to speak .... the same time.
17 .... the end, we decided that Harry was right about that matter.
18 Would you please try to be much more careful .... now on.
19 .... present, André is working on a book about rural Quebec.
20 I'm usually completely exhausted .... the end of the day.
21 .... times, I felt as though I would never be able to finish it.
22 Please submit your reports to me .... Thursday .... the latest.
23 .... first, I could hardly believe what the man had said to me.
24 I think your suggestion is probably the best one .... the long run.
25 .... the first time .... his life, he didn't argue about anything !
26 Do those men usually get paid .... the week or .... the month ?
27 I hope that these conditions will be changed .... the future.
28 .... once, not one of the students in the class made a mistake.
29 We really don't know what to expect .... one day .... the next.
30 .... the past, people did a great deal of work by hand.
31 The girls usually go for coffee .... the middle of the afternoon.

Select the correct preposition for the blank or blanks in each sentence. If there are several possibilities, explain the differences in meaning carefully.

1　The tallest building .... the world is located .... New York City.
2　The theater is .... Graham Street ..... a restaurant and a men's store.
3　Their business office is .... the fiftieth floor .... that building.
4　Our office is .... 165 Main Street. It's .... the post office.
5　I drove .... the block slowly while Suzanne ran .... the store.
6　Our friends drove .... us .... their car, but they didn't see us.
7　They'll meet us......... the corner .... St. Catherine's Street and Guy Street.
8　I always go .... work .... bus. Do you ride .... the bus too ?
9　Did Marc park his car .... front .... the house or .... the driveway ?
10　Your friend can park his car .... the alley .... our house.
11　Gordon is going .... school .... the University .... Alberta now.
12　The Booths live .... West Chestnut Street .... the university.
13　Mr. Vachon was walking .... Sherbrooke Street when I saw him.
14　Please be careful ! Walk .... the sidewalk, not .... the street.
15　They leave .... England .... the Q.E. tomorrow.
16　They'll stop .... London .... their way .... France and Italy.
17　They will arrive .... London .... Tuesday or Wednesday.
18　Are you going to go .... Quebec .... way .... the north shore ?
19　If you don't drive faster, we'll arrive .... the train station late.
20　Mr. Vocat was born .... Switzerland, but he moved .... Canada.
21　Jean and Henri drove .... Chicoutimi......... Montreal .... seven hours.
22　Mr. Perreault parked his car .... least fifteen feet .... the hydrant.
23　René's sister said he wasn't .... home. He must be .... school.
24　I believe Mr. Ratelle's ....town. He wasn't .... town last week.
25　That's right. He went .... Halifax .... a business trip last Monday.
26　Turn .... the left. Mr. Shaw's house is the third one .... the right.
27　There are people who don't care for driving .... steep hills.
28　How far is Winnipeg .... Regina .... kilometers ?
29　Mr. and Mrs. Anderson live just a few blocks .... Kevin's house.
30　If you can't get .... the house .... the door, climb .... a window.
31　There are quite a few trees .... some sections .... this city.
32　Father heard the noise and rushed .... the stairs .... the basement.
33　That student .... Joliette lives .... an apartment right .... mine.

Select the correct preposition for the blank or blanks in each sentence. If there are several possibilities, explain the differences in meaning carefully.

1   Did you put those packages .... the drawer or .... the shelf?

2   You will find much information .... the appendix .... this book.

3   Did Dorothy hear it .... the radio or see it .... television?

4   The lesson .... this page is the easiest one .... the whole book.

5   The carpenter went .... and .... the ladder three or four times.

6   What time do you usually get .... bed .... the morning?

7   Antoine's roommate hung the photograph .... the wall .... his desk.

8   A monkey escaped .... the zoo .... jumping .... a very high fence.

9   When you are away .... home, things always seem more difficult.

10 The ball fell .... the child's hand and rolled .... a chair.

11 I think that Dave's brother was .... the army .... three years.

12 He pointed .... the rope which hung .... a hook far.... our heads.

13 Catherine took her new dress .... the box very carefully.

14 He carried the box .... the stairs .... the attic .... his shoulder.

15 Yvan sits .... one side .... Marie and Serge sits .... the other.

16 Marie sits .... Yvan and Serge .... the first row .... seats.

17 The part .... the floor .... the rug needs to be washed and waxed.

18 Mr. Brown has to come .... this hallway .... the way .... his office.

19 Please move the chairs .... the aisle. They're .... my way!

20 I enjoy swimming .... the ocean, but I prefer swimming .... lakes.

21 There's some shade .... that tree. Let's sit .... it.

22 The plane flew .... the heavy clouds in order to miss the storm.

23 The man dug many small holes .... the ground .... the sidewalk.

24 You shouldn't sleep .... the ground .... night. It's much too damp.

25 He added the words ..... the bottom ..... the page.

26 The boys had to wait ..... line to get the tickets.

27 ... the dark, I couldn't read the words ... the sign.

28 Don't slip ..... the shingles and fall ..... the roof.

29 There's dust .... the edges .... those two windows.

30 Fred put the ladder ..... the side ..... the building.

31 All his friends came .....the graduation ceremony.

32 The student's relatives were .....the audience too.

33 The student looked handsome...his cap and grown.

Select the correct prepositions for the idiomatic expressions in each of the following sentences.

1 Robert resembles his grandfather .... many respects.
2 I think the conference was very successful .... the whole.
3 He works very hard, or .... any rate, he gives that impression.
4 Carol didn't seem to be excited .... the least about the news.
5 The dean said I had to take .... least twelve credits a semester.
6 .... second thought, perhaps you are right about that matter.
7 You don't like it, do you ? — .... the contrary, I love it.
8 .... best, this is only a temporary substitute for the other one.
9 Were you able to make use .... the book I lent you last week ?
10 This tool is delicate. — .... that case, we'll use it carefully.
11 .... case anyone calls for me, tell him I'll be back a little later.
12 .... the event .... trouble, call me at my office immediately.
13 I'm going to settle that matter with him once and .... all.
14 Should I start now ? Yes, ... all means. The sooner the better !
15 .... the moment, Mr. Foster is .... danger .... losing his job.
16 .... the one hand, I want to tell my boss exactly what I think.
17 .... the other hand, I don't want to lose my good position here.
18 I think that movie director has exaggerated the problem .... some extent.
19 It isn't a very good plan. .... one thing, it is too complicated.
20 .... a way, it's too bad he didn't take advantage .... the opportunity.
21 Just .... hand, I can't think of any other way to handle the matter.
22 What's the use .... telling him the truth ? He wouldn't believe it.
23 Well, ... this particular case, I believe that you are mistaken.
24 Frankly, I think that Jean-Paul's suggestion is .... the question
25 I'm sorry, but I don't have anything .... mind to suggest either.
26 .... the way, what did you think about the movie you saw yesterday ?
27 I wish he would come .... the point. He never says what he thinks.
28 Why don't we take a chance .... finding our friends at the library ?
29 Professor Moore takes a great interest .... community activities.
30 Paul said Mr. Fox was .... far the best salesman in the company.
31 My friend wants to get rid .... his car before he moves abroad.
32 All .... a sudden, the man in the car ahead.... us put on his brakes.
33 Réjean tried to translate the whole article word .... word.

Select the correct prepositions for the idiomatic expressions in the following sentences.

1 All .... all, we had a wonderful time during our vacation.
2 The elevator isn't running now. It must be .... order.
3 .... course, Ed has heard the news. .... fact, he told me about it.
4 .... long, I'm sure you will be speaking English like a native.
5 I'm always .... my worst whenever I take examinations.
6 Mr. Harrison was .... quite a hurry and couldn't wait for us.
7 Would you like to go .... a walk .... the park this afternoon ?
8 That house on the corner is .... sale. Are you interested .... it ?
9 The clerk .... that counter said those purses were .... sale.
10 First .... all, I think you should explain your idea to the director.
11 .... the time being, I think you'd better not say anything to him.
12 Aren't you glad that you went to the party with us .... all ?
13 It's always better to study vocabulary .... connection ....
    your reading.
14 Mr. Johnson said he was .... favor .... doing the work right away.
15 We had to postpone the picnic .... account .... the bad weather.
16 .... the circumstances, it was impossible to do anything about it.
17 Try to answer all .... the questions .... that page .... detail.
18 They are going to go .... Toronto .... way .... Peterborough.
19 Miss Williams makes most .... her own clothes .... hand.
20 The girls had to use newspapers .... place .... wrapping paper.
21 Frank has to work .... night .... order to earn some extra money.
22 Did Mr. Kennedy park his car .... front .... our house ?
23 We are really looking forward .... our trip .... Banff and Jasper.
24 .... mistake, I took the wrong book .... my desk this morning.
25 Professor Moore called my attention .... that particular mistake.
26 .... the most part, his explanations are quite easy to understand.
27 .... general, that is true. However, there are many exceptions.
28 The teacher said we had to learn all these expressions .... heart.
29 That is last year's telephone directory. It's .... date now.
30 What's the matter .... Howard ? He seems to be very angry.
31 I haven't been able to get .... touch .... Mr. Miller all day long.
32 Do you really think Ann threw those papers away .... purpose ?
33 Certainly not ! I'm sure that she threw them away .... accident.

Select the correct prepositions for the blank spaces in the following sentences. For additional practice, review Exercises 115 and 173.

1 You should try to cooperate .... that organization .... every way.

2 We complained .... the landlord .... the condition of the apartmen

3 Why did you quarrel .... your friends .... such a small matter ?

4 Professor Moore's friend highly recommended that book .... him.

5 Mr. Dupuis, our boss, recommended Georges .... a promotion.

6 They forced us ..... a ridiculous position ..... arguing ..... the matter.

7 My wife and I are going shopping .... a new living room carpet.

8 Mr. Johnson said he definitely disagreed ...... us ...... that matter.

9 Students often compete .... each other .... various school honors.

10 Were they unable to collect any money .... the insurance company ?

11 I think the treasurer strongly disapproves .... our new system.

12 You should submit your application .... this office before May first.

13 Mr. Green said that he had obtained the information .... a friend.

14 Don't you think you should remove the weeds ...... your garden soon ?

15 I definitely prefer traveling by air .... traveling by train or bus.

16 There's no way we can prevent people .... talking .... this matter.

17 I think it will be difficult to hide the truth .... them .... very long.

18 Those two companies import chemicals .... Sweden and Germany.

19 That corporation exports machinery .... Latin American countries.

20 Did the officials of the company express interest .... your plan ?

21 Did you finally succeed .... convincing them they were wrong ?

22 We suggested that possibility .... the members of the committee.

23 We weren't able to convince them .... the real value of the plan.

24 Don't you think you'd better consult your lawyer .... that problem ?

25 They are going to transfer him .... this department .... another on

26 I don't see how you can fit all those clothes. .... that little suitcase.

27 You'd better demand an answer .... that fellow as soon as possible

28 Guy said he planned to devote a great deal of time .... the project.

29 It was difficult for me to keep .... smiling .... his funny remark.

30 The teacher suspected the student .... cheating on the examination.

31 I think it's easy to confuse these two expressions .... the other one.

32 You really shouldn't boast .... your success .... other people.

33 I don't know why John insists .... blaming me .... all his troubles.

Select the correct prepositions for the blank spaces in the following sentences.

at
about
from
on
with
in
to
for
of

1 That man reminds me .... my grandfather.
2 I really respect that man .... his honesty.
3 Fred worries .... his brother a great deal.
4 Sometimes I wonder .... that very much.
5 We'll advise them .... our change in plans.
6 I'm going to apply .... a scholarship there.
7 She will profit .... her work in this class.
8 I'd better warn my friend .... that soon.
9 You can inquire .... that in the front office.
10 Can you account .... all the money you've spent since you arrived ?
11 I think that we'll have to eliminate some names .... those lists.
12 Since it's important, would you attend .... that matter right away ?
13 I really don't see why you object .... our suggestion so strongly.
14 Why don't you plan .... meeting us here shortly after five o'clock ?
15 Unfortunately, I couldn't think .... anything to suggest at that time.
16 You should think .... this matter carefully before making a decision.
17 I think you ought to apologize .... Thérèse .... your rude remarks.
18 George is a dependable person. You can rely .... him to help you.
19 When you read the newspapers, you should watch .... that article.
20 Father says it's hard sometimes to distinguish one make of car
     .... another.
21 I don't think that they'll approve .... getting the money in that way.
22 Luc has changed .... a poor student .... a good one overnight.
23 Some people seem to enjoy gossiping .... other people's affairs.
24 You should be able to interest those people .... your new invention.
25 Please don't lean .... that wall. There's fresh paint .... it.
26 Frankly, I don't care to argue .... you .... that particular subject.
27 A thick layer of paint will protect the wood .... the rain and snow.
28 Be sure to thank your host and hostess .... having you to their house.
29 Could you supply us .... several more copies of the announcement ?
30 Don't think .... your finances so much !
31 His friends have constantly encouraged him .... his difficult work.
32 Jacques told me he hadn't decided .... a name for his book yet.
33 After you've done this page, refer .... the answers in the appendix.

Select the correct prepositions for the blank spaces in the following sentences.

1 Were your friends successful .... getting a loan from the bank ?
2 I'm sure the explanation in the book will be quite clear .... you.
3 That type of engine is definitely superior .... any other type.
4 Mrs. Parker was very upset .... the news of her father's death.
5 I'm not familiar .... his name, but his face seems familiar .... me.
6 I certainly hope that David is aware .... all the problems involved.
7 We were very grateful .... our friends .... all of their assistance.
8 My friend Howard is very enthusiastic .... his new equipment.
9 Don't you think you should try to be friendly .... your classmates ?
10 You should try to be considerate .... other people's feelings.
11 I'm conscious .... their feelings, but I'm afraid .... offending them
12 Mr. Anderson is responsible .... hiring and firing employees.
13 That type of music is quite popular .... teen-age boys and girls.
14 At present, my daily expenses are just about equal .... my income.
15 Jérôme is capable .... doing better work than he's doing at present.
16 We were very doubtful .... his ability to finish the job by himself.
17 Are you positive .... that ? I find it extremely difficult to believe !
18 Yes, I'm certain .... it. Why do you seem to be so skeptical .... it ?
19 There's really no need for you to be afraid .... the examination.
20 The students are very anxious .... the results of the examination.
21 Alain was proud .... his good marks on the English examination.
22 My plan is similar .... yours, but it's quite different .... Frank's.
23 If this plan is satisfactory .... you, I'll present it to the committee.
24 Can you tell me how many men were absent .... work last week ?
25 Pierre says he has become quite fond .... jazz lately.
26 We're still hopeful .... hearing from our friends before Saturday.
27 After next weekend, I'll be completely free .... all my worries !
28 That fashion magazine is full .... advertising for women's clothes.
29 George is still very loyal .... his friends despite their argument.
30 That man's personality makes him unfit .... any higher position.
31 Thin gloves like these aren't very suitable .... that kind of work.
32 He's generous .... his money. He's generous .... giving to charities
33 A good basic knowledge of English is essential .... advanced work.

Select the correct prepositions for the blank spaces in the following sentences.

1 My friends and I were very happy .... the results of the election.
2 It seemed quite evident .... his behavior that he wasn't satisfied.
3 I could tell .... his face that he was very angry .... something.
4 It was certainly kind .... you to help me with that difficult work.
5 Well, you were very kind .... me when I asked you for some help.
6 I wish François would take a vacation. It would be good .... his health.
7 Mr. Archibald's a good person to work .... He's good ....
  his employees.
8 It was good .... you to come this evening to help us with our work.
9 Unfortunately, I am not good .... remembering people's names.
10 Professor Moore is always very patient .... his English students.
11 Bill should submit an application. He's eligible .... membership.
12 It's quite apparent .... me that he's eager .... a chance to do it.
13 The little boy was afraid .... the dog.
14 The salesman said that the overcoat was identical .... the other one.
15 Sharon likes that kind of soap. She says it's easy .... her hands.
16 Do you think a pantsuit is appropriate .... that kind of occasion ?
17 I can't understand why you're jealous .... your friend's success.
18 It was thoughtful .... Irène to send you a gift on your birthday.
19 Jean-Pierre said that the weather was perfect .... taking color
  photographs.
20 You should try to be more tolerant .... other people's opinions.
21 The foreman, Mr. Desjardins, is always very critical .... their work.
22 Mrs. Dubois is dependent .... her son Richard .... support.
23 At the moment, four Swiss francs are roughly equivalent .... one dollar.
24 Dogs are usually very faithful .... their masters if treated properly.
25 You'll find that this tool is very useful .... many different things.
26 That new product will be available .... the public late next year.
27 The new model is definitely inferior .... the old one in my opinion.
28 Some teachers are more liberal .... their students than others.
29 Since it was the man's first offense, the judge was lenient .... him.
30 Don't you think a small car would be adequate .... our purposes ?
31 Frankly, I think Roger is incapable .... handling such a hard job.
32 Paint is fine .... certain kinds of surfaces, but not .... this kind.
33 The police were suspicious .... the man's very peculiar behavior.

Select the correct prepositions for the blank spaces in the following sentences.

1 Albert said he was very ashamed .... his friend's bad manners.

2 Tom is very devoted .... his work. He's well qualified .... it too.

3 We feel very obligated .... our friends .... their kind assistance.

4 Although his name is the same as mine, I'm not related .... him.

5 Jeanne married a wealthy man. She got married .... him last June.

6 She was engaged .... him for ten months before they got married.

7 Now she is engaged .... decorating their new home in St. Sauveur.

8 I certainly hope Arthur is prepared .... a great deal of criticism.

9 Arthur is quite accustomed .... receiving criticism by this time.

10 The comments Arthur's friends made were not pleasing .... him.

11 That textbook is intended .... intermediate students.

12 I don't think that I'm acquainted .... that particular textbook.

13 John was so tired .... all the hard work that he could hardly move.

14 The clerk said he was tired .... hearing complaints day after day.

15 Our conference was interrupted .... telephone calls several times.

16 I was confused .... what to say .... answer .... his unusual question.

17 Barbara has been very concerned .... her mother's poor health.

18 All the executives were strongly opposed .... any radical changes.

19 When I read that article, I was reminded .... a story by Faulkner.

20 Mr. Moore is often taken .... a student because he looks so young.

21 My English teacher said he was quite satisfied .... my classwork.

22 Paul is interested .... getting some information about that college.

23 Of course, almost everyone was happy and excited .... the news.

24 Mr. Burke is employed .... a large corporation .... a consultant.

25 I don't think Mr. Anderson is convinced .... that man's honesty.

26 A large amount of money was stolen .... the bank during the night.

27 The police said a well-known criminal was involved ..... the robbery.

28 I think she was pleased .... the gift I gave her for her birthday.

29 Dr. W.K. Davis is regarded .... the leading specialist in that field.

30 That hotel is well known .... its pleasant atmosphere and fine food.

31 Mr. Miller's expense account was increased .... $2000 .... $3500.

32 Don't you think Mary's new spring coat is very becoming .... her ?

33 I am very indebted .... you .... all of your kindness and attention.

Choose *by* or *with* for each blank in the following sentences.

1 Mr. Blanc said that all those photographs had been taken .... Georges.

2 Georges took all those professional-looking photographs .... an expensive camera.

3 Alain told me that the engine had been repaired .... a very good mechanic.

4 The mechanic was able to repair the old engine ....a special tool.

5 Alain saved a lot of money .... using second-hand parts in the engine.

6 He said the engine would work just as well .... second-hand parts.

7 We were frightened ..... the loud explosion.

8 Mr. Brown's shoes were covered ..... mud.

9 He got them dirty ..... going out in the rain.

10 We flattered Jim ..... a great deal of praise.

11 We flattered him ..... telling him nice things.

12 He was very flattered .... our praise.

13 Harold annoyed us ..... his constant advice.

14 He annoyed us ..... giving us very bad advice.

15 We were annoyed ..... his monotonous voice.

16 She went to the library .... her friend, but she returned .... herself.

17 .... a little help, I'm sure that student will improve very rapidly.

18 .... practicing constantly, he will quickly become very proficient.

19 Right now, he can speak English only .... a great deal of difficulty.

20 However, he often makes himself understood .... using his hands.

21 The holes in that wall were repaired .... the carpenter yesterday.

22 The carpenter covered the holes in the wall .... pieces of wood.

23 The carpenter repaired the wall .... putting wood over the holes.

24 The auditorium was decorated .... the boys from our English class.

25 They decorated the whole auditorium .... beautiful silver ribbons.

26 The auditorium was also decorated .... pretty Japanese lanterns.

27 François thought we had offended André ....our remarks about his book.

28 Do you think André was offended .... our criticism of his book ?

29 Yes, I definitely think that we have offended him .... criticizing his book.

30 Jérôme disappointed me .... refusing to help me .... my assignment.

31 Although I was disappointed .... his refusal, I didn't argue .... him.

32 You can't injure Mr. Lamarre's reputation .... lies about his private life.

33 What do you expect to gain.... saying all those unkind things about him ?

Put the italicized indirect object after the direct object and add the preposition *to* or *for*. Review Exercises 68 and 69 before doing this exercise.

1 Ian gave *me* the box.   *Ian gave the box to me.*
2 We bought *Michelle* a gift.   *We bought a gift for Michelle.*
3 My brother is going to leave *me* some money tonight.
4 My friend John lent *me* seventeen dollars on Friday night.
5 Mrs. Farrell is getting *her young daughter* a glass of water.
6 Mr. and Mrs. Harvey gave *us* the theater tickets yesterday.
7 The director offered *the man* the best job in the department.
8 I think this new method saves *us* a lot of time and trouble.
9 That student showed *Mr. Moore* his homework before class.
10 Catherine's grandmother made *her* a beautiful evening gown.
11 Mr. Harris teaches *Yvonne and Anne-Marie* history.
12 Claude handed *me* the newspaper and pointed to the headline.
13 Mrs. Marchand bought *herself* a new spring coat and hat yesterday.
14 Robert Lafleur sold *Lucien* his old Ford three weeks ago.
15 The people gave *us* a grand demonstration when we arrived.
16 The students sang *us* some French-Canadian songs.
17 Margaret's uncle built *Paul and her* a beautiful new home.
18 Would you please bring *me* the books just as soon as possible.
19 Richard's cousin, James, found *him* a place to stay overnight.
20 I certainly regret causing *Tom and you* all of this trouble.

Choose *after* or *afterward(s)* for the blank space in each of the following sentences. Add commas to these sentences wherever necessary.

1 First of all we had dinner together. .... we went to a movie.
2 We went shopping first of all. .... that we met our friend.
3 I can go downtown with you now and finish my work ....
4 First I went to Fredericton and Moncton. .... that I drove to Halifax.
5 .... the last election we didn't hear any more about that.
6 .... I realized that they hadn't told us the truth at all.
7 .... we had argued for a while Bill finally gave in to me.
8 .... that we seldom had any trouble with our neighbors.
9 .... that fellow asked me if I really meant what I had said.
10 .... we had settled that everything else seemed to be clear.

Choose *as, such as,* or *like* for the blank space in each sentence. Indicate those sentences in which both *like* and *such* can be used. Study the four examples carefully.

1   Mr. Gagnon accompanied the president *as* a special representative.
2   This example is (just) *like* the other one which you showed us.
3   My uncle always wore dark colors *like* black, brown, and gray.
4   My uncle always wore dark colors *such as* black, brown, and gray.
5   It's difficult for a shy person .... him to meet people.
6   Close relatives .... uncles, cousins, etc. often visit us on Sundays.
7   .... all of you know, this is an extremely serious problem.
8   Childhood is .... a very beautiful day which precedes a storm.
9   Father's behavior always served .... a good example for us.
10 There is really no city in the whole world .... Montreal.
11 .... all big cities, though, Montreal has its own special problems.
12 After a while, it seemed to be the same .... it had been before.
13 I always think that people .... that are a menace to society.
14 Every day I spent on that ship seemed .... a century to me.
15 I wish you would accept this .... a token of our gratitude.
16 I enjoy all the school sports .... hockey, baseball, and so forth.
17 A good teacher never treats his students .... children.
18 .... a former officer, you are entitled to certain privileges.
19 That scientist, ... many others, left his country .... a boy.
20 Stamps .... these are really quite rare.

Choose *after* or *later* for the blank space in each of the following sentences. Add commas to these sentences wherever necessary.

1   We had a chance to speak to the men .... in the evening.
2   We spoke to those men in their office .... the meeting.
3   I will have to speak to you .... because I am busy right now.
4   I'm going to a meeting now but I can speak to you .... that.
5   A little while .... he asked me what I intended to say.
6   .... a little while he returned with a notebook in his hands.
7   .... we had discussed the matter he agreed with us completely.
8   .... the conference we mentioned that matter to him again.
9   .... he said that he would try to meet us .... the lecture.
10 .... I had said that to him I realized that I had made a mistake.

Use the correct form of each italicized verb in parentheses in the following passage.

While I (*walk*) across the campus the other day, I (*meet*) my old friend, Jean, whom I (*see, not*) for some time. Naturally, we (*stop*) (*talk*) to each other for a few minutes. I asked him how he (*do*) in his classes. He told me that he (*take*) a course in English. He said that he (*complete*) the elementary course two semesters before, and that, by next semester, he (*be*) ready (*take*) the most advanced English course (*offer*) by our college.

"Until now," he said, "I (*take, always*) the necessary credits which (*make*) up a minimum fulltime program. However, I (*enroll*) for more credits next semester. Then I (*lose, not*) so much time. You see, I (*interest*) in (*get*) my degree as soon as possible." He also said that he (*ask, already*) his advisor for permission (*take*) more credits next semester, and his advisor (*state*) that it (*be*) quite possible because he (*get*) such good marks in all of his previous English classes.

"I am glad (*hear*) that you (*make*) such good progress so far," I (*say*) to Jean. Then I asked him if he (*tell*) me the secret of his success. Before I tell you what he (*reply*), I should explain that Jean (*be, always*) a very diligent student. Of course, this will be quite obvious to you when you (*read*) the next paragraph. This is what he (*say*):

"The secret of my success is simple, Pierre. First of all, I refuse (*neglect*) my studies as some students (*do*). I am always (*prepare*) (*recite*) in class. I never pretend (*know*) those things which I (*study, not*). I never try (*avoid*) (*write*) the assignments. I never object (*study*) the finer points of English grammar. I am always interested in (*learn*) something new about the English language. I resist the temptation of (*go*) to the movies with my friends when I (*have*) a new English lesson (*study*). I always manage (*study*) at least two hours a day. I never put off (*sit down*) at my desk with my textbook. I don't hesitate (*stay up*) until very late (*finish*) my assignments. I don't mind (*give up*) my time for such an important thing as (*learn*) English. This knowledge (*prove*) (*be*) invaluable to me in the future. There! Isn't it simple!"

You probably *(think)* that I *(exaggerate)* what Jean *(say)*. However, I *(assure)* you that it *(be)* the truth. Well, I told Jean I *(be, not)* so sure that his method *(be)* simple. "But you *(deserve)* a lot of credit for *(work)* so hard," I added. "I *(think)* you are very smart *(devote)* all of your time to *(improve)* your English now. When you *(get)* into the *(advance)* section next year, you *(realize)* how important it *(be)* *(have)* a good foundation in English." Of course, I *(encourage)* Jean *(keep up)* the good work too. I gave him the name of the book I *(use)* in my English class several months earlier. I suggested that he *(buy)* it and *(read)* it. Then we *(discuss)* what my teacher *(tell)* me about the course Jean *(take)* the *(follow)* semester.

After that, I mentioned to Jean that I *(have)* a little difficulty with my course in economics at that time. I told him I *(take)* the same course the previous semester but *(fail)* *(pass)* the final examination. I admitted to him that I *(study, not)* very hard. "Now I realize how foolish that *(be)*. I wish that I *(be)* more diligent last semester," I said.

After my explanation, Jean felt sure that I *(pass)* my economics course the previous semester if I *(study)* regularly. Of course, I *(agree)* with him. Then I told him about the conversation I *(have)* with my economics teacher, Mr. Provost, just before the examination last semester. Mr. Provost *(say)*, "Mr. Lemieux, I know that you *(touch, not)* a book since the time you *(enroll)* in this course. Undoubtedly, you *(fail)* this *(come)* examination. You *(force)* *(repeat)* this course next semester. When that time *(come)*, you *(do)* much better work than you *(do)* up to now !"

After *(hear)* that, Jean said to me, "Right. Now. If I *(be)* you, I *(plan)* *(study)* every night. You *(get)* good marks when you *(be)* in high school. In fact, you *(consider)* *(be)* the best student in your class. There's no reason why you *(be able, not)* *(get)* good marks now." I *(agree)* and *(promise)* that I *(work)* harder in the future.

APPENDIX

THE CARDINAL NUMBERS

1	one	11	eleven	21	twenty-one
2	two	12	twelve	22	twenty-two
3	three	13	thirteen	30	thirty
4	four	14	fourteen	40	forty
5	five	15	fifteen	50	fifty
6	six	16	sixteen	60	sixty
7	seven	17	seventeen	70	seventy
8	eight	18	eighteen	80	eighty
9	nine	19	nineteen	90	ninety
10	ten	20	twenty	100	one hundred
					a hundred

200	two hundred	10,000	ten thousand
1000	one thousand	100,000	one hundred thousand
2000	two thousand	1,000,000	one million

THE ORDINAL NUMBERS

1st	first	11th	eleventh	21st	twenty-first
2nd	second	12th	twelfth	22nd	twenty-second
3rd	third	13th	thirteenth	30th	thirtieth
4th	fourth	14th	fourteenth	40th	fortieth
5th	fifth	15th	fifteenth	50th	fiftieth
6th	sixth	16th	sixteenth	60th	sixtieth
7th	seventh	17th	seventeenth	70th	seventieth
8th	eighth	18th	eighteenth	80th	eightieth
9th	ninth	19th	nineteenth	90th	ninetieth
10th	tenth	20th	twentieth	100th	one hundredth
					a hundreth

CANADIAN AND U.S.
MONETARY UNITS

BILLS (PAPER MONEY) :

$ 50.00 or $50	fifty dollars
$ 20.00 or $20	twenty dollars
$ 10.00 or $10	ten dollars
$ 5.00 or $5	five dollars
$ 1.00 or $1	one dollar
	a dollar

COINS (SILVER MONEY) :

$ .50	or	50¢	fifty cents
			a half dollar
$ .25	or	25¢	twenty-five cents
			a quarter
$ .10	or	10¢	ten cents
			a dime
$ .05	or	5¢	five cents
			a nickel
$ .01	or	1¢	one cent
			a penny

$ 1.25	one dollar and twenty-five cents; a dollar and a quarter
$ 2.50	two dollars and fifty cents; two and a half dollars; two fifty
$ 128.50	one hundred (and) twenty-eight dollars and fifty cents; one (hundred and) twenty-eight fifty

MEASUREMENTS :

ENGLISH AND METRIC EQUIVALENTS

LINEAR MEASURE

1 inch (in.)		= 2.54 centimeters
1 foot (ft.)	= 12 inches	= 30.48 centimeters
1 yard (yd.)	= 3 feet	= 0.914 meter
1 mile	= 1760 yards	= 1.609 kilometers
1 centimeter (cm.)	= .01 meter	= 0.3937 inch
1 meter (m.)	= 100 centimeters	= 3.2808 feet
1 kilometer (km.)	= 1000 meters	= 0.6214 mile

SQUARE MEASURE

1 square foot	= 144 square inches	= 929 square cm.
1 square yard	= 9 square feet	= 0.8361 square m.
1 acre	= 4840 square yards	= 0.4047 hectares
1 square mile	= 640 acres	= 259 hectares
1 square meter	= 10,000 square cm.	= 10.7639 square ft.
1 hectare	= 10,000 square m.	= 2.47106 acres

LIQUID MEASURE

1 ounce (oz.)		= 30 cubic cm.
1 U.S. pint (pt.)	= 16 ounces	= 0.473 liter
1 Imp. pint	= 20 ounces	= 0.591 liter
1 U.S. quart	= 2 U.S. pints	= 0.9463 liter
1 Imp. quart	= 2 Imp. pints	= 1.136 liter
1 U.S. gallon (gal.)	= 4 U.S. quarts	= 3.7853 liters
1 Imp. gallon	= 4 Imp. quarts	= 4.546 liters
1 liter (l.)	= .88 Imp. quart	= 1.0567 U.S. quarts

DRY MEASURE (WEIGHT)

1 ounce		= 28.3495 grams
1 pound	= 16 ounces	= 0.4536 kilogram
1 short ton (t.)	= 2000 pounds	= 907.18 kilograms
1 long ton	= 2240 pounds	= 1016.047 kilograms
1 gram	= 0.001 kilogram	= 0.0353 ounce
1 kilogram (kg.)	= 1000 grams	= 2.2046 pounds
1 metric ton	= 1000 kilograms	= 2204.62 pounds

TEMPERATURES :
Fahrenheit and Centigrade (Celsius) Equivalents

C	F	C	F	C	F	C	F
100	212	32.2	90	15.5	60	1.1	34
75	167	31.1	88	15	59	.5	33
50	122	30	86	14.4	58	0	32
45	113	28.9	84	13.3	56	− .5	31
40	104	27.8	82	12.2	54	− 1.1	30
39.4	103	26.7	80	11.1	52	− 2.2	28
38.9	102	25.5	78	10.5	51	− 3.3	26
38.3	101	25	77	10	50	− 5	23
37.8	100	24.4	76	8.9	48	− 6.7	20
37.2	99	23.3	74	7.8	46	− 7.8	18
36.7	98	22.2	72	6.7	44	− 8.9	16
36.1	97	21.1	70	5.5	42	− 10	14
35.5	96	20	68	5	41	− 11.1	12
35	95	18.9	66	4.4	40	− 12.2	10
34.4	94	17.8	64	3.3	38	− 15	5
33.3	92	16.7	62	2.2	36	− 17.8	0

CENTIGRADE → FAHRENHEIT   FAHRENHEIT → CENTIGRADE
Multiply by 9. Divide by 5.   Add 32   Subtract 32.   Multiply by 5. Divide by 9.

THE DAYS OF THE WEEK

Sunday	Tuesday	Thursday	Saturday
Monday	Wednesday	Friday	

THE SEASONS IN CANADA

spring	*summer*	*fall*	*winter*
April	June	September	November
May	July	October	December
	August		January
			February
			March

THE SEASONS IN THE UNITED STATES

spring	*summer*	*fall*	*winter*
March	June	September	December
April	July	October	January
May	August	November	February

HOLIDAYS IN CANADA

New Year's Day .... January 1
Easter weekend .... In March or April
Victoria Day... Third Monday in May
St. John the Baptist's Day .... June 24 (Quebec)

Dominion Day	July 1
Labor Day	First Monday in September
Thanksgiving Day	Second Monday in October
Christmas Day	December 25

HOLIDAYS IN THE UNITED STATES

New Year's Day	January 1
Lincoln's Birthday	February 12
Washington's Birthday	February 22
Easter Sunday	In March or April
Memorial Day	May 30
Independence Day	July 4
Labor Day	First Monday in September
Columbus Day	October 12
Election Day	Tuesday after first Monday in November
Veterans' Day	November 11
Thanksgiving Day	Fourth Thursday in November
Christmas Day	December 25

THE CANADIAN PROVINCES AND THEIR CAPITALS

PROVINCE	CAPITAL
Alberta (Alta.)	Edmonton
British Columbia (B.C.)	Victoria
Manitoba (Man.)	Winnipeg
New Brunswick (N.B.)	Fredericton
Newfoundland (Nfld.)	Saint John's
Nova Scotia (N.S.)	Halifax
Ontario (Ont.)	Toronto
Prince Edward Island (P.E.I.)	Charlottetown
Quebec (Que.)	Quebec City
Saskatchewan (Sask.)	Regina
North West Territories (N.W.T.)	Yellowknife
Yukon Territory (Y.T.)	Whitehorse

CANADA – 1971 CENSUS

THE PROVINCES

Province	Population	Province	Population
Ontario	7,703,103	Nova Scotia	788,960
Quebec	6,027,746	New Brunswick	634,557
British Columbia	2,184,621	Newfoundland	522,104
Alberta	1,627,874	Prince Edward Island	111,641
Manitoba	988,247	North West Territories	34,807
Saskatchewan	926,242	Yukon Territory	18,388

TEN LARGEST CITIES

Montreal	2,743,208	Hamilton	498,523
Toronto	2,628,043	Edmonton	495,702
Vancouver	1,082,352	Quebec	480,502
Ottawa	602,510	Calgary	403,319
Winnipeg	540,262	Niagara	303,429

THE 50 STATES OF THE UNITED STATES AND THEIR CAPITALS

STATE	CAPITAL		
Alabama (Ala.)	Montgomery	Montana (Mont.)	Helena
Alaska (Alas.)	Juneau	Nebraska (Neb.)	Lincoln
Arizona (Ariz.)	Phoenix	Nevada (Nev.)	Carson City
Arkansas (Ark.)	Little Rock	New Hampshire (N.H.)	Concord
California (Calif.)	Sacramento	New Jersey (N.J.)	Trenton
Colorado (Colo.)	Denver	New Mexico (N.M.)	Santa Fe
Connecticut (Conn.)	Hartford	New York (N.Y.)	Albany
Delaware (Del.)	Dover	North Carolina (N.C.)	Raleigh
Florida (Fla.)	Tallahassee	North Dakota (N.D.)	Bismarck
Georgia (Ga.)	Atlanta	Ohio	Columbus
Hawaii (Haw.)	Honolulu	Oklahoma (Okla.)	Oklahoma City
Idaho	Boise	Oregon (Ore.)	Salem
Illinois (Ill.)	Springfield	Pennsylvania (Pa.)	Harrisburg
Indiana (Ind.)	Indianapolis	Rhode Island (R.I.)	Providence
Iowa	Des Moines	South Carolina (S.C.)	Columbia
Kansas (Kans.)	Topeka	South Dakota (S.D.)	Pierre
Kentucky (Ky.)	Frankfort	Tennessee (Tenn.)	Nashville
Louisiana (La.)	Baton Rouge	Texas (Tex.)	Austin
Maine (Me.)	Augusta	Utah	Salt Lake City
Maryland (Md.)	Annapolis	Vermont (Vt.)	Montpelier
Massachusetts (Mass.)	Boston	Virginia (Va.)	Richmond
Michigan (Mich.)	Lansing	Washington (Wash.)	Olympia
Minnesota (Minn.)	St. Paul	West Virginia (W.Va.)	Charleston
Mississippi (Miss.)	Jackson	Wisconsin (Wis.)	Madison
Missouri (Mo.)	Jefferson City	Wyoming (Wyo.)	Cheyenne

THE UNITED STATES — 1970 CENSUS

THE TEN LARGEST STATES

California	19,953,134
New York	18,241,266
Pennsylvania	11,793,909
Texas	11,196,730
Illinois	11,113,976
Ohio	10,652,017
Michigan	8,875,083
New Jersey	7,168,164
Florida	6,789,443
Massachusetts	5,689,170

THE TEN LARGEST CITIES

New York, N.Y.	11,575,000
Los Angeles, Cal.	7,070,000
Chicago, Ill.	6,920,000
Philadelphia, Pa.	4,809,000
Detroit, Mich.	4,220,000
San Francisco, Cal.	3.082,000
Washington, D.C.	2,857,000
Boston, Mass.	2,655,000
Pittsburgh, Pa.	2,381,000
St. Louis, Mo.	2,358,000

ABBREVIATIONS

A.A.	Alcoholics Anonymous		Esk.	Eskimo
A.D.	Anno Domini (after the birth of Christ)		Esq.	Esquire
			E.S.T.	Eastern Standard Time
adj.	adjective		et al.	and others
adv.	adverb		etc.	*et cetera,*
advert.	advertisement			and so forth
a.m.	ante meridiem (before noon)		F.	Fahrenheit
			F.R.S.C.	Fellow of the Royal Society of Canada
anon.	anonymous			
apt.	apartment		G.I.	General Issue
Asst.	Assistant		G.M.T.	Greenwich Mean Time
b.	born		G.O.P.	Grand Old Party (Republican Party)
B.A.	Bachelor of Arts			
B.C.	Before Christ		Gov.	Governor
B.Sc.	Bachelor of Science		Govt.	Government
c.	centigrade		G.P.	General Practitioner
ca., circ.	circa (about)		G.P.O.	General Post Office
Can.	Canada		gram.	grammar, grammatical
Capt.	Captain		H.C.	House of Commons
C.B.C.	Canadian Broadcasting Corporation		Hon.	Honorable
			h.p.	horsepower
Cdn.	Canadian		hr., hrs.	hour, hours
C.E.	Civil Engineer		H.R.	House of Representatives
C.E.F.	Canadian Expeditionary Force		I.	Island
			ibid.	in the same place
cf.	compare		i.e.	that is
C.F.L.	Canadian Football League		Inc.	Incorporated
			I.O.U.	I owe you
Co.	Company		I.Q.	Intelligence quotient
C.O.D.	collect on delivery, cash on delivery		Jr.	Junior
			k.	carat
Col.	Colonel		lat.	latitude
conj.	conjunction		Lib.	Liberal
Corp.	Corporation, Corporal		LL.D.	Doctor of Laws
C.P.A.	Certified Public Accountant		log.	logarithm
cu.	cubic		long.	longitude
d.	died		Lt., Lieut.	Lieutenant
D.C.	District of Columbia		Ltd.	Limited
D.D.	Doctor of Divinity		m.	meter, married
D.D.S.	Doctor of Dental Surgery		M.A.	Master of Arts
deg.	degree(s)		Maj.	Major
Dem.	Democrat		math.	mathematics
Dept.	Department		M.D.	Doctor of Medicine
Dist.	District		M.E.	Mechanical Engineer
doz.	dozen		med.	medical, medicine
Dr.	Doctor		Mgr.	Manager
D.Sc.	Doctor of Science		M.P.	Member of Parliament Military Police
E.	East			
Ed.	Editor, edition		m.p.h.	miles per hour
E.E.C.	European Economic Community			
e.g.	for example			
Eng.	English, England			

ABBREVIATIONS (cont.)

Mr. *	A man's title	P.S.T.	Pacific Standard Time
Mrs. *	a married woman's title	Pvt.	Private
Ms. **	a woman's title	Q.C.	Queen's Counsel
ms.	manuscript	R.C.A.F.	Royal Canadian Air Force
mss.	manuscripts	R.C.M.P.	Royal Canadian Mounted Police
Mt.	Mount, Mountain	Rep.	Republican, Representative
N.	north	Rev.	Reverend
n.	noun	R.M.C.	Royal Military College
N.A.T.O.	North Atlantic Treaty Organization	R.N.	Registered Nurse
N.D.P.	New Democratic Party	R.S.V.P.	please reply
N.E.	northeast	S.	south
N.H.L.	National Hockey League	Ss.D.	Doctor of Science
no.	number	SE.	southeast
N.O.R.A.D.	North American Air Defense Command	Sgt.	Sergeant
N.W.	northwest	sing.	singular
O.K.	all right, yes, correct	sp.	spelling
p.	page	S.P.C.A.	Society for the Prevention of Cruelty to Animals
par.	paragraph	sq.	square
Parl.	Parliament	Sr.	Senior
P.C.	Progressive Conservative	St.	Saint; Street
pd.	paid	SW.	southwest
Ph.D.	Doctor of Philosophy	syn.	synonym
pkg.	package	TV.	television
pl.	plural	U.N.	the United Nations
P.M.	Prime Minister	U.P.I	United Press International
p.m.	post meridiem, (afternoon)	U.S.A.	United States of America
pp.	pages	U.S.S.R.	Union of Soviet Socialist Republics
prep.	preposition	W.H.O.	World Health Organization
pron.	pronoun		
P.S.	postscript		

ABBREVIATIONS : MONTHS AND DAYS

Jan.	=	January		Sun.	=	Sunday
Feb.	=	February		Mon.	=	Monday
Mar.	=	March		Tues.	=	Tuesday
Aug.	=	August		Wed.	=	Wednesday
Sept.	=	September		Thurs.	=	Thursday
Oct.	=	October		Fri.	=	Friday
Nov.	=	November		Sat.	=	Saturday
Dec.	=	December				

---

*It is ordinarily impolite or improper to address a man as *Mr.* or a woman as *Mrs.* without adding his or her family name. Incorrect and impolite : *May I ask you a question, Mr. ? — Do you have the time, Mrs. ?* Correct and polite : *May I ask you a question, Mr. Taylor ? — Do you have the time, Mrs. Collins ?* In English, the word *Sir* is a correct and very polite title of address for a man either older or higher in position than the speaker. For example : *May I ask you a question, Sir ?*

**Ms., like Mr., does not denote marital status.

THE PRINCIPAL PARTS OF VERBS

	1ST FORM (Present)	2ND FORM (Past)	3RD FORM (Past Participle)
REGULAR	work	worked	worked
IRREGULAR	give	gave	given

THE INFINITIVE

	ACTIVE	PASSIVE
PRESENT	(to) give	(to) be given
PERFECT	(to) have given	(to) have been given

THE "ING" FORM
(GERUND OR PARTICIPLE)

	ACTIVE	PASSIVE
PRESENT	giving	being given
PERFECT	having given	having been given

THE VERB (TO) BE

0 GENERAL FORM	be	
1 PRESENT	I am	we are
	you are	you are
	he is	they are
2 PAST (PRETERITE)	I was³	we were
	you were	you were
	he was³	they were
3 FUTURE	I will be	
4 PAST FUTURE	I would be	
5 PERFECT PRESENT	I have been (he has been)	
6 PERFECT PAST	I had been	
7 PERFECT FUTURE	I will have been	
8 PERFECT PAST FUTURE	I would have been	

THE VERB (TO) GIVE

ACTIVE

	SIMPLE	CONTINUOUS
0	give	be giving
1	I give (he gives)[1]	I am giving[2]
2	I gave	I was giving
3	I will give	I will be giving
4	I would give	I would be giving
5	I have given (he has given)[1]	I have been giving (he has been giving)[1]
6	I had given	I had been giving
7	I will have given	I will have been giving
8	I would have given	I would have been giving

PASSIVE

SIMPLE	CONTINUOUS
be given	
I am given[2]	I am being given[2]
I was given	I was being given
I will be given	
I would be given	
I have been given (he was been given)[1]	
I had been given	
I will have been given	
I would have been given	

GENERAL NOTE: Unless otherwise indicated, all persons (*I, you, he, she, it, we, they*) take the same form. For the third person singular, only *he* is given; however, this indicates that *she* and *it* take the same form. **Note 1:** The parentheses indicate that the third person singular (*he, she, it*) takes a different form from the form for the other persons. **Note 2:** The verb *be* is the auxiliary for the present and past tenses in these columns. The verb *be* takes its form according to the chart. Note that the principal part of the verb (*giving; given; being given*) does not change. **Note 3:** *I were* and *he were* after the verb *wish* and in unreal present conditional clauses after *if*.

216

PERSONAL PRONOUNS AND ADJECTIVES

	SUBJECT PRONOUNS	OBJECT PRONOUNS	POSSESSIVE PRONOUNS	POSSESSIVE ADJECTIVES	REFLEXIVE PRONOUNS
SINGULAR					
FIRST PERSON	I	me	mine	my book my books	myself
SECOND PERSON	you	you	yours	your book your books	yourself
THIRD PERSON	he	him	his	his book his books	himself
	she	her	hers	her book her books	herself
	it	it	its	its eye its eyes	itself
PLURAL					
FIRST PERSON	we	us	ours	our book our books	ourselves
SECOND PERSON	you	you	yours	your book your books	yourselves
THIRD PERSON	they	them	theirs	their book their books	themselves

IRREGULAR COMPARATIVE AND SUPERLATIVE FORMS

bad badly	worse	the worst
far	farther further	the farthest the furthest
good well	better	the best

little	less	the least
much many	more	the most

COMMONLY USED IRREGULAR VERBS

1ST FORM (Present)	2ND FORM (Past)	3RD FORM (Past Participle)	1ST FORM (Present)	2ND FORM (Past)	3RD FORM (Past Participle)
am, are, is[1]	was, were	been	hide	hid	hidden
beat	beat	beat(en)	hit	hit	hit
become	became	become	hold	held	held
begin	began	begun	hurt	hurt	hurt
bend	bent	bent	keep	kept	kept
bet	bet	bet	know	knew	known
bite	bit	bitten	lay	laid	laid
bleed	bled	bled	lead	led	led
blow	blew	blown	leave	left	left
break	broke	broken	lend	lent	lent
breed	bred	bred	let	let	let
bring	brought	brought	lose	lost	lost
build	built	built	lie	lay	lain
buy	bought	bought	make	made	made
catch	caught	caught	mean	meant	meant
choose	chose	chosen	meet	met	met
come	came	come	pay	paid	paid
cost	cost	cost	put	put	put
creep	crept	crept	quit	quit	quit
cut	cut	cut	read	read[3]	read[3]
do	did	done	ride	rode	ridden
dig	dug	dug	ring	rang	rung
draw	drew	drawn	rise	rose	risen
drink	drank	drunk	say	said	said
drive	drove	driven	see	saw	seen
eat	ate	eaten	seek	sought	sought
fall	fell	fallen	sell	sold	sold
feed	fed	fed	send	sent	sent
feel	felt	felt	set	set	set
fight	fought	fought	shake	shook	shaken
find	found	found	shoot	shot	shot
fit	fit(ted)	fit(ted)	shut	shut	shut
flee	fled	fled	sing	sang	sung
fly	flew	flown	sink	sank	sunk
forget	forgot	forgotten	sit	sat	sat
forgive	forgave	forgiven	sleep	slept	slept
freeze	froze	frozen	slide	slid	slid
get	got	got(ten)[2]	speak	spoke	spoken
give	gave	given	spend	spent	spent
go	went	gone	spin	spun	spun
grind	ground	ground	split	split	split
grow	grew	grown	spread	spread	spread
hang	hung	hung	spring	sprang	sprung
have	had	had	stand	stood	stood
hear	heard	heard	steal	stole	stolen

COMMONLY USED IRREGULAR VERBS (cont.)

1st Form (Present)	2nd Form (Past)	3rd Form (Past Participle)	1st Form (Present)	2nd Form (Past)	3rd Form (Past Participle)
stick	stuck	stuck	think	thought	thought
strike	struck	struck	throw	threw	thrown
swear	swore	sworn	understand	understood	understood
sweep	swept	swept	wake up	woke up	woken up
swim	swam	swum	wear	wore	worn
swing	swung	swung	weave	wove	woven
take	took	taken	weep	wept	wept
teach	taught	taught	win	won	won
tear	tore	torn	wind	wound	wound
tell	told	told	wring	wrung	wrung

GENERAL NOTE : The meaning of an irregular verb is sometimes changed by prefixing another word. This does not affect the form of the verb itself. Example : *undergo, underwent, undergone.* Other verbs of this type are *mislay, mislead, overhear, oversleep, overtake, overthrow, undertake, underwrite, undo, withstand.* A notable exception is the verb *welcome* which is regular in its forms : *welcome, welcomed, welcomed.*

Note 1 : The infinitive of this verb is *(to) be.* This is the only verb in English which does not take the same form for the infinitive and the first person singular of the simple present tense.

Note 2 : Since usage varies greatly on the choice of *got* or *gotten,* non-native speakers are usually confused and uncertain in using this verb. Much difficulty can be avoided by advising students to use only *got* for the past participle. Although in some cases this may conflict with local usage, the student will never be incorrect.

Note 3 : This form of the verb *(to) read* is pronounced "red".

COMMONLY USED CONTRACTIONS

I am	*I'm*	etc.	*etc.*
you are	*you're*	will not	*won't*
he is	*he's*	*I would	*I'd*
she is	*she's*	*you would	*you'd*
it is	*it's*	etc.	*etc.*
that is	*that's*	would not	*wouldn't*
there is	*there's*	should not	*shouldn't*
who is	*who's*	cannot	*can't*
what is	*what's*	could not	*couldn't*
we are	*we're*	must not	*mustn't*
you are	*you're*	*I have (gone)	*I've (gone)*
they are	*they're*	*you have (gone)	*you've (gone)*
is not	*isn't*	*he has (gone)	*he's (gone)*
are not	*aren't*	*she has (gone)	*she's (gone)*
was not	*wasn't*	*it has (gone)	*it's (gone)*
were not	*weren't*	etc.	*etc.*
do not	*don't*	have not (gone)	*haven't (gone)*
does not	*doesn't*	*I had (gone)	*I'd (gone)*
did not	*didn't*	*you had (gone)	*you'd (gone)*
*I will	*I'll*	etc.	*etc.*
*you will	*you'll*	had not (gone)	*hadn't (gone)*

*The contractions with asterisks are not normally used in negative sentences with *not.* For example, in the sentence *he will not go,* the usual contraction is *he won't go.* Also, in the sentence *he has not gone,* the usual contraction is *he hasn't gone.*

ANSWERS FOR INTERMEDIATE SECTION (EXERCISES 1-126)

2 3 works 4 work 5 has 6 have 7 writes 8 write 9 studies 10 study 11 reads 12 read 13 collect 14 collects **3** 3 He (She) reads all of the important letters. 4 He (She) studies the reports very carefully. 5 He (She) has a private secretary too. 6 He (She) usually works in the main office. 7 He (She) meets all of the important visitors. 8 He (She) gets the information from Miss Peters. 9 He (She) always gives the reports to Mr. Wilson. **5** 3 Do 4 Do 5 Does 6 Do 7 Does 8 Do 9 Do 10 Does 11 Do 12 Do 13 Do 14 Do **6** 1 I don't 2 doesn't 3 don't 4 don't 5 doesn't 6 don't 7 don't 8 doesn't 9 don't 10 don't 11 doesn't 12 don't 13 doesn't 14 doesn't **8** 3 is helping 4 are working 5 am looking 6 are listening 7 is telling 8 is talking 9 is talking and writing 10 is working 11 are studying 12 are collecting 13 are fixing 14 are also making **9** 3 is helping 4 are sitting 5 are writing 6 is working 7 am watching 8 are listening 9 is talking 10 is dictating 11 are collecting 12 is talking and writing 13 are talking and laughing **11** 3 aren't watching 4 don't watch 5 don't study 6 aren't studying 7 isn't raining 8 doesn't rain 9 isn't eating 10 doesn't always eat 11 don't see 12 don't hear 13 don't like 14 don't have **12** 3 Do 4 Are 5 Does 6 Is 7 Does 8 Is 9 Do 10 Are 11 Do 12 Does 13 Do 14 Do **13** 3 is looking 4 sleep 5 are fixing 6 speaks 7 eats 8 enjoys 9 are writing 10 works **14** 3 This 4 These 5 This 6 These 7 These 8 This 9 This 17 that 18 those 19 that 20 those 21 that 22 those 23 those **16** 3 She is studying her lesson with him. 4 They enjoy it very much. 5 He understands it completely. 6 They like them very much. 7 Do they like it ? 8 Is she explaining the lesson to them ? 9 They are talking about it. 10 He is moving it into the other room. **17** 3 Philippe's English .... 4 That girl's summer suit .... 5 The girls' new apartment .... 6 Mr. Brown's son .... 7 That man's brother ..... 8 Those men's coats ..... 9 The student's books .... 10 The students' papers .... 11 Tom's friend's sister .... 12 Fred's parents' house .... **18** 3 The doctor's office.... 4 The legs of the table.... 5 .... the price of the car ? 6 .... the boys' friend ? 7 .... the height of that wall ? 8 The women's coats .... 9 The surface of the table .... 10 The cover of the book .... **19** 3 their 4 our 5 her 6 their 7 my 8 your **20** 3 his 4 mine 5 yours 6 hers 7 theirs 8 hers **21** 1 410 Holbrook St. 2 117 Branch St. 3 206 Cedar St. 4 812 Worth St. **26** 4 They were at work. 5 It was in that drawer. 6 She was in Montreal. 7 I was very tired. 8 That was a surprise. 9 The men were angry. 10 Mr. Harris was there. **27** 2 borrowed 3 explained 4 liked 5 hired 6 studied 7 enjoyed 8 stopped. **30** 4 Did Mr. and Mrs. Wilson visit their friends in Chicoutimi ? 5 Did the teacher tell the students the answer to the question ? 6 Was that movie about birds in the Arctic interesting ? 7 Did Mr. Harris explain the meaning of the word to her ? 8 Were those men from Nova Scotia at the meeting ? **31** 4 The secretary didn't (did not) copy the names from the list carefully. 5 Alice didn't (did not) eat lunch at the cafeteria with her friends. 6 The students weren't (were not) ready for the examination. 7 Mr. Harris didn't (did not) teach at Loyola last summer. **40** 2 grew 3 chose 4 took 5 broke 6 lost 7 felt 8 sent 9 heard 10 blew 11 stood 12 met 13 fell, hurt **42** 1 knew 2 shut 3 slept 4 spoke 5 rode 6 felt 7 put 8 taught 9 spent 10 brought 11 told 12 drove 13 found **44** 1 won 2 quit 3 fit 4 cut 5 spread 6 lent 7 broke 8 threw, caught 9 stood 10 cost 11 bought 12 drove 13 brought **48** 4 will begin 5 will give 6 will read 7 will lock 8 will have **50** 5 The teacher is going to explain .... 6 We are going to attend ..... 7 I am going to study ..... 8 Mr. Wilson and Mr. Johnson are going to be .... **52** 3 Will Mr. and Mrs. Wilson arrive in Montreal on Monday ? 4 Will you finish all of the work before tomorrow ? 5 Will many people attend the meeting tomorrow night ? 6 Will there be enough food and coffee for everyone ? **53** 3 Is Gilles going to eat lunch with us today ? 4 Is Mr. Foster going to quit his job with the Sandhurst Company ? 5 Are all of the students going to go to the lecture tonight ? 6 Are you going to accept his offer for a job with that company ? **54** 3 Our friends won't (will not) go ..... 4 The Pronovosts won't (will not) leave .... 5 Mr. Johnson's secretary won't (will not) be .... 6 Réjean won't (will not) attend..... **55** 3 The Brown's aren't (are not) going to buy ... 4 I'm (I am) not going to answer ..... 5 My friend Frank isn't (is not) going to join ... 6 Miss Stewart and I aren't (are not) going to go shopping ..... **60** 1 many 2 much 3 very 4 much 5 much 6 very 7 very much 8 very much 9 very many 10 many 11 much 12 very many 13 much 14 many **63** 1 too much 2 too many 3 too much, too 4 too many, too 5 too, too many **64** 5 some 6 any 7 some 8 any 9 some 10 any 11 any (some) 12 some 13 any 14 any (some) **67** 1 no one 2 anyone 3 No one 4 anyone 5 no one 6 anyone 7 No one 8 anyone **68** (Part One) 3 The agent sold Mr. and Mrs. Hanson the house. 4 We gave Jean a birthday present yesterday. 5 Mr. Johnson sent the Apollo Company a letter. 6 Did the boy throw his friend the baseball ? (Part Two) 3 Dr. Davis gave the tickets to Charles. 4 Did the manager offer the job to that fellow ? 5 Mr. Houle told the story of his narrow escape to us. 6 Ruth and Betty sent a birthday gift to Mary last week. **69** 1 leave 2 is using 3 go 4 is preparing 5 is running 6 understands 7 are finishing 8 need 9 are watching 10 are reviewing 11 wants 12 go **74** 6 Yes, they are. 7 No, they don't. 8 Yes, they were. 9 Yes, I do. 10 No, there wasn't. 11 Yes, she did. 12 Yes, she will. 13 No, they didn't. 14 No, I'm not. 15 Yes, there were. **79** 1 Where 2 When 3 Why 4 When 5 Where 6 Why 7 Where 8 Why 9 When 10 Why 11 Where 12 When 13 Where 14 Why **87** 1 Where 2 Whose 3 What 4 How much 5 Which 6 Who 7 Whom 8 How old 9 How much 10 How 11 Which 12 What 13 When 14 How often 15 What 16 Where 17 Who 18 What 19 Who 20 How long 21 Whom 22 Why 23 How far 24 How many 25 How 26 How 27 Why 28 How long 29 How tall 30 What **89** 4 When is Bill's birthday ? 5 How many floors are there in that building ? 6 Why is John coughing ? 7 When did the Browns leave for home ? 8 What did the students study ? 9 Whose briefcase is that ? 10 How many guests were there at the party ? 11 When did Mr. Burke buy his new car ? 12 How far is Oka from there ? 13 (At) what time do their classes usually begin ? (When do their classes usually begin ?) 14 Why are you going to go ? 15 How many packs of cigarettes does that customer want ? **93** 4 has explained 5 have lived 6 has hired 7 have already mentioned 8 have followed 9 has improved 10 has copied 11 have tried 12 has never traveled 13 has increased 14 have studied **94** 4 has taken 5 has flown 6 have already done 7 have forgotten 8 has been 9 have known 10 have fallen 11 has already had 12 have already read, written 13 have had 14 have already seen, spoken **99** 3 have read 4 read 5 studied 6 has studied 7 lived 8 has lived 9 had 10 have had 11 saw 12 has seen 13 have been 14 were 15 have traveled 16 traveled **100** 1 have studied 2 has taught 3 think, is knocking 4 pays 5 have seen 6 usually rains 7 have been 8 have made 9 owes 10 am, have forgotten 11 is sitting 12 have had 13 is looking 14 comes 15 have heard **101** 7 ... was she ? No, she wasn't. 8 ... doesn't he ? Yes, he does. 9 ... did he (she) ? No, he (she) didn't. 10 ... hasn't she ? Yes, she has. 11 Won't they ? Yes, they will. 12 ... weren't there ? Yes, there were. 13 ... does she ? No, she doesn't. 14 ... didn't they ? Yes, they did. 15 ... are they ? No, they aren't. **102** 1 from 2 before 3 after 4 ago 5 before 6 from 7 before 8 ago **103** 1 at 2 at, in 3 in 4 on 5 in 6 on 7 at 8 on 9 in 10 at 11 on 12 in 13 in, at 14 on **104** 1 at 2 at 3 on 4 in 5 at 6 in 7 in 8At 9 in, at 10 on, at 11 in 12 on 13 at 14 in **106** (Part One) 1 for 2 since 3 since 4 for 5 for 6 since 7 since 8 for

(Part Three) 1 in 2 for 3 in 4 for 5 in 6 for 7 for 8 in   107   (Part One) 1 by 2 in 3 by 4 in 5 in 6 by 7 By 8 in (Part Two) 1 until 2 by 3 until 4 by 5 by 6 until 7 until 8 by (Part Three) 1 by 2 for 3 by 4 for 5 by 6 for 7 for 8 by   108   (Part One) 1 until 2 for 3 until 4 for 5 for 6 until 7 for 8 until (Part Two) 1 until 3 in 4 until 5 in 6 until 7 in 8 until (Part Three) 1 in 2 for 3 for 4 in 5 in 6 for 7 in 8 for   114   1 on 2 in 3 in 4 at, in 8 at (on) 9 in 10 at, at 11 in 12 in 13 in 14 on 15 at, on 16 in, on 17 at 18 in 19 at 20 on 21 on 22 on 23 in 24 on 25 at, in 26 at 27 in 28 in, in 29 on, in 30 in 31 on, in 32 on, in   115   1 for 2 for, in 3 for 4 about 5 to 6 about 7 to 8 for 9 for 10 in 11 at, at 12 on, for 13 from 14 to 15 with, about (over, on), at 16 about, in 17 on, to 18 for 19 on 20 of 21 on 22 of 23 for, on 24 from, into 25 at 26 to 27 to 28 on, for 29 about (of) 30 with 31 with, in 32 with, in   116   1 for 2 about (over) 3 of 4 from 5 at 6 about, toward 7 in 8 of (with) 9 about 10 for 11 with (over) 12 to 13 in, to 14 at, for 15 of (about), on 16 of, to, on 17 of 18 for, of 19 of 20 for, about 21 on, for 22 of, from 23 of (about) 24 of 25 to, from (than) 26 to 27 with 28 of, in (about) 29 to, for 30 for 31 of (about) 32 to   117   5 still 6 any more 7 still 8 any more 9 still   118   4 already 5 yet 6 already 7 yet 8 already 9 yet   119   1 already 2 yet 3 still 4 yet 5 still 6 still 7 already   120   5 too (also) 6 also 7 either 8 too (also) 9 also   121   1 doesn't 2 I'm 3 She's 4 It'll 5 She's not (She isn't) 6 Where's 7 I'm 8 didn't 9 wasn't 10 − 11 don't 12 We're 13 It's 14 wasn't 15 What's 16 There's 17 That's 18 didn't 19 Who'll 20 We've 23 − 28 won't 30 − 32 There's not (There isn't) 33 haven't   122   5 Jean-Pierre usually works ..... 6 The children are often very active .... 8 Is Mr. Rochefort usually at home .... 9 Do you always study .... 10 Dorothy and I never watch .... 11 Why doesn't that student ever write .... 12 Mr. Wilson rarely has time .... 14 Have you ever watched .... 15 The director is always in his office   124   ("place" and "time") 2 .... at Mr. Hart's house on Thursday. 3 .... down the street a few minutes ago. 4 .... on page 80 yesterday. ("place" and "manner") 2 .... to the movies with your friends ? 3 .... at the clerk doubtfully. 4 .... at the library for three hours. ("manner" and "time") 2 .... very well now. 3 .... for two hours every night. 4 .... quite early in the morning.   125   2 .... her lessons at home every evening. 3 .... my paycheck at the office every Friday. 4 .... a dress yesterday without any difficulty. 5 .... my dictionary from my desk last night. 6 .... too much coffee at breakfast this morning 7 .... lunch with them after the meeting.   126   2 .... her trip to me several times. 3 .... his wife flowers after work. 4 .... the lessons to the students in class 5 .... their daughter a bracelet for her birthday. 6 .... Mr. Moore her homework after class.

ANSWERS FOR ADVANCED SECTION (EXERCISES 127-312)

127   1 knows 2 has worked 3 are finishing 4 rains 5 has lost 6 has just graduated (has just been graduated) 7 is repairing 8 has made 9 hear 10 have seen 11 circles 12 is writing 13 has lived 14 is taking 15 have called   128   1 sold 2 has worked 3 explained 4 has been 5 spent 6 have never seen 7 returned 8 has studied 9 have spoken 10 was 11 have traveled 12 has never seen 13 have not (haven't) finished 14 had 15 have had   130   2 have been studying 3 − 4 has been feeling 5 have been waiting 6 − 7 has already been talking   132   1 beautifully 2 happy 3 good 4 usually, well 5 rapid, good 6 quietly, cautiously 7 real   134   1 carefully, smooth 2 happy 3 happily, calmly 4 beautiful, happy 5 carefully, expensive 6 ready 7 different, recently   136   1 not 2 not 3 hasn't 4 no, no, cannot (can't) 5 not (isn't) 6 not, no, don't (do not) 7 no 8 isn't, no, not 9 not 10 not 11 no 12 not 13 not, no 14 not, Don't 15 not   137   11 ... was more tactful than ... 12 ... was as nervous as ... 13 ... is the most popular man ... 14 ... is older than ... 15 ... was the clumsiest of the five players.   139   1 much 2

much 3 many 4 much 5 much 6 many 7 much 8 many 9 much   140   1 as 2 from 3 to 4 as 5 to 6 from 7 as 8 from 9 as   142   7 ... as easily as ... 8 ... more often than ... 9 ... better than ... 10 ... as thoroughly as ... 12 ... the best of ... 14 ... earlier than ... 15 ... the least of ... 16 ... worse than ... 17 ... sooner than ... 18 ... the most (least) clearly of ...   143   3 ... the most regularly of ... 4 ... as calm as ... 5 ... more (less) clearly than ... 6 ... clearer than yours. 7 ... the most (least) confident of ... 8 ... the most (least) confidently of ... 9 ... more (less) carefully than I do. 10 ... more (less) careful work ... 11 ... the wisest of ... 12 ... the most (least) wisely of ... 13 ... harder on ... 14 ... harder than ...   145   3 My secretary opened the two packages. 4 Our teacher corrects our homework. 5 That company has constructed two building. 6 She (they, etc.) didn't clean that room carefully yesterday. 7 The men are loading the truck now.   146   2 The mail is opened by the secretary every morning. 3 That proposal is being considered by the committee right now. 4 That project will be completed by Pierre Desjardins next year. 5 He has been transferred to another department by his boss. 6 Will the announcements be distributed by the company? 7 That interesting article about Montreal was written by an artist. 8 Today English is spoken by a large number of people.   147   1 was shocked 2 enjoyed 3 is taught 4 is being considered 5 happened 6 has taught 7 will divide 8 borrowed 9 has been said 10 has written 11 was promoted 12 occurred 13 will bring 14 have been used 15 will be listed   162   1 has 2 should 3 can 4 must 5 wasn't able 6 ought 7 must   163   1 buy, decide 2 to explain 3 be 4 to give 5 have said 6 wait   173   2 on doing 3 in selling 4 on getting 5 about failing 6 to using 7 of studying 8 about doing 9 on hearing 10 about (of) changing 11 from leaving 12 for making 13 for taking 14 of losing 15 in getting 16 of (about) finishing 17 of completing 18 about losing, for replacing 19 of attending 20 about (over) testifying 21 of seeing 22 on learning 23 in knowing 24 to hearing 25 of listening 26 about (over) going 27 of (for) solving 28 for not helping 29 of finding 30 by writing 31 of mentioning 32 of working harder or losing 33 by (from) investing 34 for being   174   3 studying 4 to translate 5 writing 6 to leave 7 to eliminate 8 trying 9 traveling 10 to reserve 11 hearing 12 leaving 13 to buy 14 using 15 waiting 16 to suggest 17 writing 18 to receive 19 knowing 20 to leave 21 telling 22 studying, to interrupt 23 to say 24 seeing 25 to include 26 listening 27 to risk losing 28 to be 29 interrupting 30 to give 31 to pay 32 taking   175   5 to see 7 to reveal 10 knowing 21 to tell 27 writing 28 studying 29 to know 30 to do 31 to give 32 to understand 33 to exaggerate   177   1 leaving 2 to get 3 to stay 4 to hear 5 Learning 6 to return 7 seeing 8 to criticize 9 leaving 10 to attend 11 to show 12 opening 13 Writing 14 quitting 15 to lock   178   3 have to be reserved 4 can be obtained 5 should be tried 6 must be reported 7 should be devoted 8 have to be completed   179   3 to be transferred 4 being deceived 5 to be cheated 6 being informed 7 to be promoted   180   5 Marie-Anne wasn't either. 6 We did too. 7 You should too. 8 They don't either. 9 He has too.   181   5 So does Tom. 6 Neither has she. 7 so should we. 8 Neither do they. 9 Neither can Bob.   182   4 .... but I will. 5 .... but we haven't. 6 .... but I did. 7 .... but Mr. Green doesn't. 8 .... but Mary didn't. 9 .... but Ralph can.   183   3 .... but I don't need to. 4 .... but I intend to tonight. 5 Would you like to? (Would you?) 6 .... and I don't intend to either. 7 .... but he won't be able to. 8 .... but he has to.   184   4 .... are they? No, they aren't. 5 .... can you? No, I can't. 6 .... didn't he? Yes, he did. 7 .... won't he? Yes, he will. 8 .... didn't he? Yes, he did. 9 .... didn't you? Yes, I did. 10 .... have you? No, I haven't.   185   3 When are they going to leave? 4 Why must you go to the bank? 5 Where is the bridge across the river? 6 About how long does the whole trip take? 7 How will the four packages be sent? 8

Whose bicycle can Irène borrow tomorrow ? 9 How does Mr. Séquin seem to feel this morning ? 10 How far is it to Hamilton ? **187** 3 (which you gave me) 4 (who stole the money) 5 (that were on my desk ?) 6 (that the teacher recommended.) 7 (which we made.) 8 (whose wife you met) **188** 2 (who is walking with Maurice) 3 (which we did yesterday) 4 (whom you just met) 5 (which we heard yesterday) 6 (who gets results quickly.) 7 (whose name was very unusual.) 8 (who had stolen the jewels.) **190** 3 Whom are Thomas and Frank waiting for ? For whom are Thomas and Frank waiting ? 4 Whom did that young couple get the money from ? From whom did that young couple get the money ? 5 What has Mr. Kennedy invested his money in ? In what has Mr. Kennedy invested his money ? 6 What page is that difficult exercise on ? On what page is that difficult exercise ? **191** 5 The speaker that we listened to mentioned that matter. 6 The woman that you were talking about is here now. 8 The apartment that we live in is on the twelfth floor. **193** 3 We know the man who wrote that book very well. 4 The car (which) (that) he is driving now formerly belonged to me. 5 Yesterday, I spoke to the professor who (that) teaches that subject. 6 Is this the letter (which) (that) you wanted me to deliver ? **195** 3 The fellow walking with Edward is his brother. 4 That's a book known by almost all children. 5 The answer given to this question was inadequate. 6 The message delivered by them solved the mystery. **196** 3 imported 4 running 5 dancing 6 assumed 7 existing 8 stolen **198** 3 (that Carole will be chosen.) 4 (that you didn't like that movie.) 5 (that Jacques has a new car.) 6 (that he had enough money.) **200** 3 (who told you the news.) noun clause 4 (who attended the class) adjective clause 5 (which you lent me last week.) adjective clause 6 (what you told me about it.) noun clause 7 (who is walking with Mr. Brown ?) adjective clause 8 (who had suggested that plan to them.) noun clause **201** (Part One) 1 what 2 which 3 which 4 what 5 which 6 what 7 which 8 what 9 which 10 which 11 what 12 which 13 what 14 which 15 which 16 what **202** (The word *that* cannot be omitted in sentences 3, 6, 9, and 12.) **203** 4 We tried to follow the instructions Tom had given us. 5 (The connecting word *which* cannot be omitted.) 6 The doctor I went to last week is a surgeon. **204** 1 The man who (that) is sitting by the door .... 2 (A connecting word is not required.) 3 Lots of students don't know where the Island of Majorca is located. 4 (A connecting word is not required.) 5 Please try to remember what you did .... 6 (A connecting word is not required.) 7 The butcher who (that) sold me these steaks .... 8 (A connecting word is not required.) 9 I wonder whose books and papers these are. 10 (A connecting word is not required.) **207** 7 I can't tell you when they arrived. 8 Let's ask them when they are leaving. 9 Please explain why you were absent. 10 I can't understand why you didn't return. 11 Please tell me why you bought it. 12 Can you find out who that tall fellow is ? 13 I don't know who is doing the work. 14 Can you tell me who wrote this paper ? 15 I can't imagine whom they invited. **208** 3 I knew that they always studied .... 4 My friend believed there was .... 5 The newspaper article said that the professor taught .... 6 Jean-Guy thought the students were talking .... 7 He said the members were discussing .... **209** 3 I thought that Serge had never been .... 4 François said he had forgotten .... 5 Their boss reported that they had had .... 6 I assumed that you had had .... **210** 6 Harold thought he could go .... 7 His secretary said he would return .... 8 My friend thought we should ask .... 9 Mr. Blanc said he could help .... 10 I supposed Marc would finish .... 11 John said you ought to send .... 12 The message indicated he would be .... **215** 5 Bill asked them when they were leaving. 6 I couldn't imagine what he had found. 7 He didn't know whose book that was. 8 Didn't he tell you who would help us ? 9 I didn't ask them when they could come. 10 Did he explain why he had been absent ? 11 Didn't she mention what she wanted ? 12 I couldn't remember which one was hers. 13 Laurent didn't say when we should leave. 14 Did she ask him how much it cost ? 15 I forgot to ask Ed how far it was. 216 5 said 6 telling 7 said 8 told 9 said 10 said 11 said, told 12 tell, said 13 told, tell 14 tell, said 15 said, told 217 3 I said (that) I couldn't understand those two lessons at all. 4 Catherine said (that) she knew those two girls quite well. 5 Charles told me (that) he had to leave the office before 3:00 p.m. 6 Mr. Johnson said (that) his secretary hadn't finished the work. 7 George remarked (that) he couldn't possibly finish the work by that 218 3 Her aunt asked how well Carole played the piano. 4 The agent asked when we planned to leave for Portugal. 5 The woman asked me where she could find the director's office. 6 Antoine asked me what I would offer him for that (this) camera. 7 The treasurer asked when he had to turn in that (this) report. 219 3 My friend asked me if I enjoyed my English class. My friend asked me whether or not I enjoyed my English class. 4 The driver asked if everyone would be ready to leave by ten. 5 Frank asked me if I had given the letters to Mr. Watson. Frank asked me whether or not I had given the letters to Mr. Watson. 220 3 The teacher told us to write the next two exercises. 4 The man directed us (them, her, etc.) to turn left at the corner and drive two blocks. 5 My friend asked me to show him all of the photographs. 6 Mr. Lane's wife told him not to leave his coat on the chair. 226 6 so (so that) 7 because 8 so (so that) 9 Since 10 because 228 6 so 7 so 8 such 9 so 10 such 230 3 Mr. Watkins is surprisingly active although he is quite old. 4 Although it was raining, we went for a walk in the park. 5 Although he is not well-educated, that man has a good position. 6 Our team won the hockey game although (some) key players were injured. 235 2 (while she was slicing the bread.) 3 (After I had asked the girl twice.) 4 (before the guests arrive.) 5 (When I left for work this morning,) 6 (until we're sure about that.) 237 1 Mr. Lemieux was talking to another man when I saw him today. 2 As I was crossing the street, two cars raced by me at full speed. 3 When we met the Vachons in 1970, they were living in Pierrefonds. 4 Our English teacher gave us an examination yesterday. 5 The boy fell and hurt himself while he was riding his bicycle. 6 Bill was having his breakfast when I stopped at his home this morning. 239 1 Charles was talking to Professor Moore when I saw him. 2 When the students heard the bell, they got up and left. 3 My friend Louise bought a new spring coat last week. 4 We were still eating our dinner when Mr. and Mrs. Drapeau arrived. 5 Mr. Harvey asked me about my plans the next time he saw me. 6 Just as I was leaving for home, a student stopped me in the hall. 241 1 The pharmacist had already left for home when we got to the store. 2 The Andersons moved into their new apartment last week. 3 The next time I saw George, he had a different car. 4 Dorothy signed the check and gave it to Dr. Davis yesterday. 5 When John and I got to the theater, the movie had already started. 6 Whenever it rained, Mr. Gilbert took out his old umbrella. 243 1 We will send you a telegram as soon as we arrive in Amsterdam. 2 When George comes this afternoon, he will bring his friends. 3 Mr. Green will not leave the office until you call him. 4 I will speak to you about that matter after the meeting tonight. 5 As soon as our guests arrive tonight, we will serve dinner. 245 1 will give 2 will be crossing 3 will be sitting 4 will explain 5 will be living 6 will try 246 1 met 2 was considering 3 studying 4 had forgotten 5 had learned 6, 7 wanted to learn 8 was 9 study 10 enrolled 11, 12 had finished studying 13, 14 decided to go 15 traveled 16 had never been 17, 18 enjoyed visiting 19, 20 considered staying 21, 22 would enjoy living 23 finally spent 24, 25 was forced to return 247 3 get 4 sees 5 is 6 doesn't like 7 get 8 decide 251 4 worked 5 knew 6 had 7 were 8 studied 253 3 had been 4 had asked 5 had studied 6 had not (hadn't) spent 7 had been 8 had invited 255 3 I won't bother to call you unless I hear from Mr. Brown. 4 Unless you agreed with him, Charles wouldn't even suggest it. 5 We can't write to Mr. Girouard unless he sends us his address. 6 Unless you study harder, you're going to fail the examination. 256 4 had 5 had studied 6 would offer 7 had been 260 3 did study 4 does attend 5 did finish 6 did give 7 do wear 8 did speak 277 3 We had that old chair repaired several days ago. 4 Georges finally got his car fixed. 5 I'll have the holes in that wall covered tomorrow. 6 Mrs. Kelly got the meat cut into small pieces. 7 We usually have our car washed once a week. 8 I'm going to get those reports checked very carefully. 278 1 cut down -reduce 2 think over -consider. 3 put up -erect 4 tear down -demolish 5 take after -resemble 6 look over -examine, cross out -delete 7 take up -occupy 8 call off -cancel 9 call for -require 10 take back -return 11 made up -prepare, leave out -omit 12 turn in -submit 13 show off -display 14 came across -discovered 15 talk over -discuss -16 carry out -execute 17 turn down -reject 18 go over -review, put off -postpone 19 show up -appear 20 hold up -delay 21 pick out -select 22 went on -continued 23 cut out -stop 24 stand for -represent 25 stand for -tolerate 279 3 turned it down 4 held us up 5 stand for it 6 find it out, look it up 7 make them up 8 try it on 9 get over it 10 fill it out 11 break them in 12 care for it 13 figure it out 14 handed it in 15 gave it up 16 take it off 17 put them off 18 wait on you 19 used it up 20 cross it out 21 pointed them out 22 call for you 23 bring it up 24 wear it out 25 look it up 26 go over it 27 run across them 28 count on him 280 1 to 2 with 3 for 4 on 5 with 6 from 7 on 8 with 9 from 10 with 11 of 12 from 13 to 14 to 15 on (upon) 16 with 17 with 18 with 19 with 20 for 21 to 22 with 23 for 24 to 25 of 26 with (in) 27 to 28 with 29 on 30 from, from 31 with 281 1 little green 2 square plastic 3 unusual modern 4 valuable ancient Egyptian 5 long bamboo fishing 6 friend's three sons 7 those books to the library promptly 8 the leaves from the trees in the fall 12 short sentences to us in class 14 the bill collector the money reluctantly 16 in the Yukon for two months last year 18 in a factory in St. Boniface for one summer 20 the tenants for the rent in advance 21 the train to Ottawa with my friend 22 two years to finish it completely 23 to improve my English quickly 24 quite cool downtown yesterday 26 quite unimportant to me at first 27 for me to speak English correctly 28 the man didn't say 29 will your friends say 30 car that is 31 they were in Paris 32 have all the students gone 282 1 movies better than television 3 has never been tried 9 the part about verbs to me again 10 haven't you ever been 13 tall enough to reach that shelf 15 of any way at all to improve your plan 18 could they possibly know 19 they could possibly know 20 about that at the desk by the door 21 two well-organized bus 22 today's lesson is 25 hard square object wrapped in cloth 30 Shakespeare, a poet known by everyone 32 husbands have all the responsibilities 283 2 How long will those fellows remain in Washington, D.C. ? 3 The two men asked an official a question about this rule. 4 Remarque, who is a famous writer, lived in Switzerland at that time. 5 It's wonderful to see the flowers come to life in the spring. 6 The purse with the handle and the coat with the red collar are mine. 7 Please tell me why you don't enjoy this fine sport. 8 That bird lives in this part of the country only in the winter. 9 They sent a bracelet to their daughter for her birthday. 10 My wife seldom watches television during the afternoon. 284 1 ... Albert almost got lost ... 2 ... are all abstract words. 3 How can you possibly consider ... 4 We rarely attend ... 5 There is still a strike ... 6 I am only trying ... 7 Does their teacher always ask ... 8 ... later in the summer. 9 ... really believe ... 10 ... he even wrote ... (... even before Flaubert.) 11 Those students never used to complain ... 12 ... not to smoke ... 15 We could hardly see ... 16 Always plan ... 17 ... our own customs better. 18 I still don't agree ... 19 ... they both contain ... 20 There is just one more thing ... 24 Not many people ... **285** (Only those words or names which require the definite article have been included here.) the world, the thickest jungles, the upper regions of the Amazon, the Taj Mahal, the Vatican, the Leaning Tower, the Seven Wonders of the World, the names of the seven great structures, the Philippine Islands, the Soviet Union, the top of the Empire State Building, the peak, the whole range of the Rocky Mountains, the Rhine River, the Atlantic Ocean, the Caribbean Sea, the Gulf, the streets, the Balkans, the Near East, the Scandinavian Peninsula, the House, the White House, the Kremlin, the Coliseum, the Acropolis, the Louvre, the Statue, the northernmost state, the Republic, the Panama Canal, the Orient, the length, the St. Lawrence River, the Island, the entire Australian Continent, the United Nations Building, the Imperial Japanese Palace, all the countries, all the cities, the British Commonwealth to the other, the Sorbonne, the University, *the wind.* **286** (Only those words or names which require a definite or indefinite article have been included here.) a small house in the country, a small city, a few miles, to the city, in a hurry, a bus, the little gas station, the driver of the bus, a watch, the printed schedule, an appointment or (an) important engagement, the Weston Transportation Company, the name of the bus line, a week ago, the city, a suit, a guest, the evening, the house, the city. **290** (Only those words or names which require the definite or indefinite article have been included here.) the southwestern part of the United States, along the ground, the spotted jaguar, the greatest hunter, the largest member of the cat family on the American Continent, a favorite food, the favorite food of the jaguar, the wild pig, a group, a story, the courage and (the) strength, the story, as a result, the jaguar, a wild pig, a pack, the wild pig. **291** (Only those words or names which require definite or indefinite articles have been included here.) the most important plant products. The word sugar, with a scientific name. The sugar most commonly obtained, the sugar obtained from the sap of the maple tree, the sugar derived from the juice of the sugar beet, the difference, the two forms, the Americas. **295** 1 any other 2 another 3 another, the other 4 any other 5 another 6 some other (another) 7 any other 8 the other 9 other 10 another 11 the others 12 other **296** 1 in 2 on 3 since 4 for 5 by 6 until 7 since 8 during 9 on 10 by 11 for 12 in **297** 1 at 2 from, to 3 in, at 4 at 5 in 6 by 7 for 8 at 9 in 10 in 11 on 12 at 13 at 14 in 15 on 16 at 17 in 18 from 19 at 20 by (at) 21 at 22 by, at 23 at 24 in 25 for, in 26 by, by 27 in 28 for 29 from, to 30 in 31 in **298** 1 in, in 2 on, between 3 on, of (in) 4 at, by (near, opposite) 5 around, into (in) 6 by (past), in 7 at (on), of 8 to, by, on 9 in, of, in 10 in, behind 11 to, at, of 12 on, by (near, opposite) 13 along (up, down) 14 on, in 15 for, on 16 in, on to 17 in, on 18 to, by, of 19 at 20 in, to 21 from, to, in 22 at, from 23 at, at 24 out of, in 25 to, on 26 to, on 27 down 28 from, in 29 from 30 into (in) through, through (in) 31 in, of 32 down, to (up, from) 33 from, in, opposite (above, over, below, under) **299** 1 in, on 2 in, of 3 on (over), on 4 on, in 5 up, down 6 out of, in 7 on, above (over, near, by) 8 from, by, over 9 from 10 out of, under (underneath) 11 in, for 12 to (at), from, above 13 out of 14 up, to (down, from), on 15 on, of, on 16 between, in, of 17 of, under (underneath) 18 through (down), on, to (from) 19 out of, in 20 in, in 21 under (underneath), in 22 above (over, around) 23 in, along (near, by) 24 on, at 25 at, of 26 in (on) 27 in, on 28 on, off (from) 29 along (on), of 30 against, of 31 to 32 in 33 in **300** 1 in 2 on 3 at 4 in 5 at 6 on 7 on 8 at 9 of 10 in 11 in 12 in, of 13 for 14 by 15 at, in, of 16 on 18 on 18 to 19 for 20 in, of 21 off 22 of 23 in 24 out of 25 in 26 by 27 to 28 on 29 in 30 by 31 of 32 of, of 33 for **301** 1 in 2 out of 3 of, in 4 before 5 at 6 in 7 for, in (through) 8 for, in 9 at (behind), on 10 of 11 for 12 after 13 in, with 14 in, of 15 on, of 16 in 17 of, on, in 18 to, by, of 19 of by 20 in, of 21 at, in 22 in, of 23 to, to 24 by, from 25 to 26 for 27 in 28 by 29 out of 30 with 31 in, with 32 on 33 by **302** 1 with, in 2 to, about (over) 3 with, about (over) 4 to 5 for 6 into, by about (over) 7 for 8 with, about (over, in on) 9 with (against), for 10 from 11 of 12 to 13 from, (for) 14 from 15 to 16 from, about 17 from, for 18 from 19 to 20 in 21 in 22 to 23 of 24 about 25 from, to 26 into (in) 27 from 28 to 29 from, about (at) 30 of 31 with 32 about (of) to 33 on, for **303** 1 of 2 for 3 about (over) 4 about 5 about (of) 6 for 7 from 8 about (of) 9 about 10 for 11 from 12 to 13 to 14 on 15 of 16 about 17 to, for 18 on 19 for 20 from 21 of 22 from, to (into) 23 about 24 in 25 on (against), on 26 with, about (over) 27 from 28 for 29 with 30 about 31 in 32 on 33 to **304** 1 in 2 to 3 to 4 over (about) 5 with, to 6 of 7 to, for 8 about (over) 9 with 10 of 11 of, of 12 for 13 with 14 to 15 of 16 of (about) 17 of 18 of (about), of (about) 19 of 20 about (over) 21 of 22 to, from (than) 23 to (with) 24 from 25 of 26 of 27 from (of) 28 of 29 to 30 for 31 for 32 with, about (in) 33 for (to) **305** 1 about (over) 2 from 3 from (by), about (over) 4 of 5 to 6 for 7 for, to 8 of 9 at 10 with 11 for 12 to, for 13 of 14 to 15 on 16 for 17 of (over, about) 18 of 19 for 20 of 21 of 22 on, for 23 to 24 to 25 for 26 to 27 to 28 with 29 with 30 for 31 of 32 for, for 33 of (about) **306** 1 of (over) 2 to, for 3 to, for 4 to 5 to 6 to 7 in 8 for 9 to 10 to 11 for 12 with 13 from 14 of 15 by 16 about (over), in, to 17 about (over) 18 to 19 of 20 for 21 with 22 in 23 about (over) 24 by, as 25 of 26 from 27 in 28 with 29 as 30 for 31 from, to 32 to 33 to, for **307** 1 by 2 with 3 by 4 with 5 by 6 with 7 by 8 with 9 by 10 with 11 by 12 by 13 with 14 by 15 by **308** 3 My brother is going to leave some money for me tonight. 4 My friend John lent seventeen dollars to me on Friday night. 5 Mrs. Farrell is getting a glass of water for her young daughter. 6 M. and Mrs. Harvey gave the theater tickets to us yesterday. 7 The director offered the best job in the department to the man. 8 I think this new method saves a lot of time and trouble for us. 9 That student showed his homework to Mr. Moore before class. 10 Catherine's grandmother made a beautiful evening gown for her. **309** 1 afterwards 2 after 3 afterwards 4 after 5 after 6 afterwards 7 after 8 after 9 afterwards 10 after **310** 5 like 6 such as (like) 7 as 8 like 9 as 10 like 11 like 12 as **311** 1 later 2 after 3 later 4 after 5 later 6 after 7 after 8 after 9 later, after 10 after.